Bhagavad Gita and Hinduism

BHAGAVAD GITA
AND
HINDUISM

Dr. Kapil Khanna

This edition published in 2021 by
Empty Canvas Publishers

Registered Office
119 C, Block AP, Pitampura
Delhi-110034 (India)

Corporate Office
4435-36/7, First Floor, Ansari Road
Daryaganj, New Delhi - 110002
E-mail: emptycanvaspublishers@gmail.com

Book Design & Typesetting

Bhagavad Gita and Hinduism
Author: Dr. Kapil Khanna

ISBN : 978-81-949219-6-7

Printed and Bound in India by Thomson Press India Ltd.

Preface

The Bhagavad Gita presents a synthesis of Brahmanical concept of Dharma, theistic bhakti, the yogic ideals of moksha through jnana, bhakti, karma, and Raja Yoga (spoken of in the 6th chapter). and Samkhyaphilosophy.

The Bhagavad Gita is one of the supreme works of Sanskrit and indeed of all world literature. It is the most well-known and widely translated part of the Sanskrit Mahabharata (constituting chapters 6.23 to 6.40 in the Poona edition of the Mahabharata). In the great Mahabharata war, on the battlefield of Kuruksetra (Kuru's field), Kuru's descendants, split into two sides, fight over the ancestral kingdom. Arjuna Pandava is the most brilliant warrior on the winning side, and his chariot driver is his maternal cousin, brother-in-law, and great friend Krishna Vasudeva, who is also, as Arjuna comes to realize, the great god Vishnu Narayana in human form. Just before the war commences, Arjuna asks Krishna to drive him out between the massed armies, and at the sight of those opposing him, he suffers an existential collapse and declares he will not fight.

The Gita is set in a narrative framework of a dialogue between Pandava prince Arjuna and his guide and charioteer Krishna. Doing the duty of a warrior to fight the Dharma Yudhha or righteous war between Pandavas and Kauravas, Arjuna is counselled by Krishna to "fulfill his Kshatriya (warrior) duty as a warrior and establishing Dharma." Inserted in this appeal to kshatriya dharma (chivalry) is "a dialogue [...] between diverging attitudes concerning and methods toward the attainment of liberation (moksha)". The Bhagavad Gita was exposed to the world through Sanjaya. Sanjaya is Dhritarashtra's advisor and also his charioteer.

Hinduism poses a particular challenge for several facts when exploring chief figures. Firstly, it is impossible to trace the exact beginning. It has no single founder, but comprises a number of leaders who reformed and revived existing customs, either breaking them into innumerable sub-groups or consolidating them. The rather vague boundary between man and the immortal makes the subject even more complex.

Among all the surviving customs Hinduism is the longest surviving philosophical custom in India. We can recognize several historical stages. The earliest, from around 700 BC, was the proto-philosophical period, when karma and liberation theories arose, and the proto-scientific ontological lists in the Upanishads were compiled. Next came the classical period, spanning the first millennium ad, in which there was constant philosophical exchange between various Hindu, Buddhist and Jaina schools. During this period, some schools, such as Sankhya, Yoga and Vaisesika, fell into oblivion and others, such as Kashmir Saivism, emerged. At last, after the classical period only two or three schools remained active. The political and economic disturbances caused by repeated Muslim invasions hampered intellectual growth. The schools that survived were the Logic school (Nyaya), especially New Logic (Navya-Nyaya), the grammarians and, above all, the Vedanta schools. The chief concerns of the Hindu philosophers were metaphysics, epistemological issues, philosophy of language, and moral philosophy.

This is a reference book. All the matter is just compiled and edited in nature, taken from the various sources which are in public domain.

The Bhagavad Gita is the sealing achievement of this Hindu synthesis, incorporating various religious traditions. According to Hiltebeitel, bhakti forms an essential ingredient of this synthesis, which incorporates bhakti into the Brahmanical fold. According to Deutsch and Dalvi, the Bhagavad Gita attempts "to forge a harmony" between different strands of Indian thought: jnana, dharma and bhakti.

—Editor

Contents

CHAPTER

1

Bhagavad Gita

The *Bhagavad Gita*, referred to as simply the Gita, is a 700-verse Hindu scripture in Sanskrit that is part of the Hindu epic *Mahabharata*.

The *Gita* is set in a narrative framework of a dialogue between Pandava prince Arjuna and his guide and charioteer Krishna. Doing the duty of a warrior to fight the Dharma Yudhha or righteous war between Pandavas and Kauravas, Arjuna is counselled by Krishna to "fulfill his Kshatriya (warrior) duty as a warrior and establishing Dharma." Inserted in this appeal to *kshatriya dharma* (chivalry) is "a dialogue [...] between diverging attitudes concerning and methods toward the attainment of liberation (*moksha*)". The *Bhagavad Gita* was exposed to the world through Sanjaya. Sanjaya is Dhritarashtra's advisor and also his charioteer.

The *Bhagavad Gita* presents a synthesis of Brahmanical concept of Dharma, theistic bhakti, the yogic ideals of moksha through jnana, bhakti, karma, and Raja Yoga (spoken of in the 6th chapter). and Samkhyaphilosophy.

Numerous commentaries have been written on the *Bhagavad Gita* with widely differing views on the essentials. Vedanta commentators read varying relations between the Self and the Brahman in the text: Advaita Vedanta sees the non-dualism of Atman (soul) and Brahman as its essence, whereas Bhedabheda and Vishishtadvaita see Atman and Brahman as both different and non-different, and Dvaita sees them as different. The setting of the *Gita* in a battlefield has been interpreted as an allegory for the ethical and moral struggles of the human life. The *Bhagavad Gita*'s call for selfless action inspired many leaders of the Indian independence movement including Bal Gangadhar Tilak and Mohandas Karamchand Gandhi. Gandhi referred to the *Gita* as his "spiritual dictionary".

CONTENT

Narrative

In the epic *Mahabharata,* after Sanjaya—counsellor of the Kuru king Dhritarashtra—returns from the battlefield to announce the death of Bhisma, he begins recounting the details of the *Mahabharata* war. *Bhagavad Gita* forms the content of this recollection. The *Gita* begins before the start of the climactic Kurukshetra War, where the Pandava prince Arjuna is filled with doubt on the battlefield. Realizing that his enemies are his own relatives, beloved friends, and revered teachers, he turns to his charioteer and guide, God's Incarnation Lord Shri Krishna, for advice. Responding to Arjuna's confusion and moral dilemma, Krishna explains to Arjuna his duties as a warrior and prince, elaborating on a variety of philosophical concepts.

Characters

- Arjuna, one of the Pandavas
- Lord Shri Krishna, Arjuna's charioteer and guru who was actually incarnation of God
- Sanjaya, counsellor of the Kuru king Dhritarashtra
- Dhritarashtra, Kuru king.

Overview of Chapters

Bhagavad Gita comprises 18 chapters (section 25 to 42) in the *Bhishma Parva* of the epic *Mahabharata* and consists of 700 verses. Because of differences in recensions, the verses of the *Gita* may be numbered in the full text of the *Mahabharata* as chapters 6.25–42 or as chapters 6.23–40. According to the recension of the *Gita* commented on by Adi Shankara, a prominent philosopher of the Vedanta school, the number of verses is 700, but there is evidence to show that old manuscripts had 745 verses. The verses themselves, composed with similes and metaphors, are poetic in nature. The verses mostly employ the range and style of the Sanskrit Anustubh meter (*chhandas*), and in a few expressive verses the Tristubh meter is used.

The Sanskrit editions of the *Gita* name each chapter as a particular form of yoga. However, these chapter titles do not appear in the Sanskrit text of the *Mahabharata*. Swami Chidbhavananda explains that each of the eighteen chapters is designated as a separate yoga because each chapter, like yoga, "trains the body and the mind". He labels the first chapter "Arjuna Vishada Yogam" or the "Yoga of Arjuna's Dejection". Sir Edwin Arnold translates this chapter as "The Distress of Arjuna"

Gita Dhyanam: (contains 9 verses) The *Gita Dhyanam* is not a part of the main Bhagavad Gita, but it is commonly published with the Gîtâ as a prefix.

The verses of the *Gita Dhyanam* (also called *Gîtâ Dhyâna* or *Dhyâna Slokas*) offer salutations to a variety of sacred scriptures, figures, and entities, characterise the relationship of the Gîtâ to the Upanishads, and affirm the power of divine assistance. It is a common practice to recite these before reading the *Gita*.

1. Arjuna–Visada yoga (*The Distress of Arjuna* contains 46 verses): Arjuna has requested Krishna to move his chariot between the two armies. His growing dejection is described as he fears losing friends and relatives as a consequence of war.
2. Sankhya yoga (*The Book of Doctrines* contains 72 verses): After asking Krishna for help, Arjuna is instructed into various subjects such as, Karma yoga, Gyaana yoga, Sankhya yoga, Buddhi yoga and the immortal nature of the soul. This chapter is often considered the summary of the entire *Bhagavad Gita*.

3. Karma yoga (*Virtue in Work* contains 43 verses): Krishna explains how Karma yoga, i.e. performance of prescribed duties, but without attachment to results, is the appropriate course of action for Arjuna.
4. Gyaana-Karma-Sanyasa yoga (*The Religion of Knowledge* contains 42 verses): Krishna reveals that he has lived through many births, always teaching yoga for the protection of the pious and the destruction of the impious and stresses the importance of accepting a guru.
5. Karma-Sanyasa yoga (*Religion by Renouncing Fruits of Works* contains 29 verses): Arjuna asks Krishna if it is better to forgo action or to act ("renunciation or discipline of action"). Krishna answers that both are ways to the same goal, but that acting in Karma yoga is superior.
6. Dhyan yoga or Atmasanyam yoga (*Religion by Self-Restraint* contains 47 verses): Krishna describes theAshtanga yoga. He further elucidates the difficulties of the mind and the techniques by which mastery of the mind might be gained.
7. Gyaana-ViGyaana yoga (*Religion by Discernment* contains 30 verses): Krishna describes the absolute reality and its illusory energy Maya.
8. Aksara-Brahma yoga (*Religion by Devotion to the One Supreme God* contains 28 verses): This chapter containseschatology of the *Bhagavad Gita*. Importance of the last thought before death, differences between material and spiritual worlds, and light and dark paths that a soul takes after death are described.
9. Raja-Vidya-Raja-Guhya yoga (*Religion by the Kingly Knowledge and the Kingly Mystery* contains 34 verses): Krishna explains how His eternal energy pervades, creates, preserves, and destroys the entire universe. According to theologian Christopher Southgate, verses

of this chapter of the *Gita* are panentheistic, while German physicist and philosopher Max Bernhard Weinstein deems the work pandeistic.

10. Vibhuti-Vistara-yoga (*Religion by the Heavenly Perfections* contains 42 verses): Krishna is described as the ultimate cause of all material and spiritual existence. Arjuna accepts Krishna as the Supreme Being, quoting great sages who have also done so.
11. Visvarupa-Darsana yoga (*The Manifesting of the One and Manifold* contains 55 verses): On Arjuna's request, Krishna displays his "universal form" (*Visvarspa*), a theophany of a being facing every way and emitting the radiance of a thousand suns, containing all other beings and material in existence.
12. Bhakti yoga (*The Religion of Faith* contains 20 verses): In this chapter Krishna glorifies the path of devotion to God. Krishna describes the process of devotional service (Bhakti yoga). He also explains different forms of spiritual disciplines.
13. Ksetra-Ksetrajna Vibhaga yoga (*Religion by Separation of Matter and Spirit* contains 35 verses): The difference between transient perishable physical body and the immutable eternal soul is described. The difference between individual consciousness and universal consciousness is also made clear.
14. Gunatraya-Vibhaga yoga (*Religion by Separation from the Qualities* contains 27 verses): Krishna explains the three modes (gunas) of material nature pertaining to goodness, passion, and nescience. Their causes, characteristics, and influence on a living entity are also described.
15. Purusottama yoga (*Religion by Attaining the Supreme* contains 20 verses): Krishna identifies the transcendental characteristics of God such as, omnipotence, omniscience, and omnipresence. Krishna also describes

a symbolic tree (representing material existence), which has its roots in the heavens and its foliage on earth. Krishna explains that this tree should be felled with the "axe of detachment", after which one can go beyond to his *supreme abode*.

16. Daivasura-Sampad-Vibhaga yoga (*The Separateness of the Divine and Undivine* contains 24 verses): Krishna identifies the human traits of the divine and the demonic natures. He counsels that to attain the supreme destination one must give up lust, anger, greed, and discern between right and wrong action by discernment through Buddhi and evidence from the scriptures.
17. Sraddhatraya-Vibhaga yoga (*Religion by the Threefold Kinds of Faith* contains 28 verses): Krishna qualifies the three divisions of faith, thoughts, deeds, and even eating habits corresponding to the three modes (gunas).
18. Moksha-Sanyasa yoga (*Religion by Deliverance and Renunciation* contains 78 verses): In this chapter, the conclusions of previous seventeen chapters are summed up. Krishna asks Arjuna to abandon all forms of dharma and simply surrender unto him and describes this as the ultimate perfection of life.

THEMES

Dharma

The term *dharma* has a number of meanings. Fundamentally, it means "what is right". Early in the text, responding to Arjuna's despondency, Krishna asks him to follow his *swadharma,* "the *dharma* that belongs to a particular man (Arjuna) as a member of a particular *varna,* (i.e., the *ksatriya*)."

According to Vivekananda:

If one reads this one Shloka, one gets all the merits of reading the entire Gita; for in this one Shloka lies imbedded the whole Message of the Gita."

> ***klaibhyam mâ sma gamah pârtha naitattvayyupapadyate, ksudram hrdayadaurbhalyam tyaktvottistha paramtapa.***

Do not yield to unmanliness, O son of Prithâ. It does not become you. Shake off this base faint-heartedness and arise, O scorcher of enemies! (2.3)

Dharma and Heroism

The *Bhagavad Gita* is set in the narrative frame of the *Mahabharata,* which value-s*heroism,* "energy, dedication and self-sacrifice", as the *dharma,* "holy duty" of the Ksatriya (warrior). Axel Michaels in his book *Hinduism: Past and Present*writes that in the *Bhagavad Gita,* Arjuna is "exhorted by his charioteer, Krsna, among others, to stop hesitating and fulfill his Kshatriya (warrior) duty as a warrior and kill."

According to Malinar, the dispute between the two parties in the *Mahabharata*centers on the question how to define "the law of heroism". Malinar gives a description of the *dharma* of a Ksatriya (warrior) based on the *Udyogaparvan*, the fifth book of the *Mahabharata*:

This duty consists first of all in standing one's ground and fighting for status. The main duty of a warrior is never to submit to anybody. A warrior must resist any impulse to self-preservation that would make him avoid a fight. In brief, he ought to be a man (*puruso bhava;* cf. 5.157.6; 13;15). Some of the most vigorous formulations of what called the "heart" or the "essence" of heroism (*ksatrahrdaya*) come from the ladies of the family. They bare shown most unforgiving with regard to the humiliations they have gone through, the loss of their status and honour, not to speak of the shame of having a weak man in the house, whether husband, son or brother.

Michaels defines heroism as "power assimilated with interest in salvation". According to Michaels:

> ***Even though the frame story of the Mahabharata is rather simple, the epic has an outstanding significance***

for Hindu heroism. The heroism of the Pandavas, the ideals of honor and courage in battle, are constant sources of treatises in which it is not sacrifice, renunciation of the world, or erudition that is valued, but energy, dedication and self-sacrifice. The Bhagavad Gita, inserted in the sixth book (Bhismaparvan), and probably completed in the second century A.D., is such a text, that is, a philosophical and theistic treatise, with which the Pandava is exhorted by his charioteer, Krishna, among others, to stop hesitating and fulfill his Kshatriya (warrior) duty as a warrior and kill.

According to Malinar, "Arjuna's crisis and some of the arguments put forward to call him to action are connected to the debates on war and peace in the *UdP* [Udyoga Parva]". According to Malinar, the *UdP* emphasizes that one must put up with fate and, the *BhG* personalises the surrender one's personal interests to the power of destiny by "propagating the view that accepting and enacting the fatal course of events is an act of devotion to this god [Krsna] and his cause."

Modern Interpretations of Dharma

Svadharma and Svabhava

The eighteenth chapter of the *Gita* examines the relationship between *svadharma* and *svabhava*. This chapter uses the gunas of Shankhya philosophy to present a series of typologies, and uses the same term to characterise the specific activities of the four *varnas*, which are distinguished by the "gunas proceeding from their nature."

Aurobindo modernizes the concept of *dharma* and *svabhava* by internalizing it, away from the social order and its duties toward one's personal capacities, which leads to a radical individualism, "finding the fulfillment of the purpose of existence in the individual alone." He deduced from the *Gita* the doctrine that "the functions of a man ought to be determined by his natural turn, gift, and capacities", that the individual should "develop freely" and thereby, would be best able to serve society. Gandhi's view differed from Aurobindo's view. He recognized in the concept of *swadharma* his idea of *swadeshi*, the idea that "man owes his service above all to those who are nearest to him by birth and situation." To him, *swadeshi* was "*swadharma* applied to one's immediate environment."

The Field of Dharma

The first reference to *dharma* in the *Bhagavad Gita* occurs in its first verse, where Dhritarashtra refers to the Kurukshetra, the location of the battlefield, as the *Field of Dharma*, "The Field of Righteousness or Truth". According to Fowler, *dharma* in this verse may refer to the *sanatana dharma*, "what Hindus understand as their religion, for it is a term that encompasses wide aspects of religious and traditional thought and is more readily used for ""religion". Therefore, 'Field of action' implies the field of righteousness, where truth will eventually triumph.

"The Field of Dharma" is also called the "Field of action" by Sri Aurobindo, a freedom fighter and philosopher. Sarvapalli Radhakrishnan, a philosopher and the second president of India, saw the "The Field of Dharma" as the world (Bhavsagar), which is a "battleground for moral struggle".

Allegory of War

Unlike any other religious scripture, the *Bhagavad Gita* broadcasts its message in the centre of the battlefield. The choice of such an unholy ambience for the delivery of a philosophical discourse has been an enigma to many commentators. Several modern Indian writers have interpreted the battlefield setting as an allegory of "the war within".

Eknath Easwaran writes that the *Gita* ' s subject is "the war within, the struggle for self-mastery that every human being must wage if he or she is to emerge from life victorious", and that "The language of battle is often found in the scriptures, for it conveys the strenuous, long, drawn-out campaign we must wage to free ourselves from the tyranny of the ego, the cause of all our suffering and sorrow."

Ṡwami Nikhilananda, takes Arjuna as an allegory of Âtman, Krishna as an allegory of*Brahman*, Arjuna's chariot as the body, and Dhritarashtra as the ignorance filled mind.

Mohandas Karamchand Gandhi, in his commentary on the *Gita*, interprets the battle as "an allegory in which the battlefield is the soul and Arjuna, man's higher impulses struggling against evil".

Swami Vivekananda also emphasised that the first discourse in the *Gita* related to the war could be taken allegorically. Vivekananda further remarked,

This Kurukshetra War is only an allegory. When we sum up its esoteric significance, it means the war which is constantly going on within man between the tendencies of good and evil.

In Aurobindo's view, Krishna was a historical figure, but his significance in the *Gita* is as a "symbol of the divine dealings with humanity", while Arjuna typifies a "struggling human soul". However, Aurobindo rejected the interpretation that the Gita, and the *Mahabharata* by extension, is "an allegory of the inner life, and has nothing to do with our outward human life and actions":

...That is a view which the general character and the actual language of the epic does not justify and, if pressed, would turn the straightforward philosophical language of the *Gita* into a constant, laborious and somewhat puerile mystification....the *Gita* is written in plain terms and professes to solve the great ethical and spiritual difficulties which the life of man raises, and it will not do to go behind this plain language and thought and wrest them to the service of our fancy. But there is this much of truth in the view, that the setting of the doctrine though not symbolical, is certainly typical.

Swami Chinmayananda writes:

Here in the Bhagavad Gita, we find a practical handbook of instruction on how best we can re-organise our inner ways of thinking, feeling, and acting in our everyday

life and draw from ourselves a larger gush of productivity to enrich the life around us, and to emblazon the subjective life within us.

Moksha: Liberation

Liberation or *moksha* in Vedanta philosophy is not something that can be acquired or reached. *Âtman* (Soul), the goal of*moksha,* is something that is always present as the essence of the self, and can be revealed by deep intuitive knowledge. While the Upanishads largely uphold such a monistic viewpoint of liberation, the *Bhagavad Gita* also accommodates the dualistic and theistic aspects of *moksha*.

The *Gita,* while occasionally hinting at impersonal *Brahman* as the goal, revolves around the relationship between the Self and a personal God or *Saguna Brahman*. A synthesis of knowledge, devotion, and desireless action is given as a prescription for Arjuna's despondence; the same combination is suggested as a way to moksha. Winthrop Sargeant further explains, "In the model presented by the *Bhagavad Gîtâ*, every aspect of life is in fact a way of salvation."

Yoga

Yoga in the *Bhagavad Gita* refers to the skill of union with the ultimate reality or the Absolute. In his commentary, Zaehnersays that the root meaning of yoga is "yoking" or "preparation"; he proposes the basic meaning "spiritual exercise", which conveys the various nuances in the best way.

Sivananda's commentary regards the eighteen chapters of the *Bhagavad Gita* as having a progressive order, by which Krishna leads "Arjuna up the ladder of Yoga from one rung to another." The influential commentator Madhusudana Sarasvati divided the *Gita* ' s eighteen chapters into three sections of six chapters each. Swami Gambhirananda characterises Madhusudana Sarasvati's system as a successive approach in which Karma yoga leads to Bhakti yoga, which in turn leads to Gyaana yoga:

- Chapters 1–6 = Karma yoga, the means to the final goal
- Chapters 7–12 = Bhakti yoga or devotion
- Chapters 13–18 = Gyaana yoga or knowledge, the goal itself.

Karma Yoga

As noted by various commentators, the *Bhagavad Gita* offers a practical approach to liberation in the form of Karma yoga. The path of Karma yoga upholds the necessity of action. However, this action is to be undertaken without any attachment to the work or desire for results.

Bhagavad Gita terms this "inaction in action and action in inaction (4.18)". The concept of such detached action is also called *Nishkam Karma,* a term not used in the *Gita*. Lord Krishna, in the following verses, elaborates on the role actions, performed without desire and attachment, play in attaining freedom from material bondage and transmigration:

To action alone hast thou a right and never at all to its fruits; let not the fruits of action be thy motive; neither let there be in thee any attachment to inaction.

Fixed in yoga, do thy work, O Winner of wealth (Arjuna), abandoning attachment, with an even mind in success and failure, for evenness of mind is called yoga. (2.47-8)

With the body, with the mind, with the intellect, even merely with the senses, the Yogis perform action toward self-purification, having abandoned attachment. He who is disciplined in Yoga, having abandoned the fruit of action, attains steady peace. (5.11)

Mohandas Karamchand Gandhi writes, "The object of the *Gita* appears to me to be that of showing the most excellent way to attain self-realization", and this can be achieved by selfless action, "By desireless action; by renouncing fruits of action; by dedicating all activities to God, i.e., by surrendering oneself to Him body and soul." Gandhi called the *Gita* "The Gospel of Selfless Action". To achieve true liberation, it is important to control all mental desires and tendencies to enjoy sense pleasures. The following verses illustrate this:

When a man dwells in his mind on the object of sense, attachment to them is produced. From attachment springs desire and from desire comes anger.

From anger arises bewilderment, from bewilderment loss of memory; and from loss of memory, the destruction of intelligence and from the destruction of intelligence he perishes. (2.62-3)

Bhakti Yoga

The introduction to chapter seven of the *Bhagavad Gita* explains *bhakti* as a mode of worship which consists of unceasing and loving remembrance of God. Faith (*Sraddhâ*) and total surrender to a chosen God (*Ishta-deva*) are considered to be important aspects of *bhakti*. Theologian Catherine Cornille writes, "The text [of the *Gita*] offers a survey of the different possible disciplines for attaining liberation through knowledge (*Gyaana*), action (*karma*), and loving devotion to God (*bhakti*), focusing on the latter as both the easiest and the highest path to salvation." M. R. Sampatkumaran, a *Bhagavad Gita* scholar, explains in his overview of Ramanuja's commentary on the *Gita*, "The point is that mere knowledge of the scriptures cannot lead to final release. Devotion, meditation, and worship are essential." Ramakrishna believed that the essential message of the *Gita* could be obtained by repeating the word *Gita* several times, "'Gita, Gita, Gita', you begin, but then find yourself saying 'ta-Gi, ta-Gi, ta-Gi'. *Tagi* means one who has renounced everything for God." In the following verses, Krishna elucidates the importance of bhakti:

And of all yogins, he who full of faith worships Me, with his inner self abiding in Me, him, I hold to be the most attuned (to me in Yoga). (6.47)

... those who, renouncing all actions in Me, and regarding Me as the Supreme, worship Me... For those whose thoughts have entered into Me, I am soon the deliverer from the ocean of death and transmigration, Arjuna. Keep your mind on Me alone, your intellect on Me. Thus you shall dwell in Me hereafter. (12.6)

Radhakrishnan writes that the verse 11.55 is "the essence of bhakti" and the "substance of the whole teaching of the *Gita*":

Those who make me the supreme goal of all their work and act without selfish attachment, who devote themselves to me completely and are free from ill will for any creature, enter into me.(11.55)

Jnana Yoga

Jnana yoga is the path of wisdom, knowledge, and direct experience of *Brahman* as the ultimate reality. The path renounces both desires and actions, and is therefore depicted as being steep and very difficult in the *Bhagavad Gita*. This path is often associated with the non-dualistic Vedantic belief of the identity of the *Âtman* with the *Brahman*. For the followers of this path, the realisation of the identity of *Âtman* and *Brahman* is held as the key to liberation.

When a sensible man ceases to see different identities due to different material bodies and he sees how beings are expanded everywhere, he attains to the *Brahman* conception. (13.31)

Those who see with eyes of knowledge the difference between the body and the knower of the body, and can also understand the process of liberation from bondage in material nature, attain to the supreme goal. (13.35)

COMPOSITION AND SIGNIFICANCE

Authorship

The epic *Mahabharata* is traditionally ascribed to the Sage Ved Vyasa; the *Bhagavad Gita*, being a part of the *Mahabharata*'s *Bhisma Parva*, is also ascribed to him.

Date of Composition

Theories on the date of composition of the *Gita* vary considerably. Scholars accept dates from the fifth century to the second century BCE as the probable range. Professor Jeaneane Fowler, in her commentary on the *Gita*, considers second century BCE to be the likely date of composition. Kashi Nath Upadhyaya, a *Gita*s scholar, on the basis of the estimated dates of *Mahabharata*, Brahma sutras, and other independent sources, concludes that the *Bhagavad Gita* was composed in the fifth or fourth century BCE.

It is generally agreed that, "Unlike the Vedas, which have to be preserved letter-perfect, the *Gita* was a popular work whose reciters would inevitably conform to changes in language and style", so the earliest "surviving" components of this dynamic text are believed to be no older than the earliest "external" references we have to the *Mahabharata* epic, which may include an allusion in Panini's fourth century BCE grammar. It is estimated that the text probably reached something of a "final form" by the early Gupta period (about the 4th century CE). The actual dates of composition of the *Gita* remain unresolved.

Hindu Synthesis and Smriti

Due to its presence in the *Mahabharata*, the *Bhagavad Gita* is classified as a Smriti text or "that which is remembered". The *Smriti* texts of the period between 200 BCE-100 CE belong to the emerging "Hindu synthesis", proclaiming the authority of the Vedas while integrating various Indian traditions and religions. Acceptance of the Vedas became a central criterion for defining Hinduism over and against the heterodoxies, which rejected the Vedas.

The so-called "Hindu synthesis" emerged during the early Classical period (200 BCE-300 CE) of Hinduism. According to Alf Hiltebeitel, a period of consolidation in the development of Hinduism took place between the time of the late Vedic Upanishad (ca. 500 BCE) and the period of the rise of the

Guptas (ca. 320–467 CE) which he calls the "Hindu synthesis", "Brahmanic synthesis", or "Orthodox synthesis". It developed in interaction with other religions and peoples:

The emerging self-definitions of Hinduism were forged in the context of continuous interaction with heterodox religions (Buddhists, Jains, Ajivikas) throughout this whole period, and with foreign people (Yavanas, or Greeks; Sakas, or Scythians; Pahlavas, or Parthians; and Kusanas, or Kushans) from the third phase on [between the Mauryan empire and the rise of the Guptas].

The *Bhagavad Gita* is the sealing achievement of this Hindu synthesis, incorporating various religious traditions. According to Hiltebeitel, *bhakti* forms an essential ingredient of this synthesis, which incorporates *bhakti* into the Brahmanical fold. According to Deutsch and Dalvi, the *Bhagavad Gita* attempts "to forge a harmony" between different strands of Indian thought: jnana, dharma and bhakti.

Deutsch and Dalvi note that the authors of the *Bhagavad Gita* "must have seen the appeal of the soteriologies both of the "heterodox" traditions of Buddhism and Jainism and of the more "orthodox" ones of Samkhya and Yoga", while the Brahmanic tradition emphasised "the significance of *dharma* as the instrument of goodness".

Scheepers mentions the *Bhagavat Gita* as a Brahmanical text which uses the Ashramanic and Yogic terminology to spread the Brahmanic idea of living according to one's duty or *dharma,* in contrast to the yogic ideal of liberation from the workings of karma. According to Basham,

The *Bhagavadgita* combines many different elements from Samkhya and Vedanta philosophy. In matters of religion, its important contribution was the new emphasis placed on devotion, which has since remained a central path in Hinduism. In addition, the popular theism expressed elsewhere in the *Mahabharata* and the transcendentalism of the Upanishads converge, and a God of personal characteristics is identified with the brahman of the Vedic tradition. The *Bhagavadgita* thus gives a typology of the three dominant trends of Indian religion: dharma-based householder life, enlightenment-based renunciation, and devotion-based theism.

Raju too sees the *Bhagavad Gita* as a synthesis:

The Bhagavadgita may be treated as a great synthesis of the ideas of the impersonal spiritual monism with personalistic monotheism, of the yoga of action with the yoga of transcendence of action, and these again withyogas of devotion and knowledge.

The influence of the *Bhagavad Gita* was such, that its synthesis was adapted to and incorporated into specific Indian traditions. Nicholson mentions the *Shiva Gita* as an adaptation of the Vishnu-oriented *Bhagavat Gita* into Shiva-oriented terminology, and the *Isvara Gita* as borrowing entire verses from the Krishna-oriented *Bhagavad Gita* and placing them into a new Shiva-oriented context.

Status

The *Bhagavad Gita* is part of the Prasthanatrayi, which also includes the Upanishads and Brahma sutras. These are the key texts for the Vedanta, which interprets these texts to give a unified meaning.

Advaita Vedanta sees the non-dualism of Atman and Brahman as its essence, whereas Bhedabheda and Vishishtadvaita see Atman and Brahman as both different and non-different, and Dvaita sees them as different. In recent times the Advaita interpretation has gained worldwide popularity, due to the Neo-Vedanta of Vivekananda and Radhakrishnan, while the Achintya Bheda Abedha Interpretation has gained worldwide popularity via the Hare Krishnas, a branch of Gaudiya Vaishnavism.

Although early Vedanta gives an interpretation of the *sruti* texts of the Upanishads, and its main commentary the Brahman Sutras, the popularity of the *Bhagavad Gita* was such that it could not be neglected. It is referred to in the Brahman Sutras, and Shankara, Bhaskara and Ramanuja all three wrote commentaries on it. The *Bhagavad Gita* is different from the Upanishads in format and content, and accessible to all, in contrast to the *Sruti,* which are only to be read and heard by the higher castes. Some branches of Hinduism give it the status of an Upanishad, and consider it to be a Œruti or "revealed text". According to Pandit, who gives a modern-orthodox interpretation of Hinduism, "since the *Bhagavad Gita* represents a summary of the Upanishadic teachings, it is sometimes called 'the Upanishad of the Upanishads'."

COMMENTARIES AND TRANSLATIONS

Bhagavad Gita integrates various schools of thought, notably Vedanta, Samkhya and Yoga, and other theistic ideas. It remains a popular text for commentators belonging to various philosophical schools. However, its composite nature also leads to varying interpretations of the text. In the words of Mysore Hiriyanna,

[The *Gita*] is one of the hardest books to interpret, which accounts for the numerous commentaries on it–each differing from the rest in one essential point or the other.

Different translators and commentators have widely differing views on what multi-layered Sanskrit words and passages signify, and their presentation in English depending on the sampradaya they are affiliated to.

Richard H. Davis cites Callewaert & Hemraj's 1982 count of 1891 BG translations in 75 languages, including 273 in English.

Classical commentaries

The oldest and most influential medieval commentary was that of Adi Shankara (788–820 A. D.), also known as Shankaracharya (Sanskrit: Samkarâcârya). Shankara's commentary was based on a recension of the *Gita* containing 700 verses, and that recension has been widely adopted by others.

Ramanujacharya's commentary chiefly seeks to show that the discipline of devotion to God (Bhakti yoga) is the way of salvation.

Madhva, a commentator of the Vedanta school, whose dates are given either as (1199–1276 CE) or as (1238–1317 CE), also known as Madhvacharya, wrote a commentary on the *Bhagavad Gita*, which exemplifies the thinking of the "dualist" school. Winthrop Sargeant quotes a dualistic assertion of the Madhva's school that there is "an eternal and complete distinction between the Supreme, the many souls, and matter and its divisions". His commentary on the *Gita* is called *Gita Bhâshya*. It has been annotated on by many ancient pontiffs of Dvaita Vedanta school like Padmanabha Tirtha, Jayatirtha, and Raghavendra Tirtha.

In the Shaiva tradition, the renowned philosopher Abhinavagupta (10–11th century CE) has written a commentary on a slightly variant recension called *Gitartha-Samgraha*. Other classical commentators include Nimbarka (1162 CE), Vidyadhiraja Tirtha, Vallabha (1479 CE)., Madhusudana Saraswati, Raghavendra Tirtha, Vanamali Mishra, Chaitanya Mahaprabhu (1486 CE), while Dnyaneshwar (1275–1296 CE) translated and commented on the *Gita* in Marathi, in his book *Dnyaneshwari*.

Independence Movement

At a time when Indian nationalists were seeking an indigenous basis for social and political action, *Bhagavad Gita* provided them with a rationale for their activism and fight against injustice. Among nationalists, notable commentaries were written by Bal Gangadhar Tilak and Mahatma Gandhi, who used the text to help inspire the Indian independence movement. Tilak wrote his commentary Shrimadh Bhagvad Gita Rahasya while in jail during the period 1910–1911 serving a six-year sentence imposed by the British colonial government in India for sedition. While noting that the *Gita* teaches possible paths to liberation, his commentary places most emphasis on

Karma yoga. No book was more central to Gandhi's life and thought than the *Bhagavad Gita,* which he referred to as his "spiritual dictionary". During his stay in Yeravda jail in 1929, Gandhi wrote a commentary on the *Bhagavad Gita* in Gujarati. The Gujarati manuscript was translated into English by Mahadev Desai, who provided an additional introduction and commentary. It was published with a foreword by Gandhi in 1946. Mahatma Gandhi expressed his love for the *Gita* in these words:

I find a solace in the *Bhagavadgîtâ* that I miss even in the Sermon on the Mount. When disappointment stares me in the face and all alone I see not one ray of light, I go back to the *Bhagavadgîtâ.* I find a verse here and a verse there and I immediately begin to smile in the midst of overwhelming tragedies - and my life has been full of external tragedies - and if they have left no visible, no indelible scar on me, I owe it all to the teaching of*Bhagavadgîtâ.*

Hindu Revivalism

Although Vivekananda did not write any commentaries on the *Bhagavad Gita,* his works contained numerous references to the *Gita,* such as his lectures on the four yogas - Bhakti, Gyaana, Karma, and Raja. Through the message of the *Gita,* Vivekananda sought to energise the people of India to claim their own dormant but strong identity. Bankim Chandra Chattopadhyay thought that the answer to the problems that beset Hindu society was a revival of Hinduism in its purity, which lay in the reinterpretation of *Bhagavad Gita* for a new India. Aurobindo saw *Bhagavad Gita* as a "scripture of the future religion" and suggested that Hinduism had acquired a much wider relevance through the *Gita.* Sivananda called *Bhagavad Gita* "the most precious jewel of Hindu literature" and suggested its introduction into the curriculum of Indian schools and colleges. In the lectures Chinmayananda gave, during tours undertaken to revive of moral and spiritual values of the Hindus, he borrowed the concept of *Gyaana yajna,* or the worship to invoke divine wisdom, from the *Gita.* He viewed the *Gita* as a universal scripture to turn a person from a state of agitation and confusion to a state of complete vision, inner contentment, and dynamic action. Teachings of International Society for Krishna Consciousness (ISKCON), a Gaudiya Vaishnava religious organisation which spread rapidly in North America in the 1970s and 1980s, are based on a translation of the *Gita* called *Bhagavad-Gîtâ As It Is* by His Divine Grace A.C. Bhaktivedanta Swami Prabhupada.

Other Modern Commentaries

Among notable modern commentators of the *Bhagavad Gita* are Bal Gangadhar Tilak, Vinoba Bhave, Mohandas Karamchand Gandhi, Sri Aurobindo , Sarvepalli Radhakrishnan, Chinmayananda, etc. Chinmayananda took a syncretistic approach to interpret the text of the Gita.

Paramahansa Yogananda's two volume commentary on the *Bhagavad Gita*, called *God Talks With Arjuna: The Bhagavad Gita*, was released in 1995.

Eknath Easwaran has also written a commentary on the *Bhagavad Gita*. It examines the applicability of the principles of *Gita*to the problems of modern life.

Other notable commentators include Jeaneane Fowler, Ithamar Theodor, Maharishi Mahesh Yogi, and Sadly Vasvani.

Scholarly Translations

The first English translation of the *Bhagavad Gita* was done by Charles Wilkins in 1785. In 1981, Larson listed more than 40 English translations of the *Gita*, stating that "A complete listing of *Gita* translations and a related secondary bibliography would be nearly endless". He stated that "Overall... there is a massive translational tradition in English, pioneered by the British, solidly grounded philologically by the French and Germans, provided with its indigenous roots by a rich heritage of modern Indian comment and reflection, extended into various disciplinary areas by Americans, and having generated in our time a broadly based cross-cultural awareness of the importance of the *Bhagavad Gita* both as an expression of a specifically Indian spirituality and as one of the great religious "classics" of all time." Sanskrit scholar Barbara Stoler Miller produced a translation in 1986 intended to emphasise the poem's influence and current context within English Literature, especially the works of T.S. Eliot, Henry David Thoreau and Ralph Waldo Emerson. The translation was praised by scholars as well as literary critics and became one of most continually popular translations to date.

The *Gita* has also been translated into other European languages. In 1808, passages from the *Gita* were part of the first direct translation of Sanskrit into German, appearing in a book through which Friedrich Schlegel became known as the founder of Indian philology in Germany. Swami Rambhadracharya released the first Braille version of the scripture, with the original Sanskrit text and a Hindi commentary, on 30 November 2007. The former Turkish Scholar-Politician,Bulent Ecevit translated several Sanskrit scriptures including the *Gita* into Turkish language. Mahavidwan R. Raghava Iyengar translated the *Gita* in Tamil in sandam metre poetic form.

CONTEMPORARY POPULARITY

With the translation and study of the *Bhagavad Gita* by Western scholars beginning in the early 18th century, the *Bhagavad Gita* gained a growing appreciation and popularity. According to the well-known Indian historian and writer Khushwant Singh, Rudyard Kipling's famous poem "If—" is "the essence of the message of *The Gita* in English."

Appraisal

The *Bhagavad Gita* has been highly praised, not only by prominent Indians including Mohandas Karamchand Gandhi and Sarvepalli Radhakrishnan, but also by Aldous Huxley, Henry David Thoreau, J. Robert Oppenheimer, Ralph Waldo Emerson, Carl Jung, Herman Hesse, Bulent Ecevit and others.

The *Gita* ' s emphasis on selfless service was a prime source of inspiration for Gandhi, who said: When doubts haunt me, when disappointments stare me in the face, and I see not a single ray of hope on the horizon, I turn to *Bhagavad-Gita* and find a verse to comfort me; and I immediately begin to smile in the midst of overwhelming sorrow. My life has been full of external tragedies and if they have not left any visible or invisible effect on me, I owe it to the teaching of the *Bhagavad Gita*.

Jawaharlal Nehru, the first Prime Minister of independent India, commented on the *Gita*: The *Bhagavad-Gita* deals essentially with the spiritual foundation of human existence. It is a call of action to meet the obligations and duties of life; yet keeping in view the spiritual nature and grander purpose of the universe.

J. Robert Oppenheimer, American physicist and director of the Manhattan Project, learned Sanskrit in 1933 and read the *Bhagavad Gita* in the original form, citing it later as one of the most influential books to shape his philosophy of life. Upon witnessing the world's first nuclear test in 1945, he later said he had thought of the quotation "Now I am become Death, the destroyer of worlds", verse 32 from chapter 11 of the *Bhagavad Gita*.

Adaptations

Philip Glass retold the story of Gandhi's early development as an activist in South Africa through the text of the *Gita* in the opera *Satyagraha* (1979). The entire libretto of the opera consists of sayings from the *Gita* sung in the original Sanskrit. In Douglas Cuomo's *Arjuna's dilemma*, the philosophical dilemma faced by Arjuna is dramatised in operatic form with a blend of Indian and Western music styles. The 1993 Sanskrit film, *Bhagavad Gita*, directed by G. V. Iyerwon the 1993 National Film Award for Best Film.

The 1995 novel and 2000 golf movie *The Legend of Bagger Vance* are roughly based on the *Bhagavad Gita*.

CHAPTER

2

Hindu Religion and Bhagavad Gita

The most sacred text of the Hindu religion Bhagavad Gita is a self-contained episode of seven hundred verses embedded in one book of the great Sanskrit epic, the Mahabharata. It is also the archetype of that necessarily modern phenomenon, the classic of world spirituality. Over the same period the Gita has assumed for a number of Hindus a universal status, so that it is regarded not only as the quintessential Hindu religious text, but also as a charter for all types of frequently contravening social and political action. One fact for the Gita's universality is its capacity to bear almost any shade of interpretation, because of the variegated nature of its contents. While this shows the fact that the Gita is and always has been a live religious text, with an obviously limitless capacity to inspire new and necessarily valid meanings, from the perspective of the custom in which they are coined, it does not imply that all interpretations are equally convincing from the historical and philological perspectives; far from it. Nevertheless, it is often easier for scholarly exegetes and historians (themselves not always immune to bias) to reject other interpretations than to provide completely convincing substitutes.

In original Gita is a religious text, not a philosophical tract. Its motive is to engender and consolidate certain attitudes in its audience, in much the same way as the 'Lord' of the title, Krishna, attempts in a number of ways to lead his interlocutor, Arjuna, from perplexity to understanding and correct action.

Although, in the context of the Mahabharata the problem is faced by one of the protagonists, Arjuna, and its resolution allows the action to proceed, for most Hindus the Gita is not simply part of the epic story but a religious teaching, transmitted to them personally by the guru-God Krishna. The problem hence is not remote or fictional but imminent, and the solution, through the grace of God, is equally accessible. That it is thought to be the word of God and also part of a narrative encompassing, in the words of a Western theatrical adaptation of the Mahabharata, 'the poetical history of mankind', helps us to understand what seems to be a paradoxical fact about the Gita, in the light of its recent history.

Although it has been revered and the object of much exegesis from early in its existence, detailed knowledge of its contents seems not to have penetrated beyond scholarly circles in India until the last hundred years. One fact for this is that the original language of the Gita, Sanskrit, was known only to a relatively small number of pandits; moreover, translations into modern Indian languages, even if regarded desirable, would have necessitated a readership, which in turn necessitated education. Literacy of that kind commenced to come out in India on a significant scale only in the nineteenth century, initially through the medium of English. Moreover, it was not until this period that printing presses were introduced, creating the possibility of the widespread distribution of written material. Before this change, it seems likely that most Indians, if they knew the Gita at all, knew it as part of an orally transmitted and flexible narrative custom, as an adjunct to various rituals, and as material for recitation in a devotional context.

In other words, they might have known and been able to recite certain verses, but they would have had no theological overview of the text. Indeed, for a number of Hindus the situation may not be so very various today: what the Gita is (the word of God) or what it is perceived to represent (the values inherent in Hindu culture) may be more significant than its literal, verse by verse meaning. Moreover, its primary meaning may not be in its metaphysical or philosophical content at all, but in the story it tells, and in the relationship it dramatizes between God and human beings. This is not intended as a denial of the evident fact that some of the Gita's teachings have, in a generalized form, become cornerstones of belief for a number of, if not most Hindus.

But it may serve as a warning to the modern Westerner, catching a book called The Bhagavad Gita and reading it from cover to cover, not to assume that she or he is using, understanding, or valuing the text in ways that are necessarily like to those employed in the custom from which it derives.

Even within scholarly Sanskritic circles, there have been almost as a number of interpretations as interpreters or schools of thought. The history of the meaning of the text, so far as we can trace it, has hence always been that of its commentaries and interpretations, whatever their level of sophistication. Before the modern period, any systematic study of the Gita would always have been from within a particular commentarial custom. This method of approaching the text has been to some extent obscured by recent attempts to present the Gita 'as it is'. But for all their claims, the 'fundamentalists' responsible are of course no freer of interpretative frameworks and presuppositions than their forerunners, who were usually their superiors in rigour and sophistication.

Due to its role in the history of modern Indian culture and its pivotal position in the interaction which has taken place between Indian religions and the West in the last two centuries, study of the Gita continues to be instructive. But there are other, perhaps more significant reasons for the impartial reader to engage with it. (I leave aside what for some may be the most compelling consideration – the question of whether it has some universally valid spiritual or religious value.) Even in translation, even cut loose from a specific custom of commentary, the Gita touches on and develops in its own way a number of key themes from the history of Indian religions, and raises questions that are still debated.

As we shall see, it is the product of a time of transition, and it attempts to reconcile diverging world views. Maybe in that—in Arjuna's predicament, if not the solution to it—lies some of the Gita's appeal to our own age. The Mahabharata, the great epic which provides the Gita with its literary context, has no single author (if one discounts the mythical Vyasa). It belongs to an oral custom that may have its origins in the eighth or ninth century BC. Succeeding generations of reciter-poets added to, expanded on, and elaborated the basic material, which tells of a cataclysmic war between two branches of the same family and their followers. Like a snowball, the epic picked up and incorporated all the significant religious, philosophical, and social changes through which it passed, often juxtaposing layers with little or no attempt at reconciliation.

Nevertheless, certain themes, because they had come to preoccupy Indian religion and culture generally, began to dominate its 'poetical history': the question of what makes up Dharma or the Law (the way things really are and hence the way they should be), how men and women can assume knowledge of that truth, and how they should act in relation to it. By the time the Gita had been incorporated into or crystallized out of the epic (scholars are divided on which is the correct description)—perhaps in some form in the third century BC.

A number of these questions had become acutely significant for what we have come to call the 'Hindu' custom. In fact for this period that custom is more accurately termed 'Brahminical', after the hereditary priestly class or estate which had established itself and its sacred body of knowledge, the Veda, as the arbiters of orthoprax and orthodox socio-religious conduct and values. This dominance is reflected both in the epic as we now have it and in the Gita.

The fact that the chief protagonists of the Gita are not brahmins at all but members of the equally hereditary warrior or ruling class should not blind us to this. To refer to the Brahminical custom is perhaps misleading, unless it is realized that by the time of the Gita there were a number of movements or tendencies within that custom, not all of them evidently compatible. This led to tensions, the most significant being between those (portrayed as customalists) who enjoined the fulfilment of one's prescribed social and religious duties as a member of the class into which one had been born, and those who recommended resigning that ascribed status altogether in favour of a life of homelessness and spiritual discipline.

In the context of Brahminical texts this divergence had first come to formal light in the early Upanishads (a category of late Vedic texts). It was there too that the essentials of the well-known doctrine of karma and rebirth made their initial seem ance. It is easy to suppose that such a doctrine developed naturally out of the ritualists' world view. The sacrifice is a mechanism for producing a result. Sacrificial action (the Sanskrit word for 'action' is karman), if performed correctly, produces future benefits for the sacrificer. It is hence possible to sacrifice in order to attain a place in another world after death. The responsibility for the correct performance of the ritual lies with the brahmins, the technicians of the sacrifice, who perform the ritual on behalf of the person who desires the result. The effects of the sacrifice are, however, finite, and it has to be continually renewed. So it is not hard to infer that the sacrificially created merit (or food), which was supposed to sustain life in the other world after death, would eventually run out.

At that point one would die again, returning through several natural stages to be reborn in this world, not necessarily as a human being. The cycle is potentially endless, and from this it is a relatively short step to the conclusion that action (karma) pursued for a motive of whatever kind results in a relatively better or worse rebirth, life after life. At about the same time there arose the perception that since embodied existence in this world, or any other, was necessarily impermanent and subject to various ills, then even if some individuals were not suffering now they soon would be, and death was both inevitable and unpleasant.

To be caught in the cycle of death and rebirth was hence not viewed positively, as a form of immortality, but negatively as suffering, and the object was to find a way to escape it. This was not annihilationism, for against continual rebirth was postulated a goal of permanent liberation and bliss, free of physical imperfection and impermanence. The way to this new goal was first formulated in the late Vedic texts in terms of knowledge of the inner meaning of the sacrifice—what holds it together and enables it to work. Presently this was extended to everything that exists: the same principle informs and underlies all things, including the embodied or essential self. The term that was eventually settled on to designate this principle was 'Brahman'.

As per this line of thought, there was essentially no difference between the essence of the individual and Brahman, the principle underlying all things. Consequently, liberation from the cycle of death and rebirth was a matter of gnosis, for by knowing or realizing Brahman (one's own true nature) one would go to Brahman, a permanent, unchanging, and blissful state—a line of thought reiterated in the Gita. Motiveful sacrificial action, indeed, motiveful action of any kind could not help in this; on the contrary, because such actions were linked with a personal desire for specific results, they merely bound one more firmly to the cycle of death and rebirth.

In line with this, the Gita itself defines Yoga as 'evenness of mind', the cultivation of an attitude of non-attachment, based on knowledge of the way things really are, which leads to 'skill in actions', that is, the ability to act without desire. As per the Brahminical orthodoxy, to fulfil one's duty in one of the three higher estates it was necessary to be a sacrificer, and to be a sacrificer it was necessary to be married and take a full part in the social world, the world of desire and motiveful action. Yet as we have seen, as per the the Upanishadic analysis this was not conducive to liberation from rebirth and suffering. Only renunciation of the sacrificial and social world would enable the individual to approach that goal. Brahminical orthodoxy came to terms with this challenge by attempting to institutionalize renunciation as an alternative way of life that one could choose to follow after one had served one's apprenticeship as a Vedic student.

This later hardened into a compulsory progression from stage to stage, with renunciation taking place only after one had fulfilled one's duties as a householder and sacrificer. When the Gita was formulated, however, there was clearly still an element of choice. In the broader Indian context, neither was it a matter of a simple choice between orthodox Brahmanical renunciation and life as a ritually bound householder. Other routes, other modes of life were also available to those seeking personal liberation, chief among them the heterodox systems of Jainism and Buddhism, with their rival views of what constituted Dharma (correct behaviour in the light of the way things really are).

Indeed, it was in these heterodox systems that the doctrine of karma first became fully ethicized as a moral law that was universally applicable, regardless of birth, social status, or occupation. And whether to conform to it or not was a matter for the individual alone to decide. A cornerstone of this renunciatory morality was that deliberate injury done to other living beings was wrong and had bad karmic effects for the person doing the injury. This is an ethical stance which provides a direct challenge to Brahminical values for, as we have seen, Brahminical society is divided into four classes or estates, and members of each estate have their own inherent dutyor Dharma.

Persons born into a particular estate follow the inherent duty of that estate. By doing so they help to maintain the natural order of existence and automatically accrue good results; should they deviate from their inherent duty, however, the results will be bad for them personally and for society as a whole. One of the four estates is that of the warrior or ruler, and it is a warrior's duty to fight. This is clearly antithetical to the renunciatory ideal of nonviolence.

From one perspective, therefore, to refrain from violence will bring bad results, but from the other, to engage in it will be similarly disastrous. We are brought back to the Gita, for this is precisely Arjuna's dilemma: to conform to his inherent duty as a warrior and fight, and by doing so slaughter his enemies who are also his kinsmen, or to lay down his arms and disrupt the natural and social order. In other words, the Gita, through Arjuna, addresses the problem of the age: the problem of choice—of how to choose rightly. One of the Gita's chief projects, therefore, is to reconcile or synthesize the discordant ideologies of orthodox Brahminism and renunciation—a discord that is dramatized and personified in the person of Arjuna, who finds himself caught, like Hamlet, between two world-views and two sets of values.

The answer of this difference of opinion is put into the mouth of Krishna, Arjuna's charioteer, comrade-in-arms, teacher, and, as revealed in the Gita, God omnipotent. Krishna offers the distraught warrior what seems like a tier or nest of solutions. What they have in common is that they are all presented as justifications for fighting—hat is to say, for acting in the world, conforming to one's inherent duty, and perpetuating the socioreligious status quo. From the social perspective this is deeply conservative, although what Krishna is Offering in fact is a compromise. He tells Arjuna to act, but to do so without attachment to the results or fruits of his actions. In other words, he must act without desire, and that will ensure that, whatever its immediate physical consequences, the action will have no karmic repercussions for him as the apparent agent of the action. In this way it is possible to experience the soteriological benefits of renunciation without leaving society or abandoning one's inherent duty.

In fact, as per the Krishna, this internal renunciation is really the only way one can renounce, for the nature of material existence is such that it is impossible not to act. Yet, in rejecting the way of the renouncer, Krishna is not thereby necessarily fully endorsing mainstream ritual Brahminism, His prescription to act without attachment to the fruits of action devalues the Brahminical soteriological goal of heaven, which for the orthodox is something to be attained through motiveful ritual. In other words, sacrifice as a means to personal salvation, as opposed to cosmic and social regulation, is rejected by the Gita.

Indeed, if one is constrained to act, then the action in itself becomes soteriologically irrelevant: it is one's accompanying internal attitude that is crucial, whether one acts out of desire or out of duty. From a soteriological as opposed to a social perspective, this is subversive of orthodox values, since it implies that, regardless of gender or class, anyone at all, simply by conforming to their class duty without attachment, can hope for salvation. At another but related level of justification, Krishna tells Arjuna that what is permanent in the individual, the self, neither acts nor suffers the effects of action, hence one cannot really kill or be killed. Furthermore, unlike embodied beings, Krishna as God is not constrained to act; nevertheless, he does so to maintain the world, and those who are wise will follow his instance. Krishna thus has a positive view of the world and the prevailing social order, for he is concerned to maintain it, and indeed intervenes by descending into the world whenever that order is threatened. Again this is an orthodox Brahminical idea somewhat recast, for the general function of sacrificial ritual is to keep the world from sliding into disorder.

There is, however, another fact why Krishna should view the world positively, since by activating his lower or material nature, it is Krishna himself who has brought the universe into being, along with everything else. He is both the source and essence of all things, and the dispassionate observer of his own creation. World renunciation of the kind undertaken by 'atheistic' Jains and Buddhists, and orthodox Brahminical renouncers (with their predilection for an impersonal monism derived from speculation on the meaning of the sacrifice), seems largely incompatible with monotheism of this type.

To renounce the world would be tantamount to renouncing (part of) God. Moreover, Krishna specifically states that he has created not just the material world but the social order as well, the four estates. The solution to Arjuna's problem, therefore, is to act without attachment to the results—to fight because it is his inherent duty to fight. But in a modification of this, Krishna instructs the warrior that the results of any action whatsoever should be made over to God (i.e. Krishna). And in that way one will come to God. In terms of the ideology of sacrifice, of which again this is a reformulation, this necessitates that both the action and its results should be offered as a sacrifice to God. In a Brahminical sacrifice the results accrue to the agent, the patron of the sacrifice, but here the results accrue to God.

Whereas Brahminical ideology is anthropocentric, the Gita is theocentric, and in a further tier of the Gita's teaching it becomes clear that the only real agent, the only real actor with regard to any and every action, is God. Therefore, by making over one's actions and their karmic consequences to God, one is merely conforming to the way things really are. In the Gita God and the self, or the essence of the individual, are perhaps still near enough to being identical for God's agency not yet to be fatal to a sense of human effort and responsibility. Nevertheless, one thing that the spectacular and, for Arjuna, the overwhelming theophany makes clear is that God is the only true actor and humans merely the instruments of his action. Sub specie aeternitatis Arjuna's adversaries have already been destroyed by God: the warrior's only responsibility, therefore, is to be God's instrument in bringing about what, from this perspective, has already happened. In other words, it will come about regardless of Arjuna's intention.

Acting with desire and attachment to the results of action is hence not merely deluded but meaningless. Where does this leave the person seeking liberation from suffering, or salvation? Krishna has already said that those who make over the results of their actions to God go to Him, and indeed that all actions should be sacrificed to Him. But beyond that, one should make such offerings with devotion to God: 'whoever shares in me with single-minded devotion, they are in me and I am in them.' No devotee of Krishna's, regardless of social status or gender, is lost. (Again there is a change in soteriological perspective without the kind of threat to orthodox Brahminical supremacy that external, social renunciation offers.) By thinking on God, by sacrificing one's actions to Him in a spirit of egoless non-attachment, one can earn God's grace, and through that grace one will attain supreme peace. In effect it is possible to please God by conforming to one's class duty and doing the things one has always done; yet such a strategy can only be theologically effective if accompanied by a radical change of attitude towards those same duty-bound actions, so that they come to be regarded not as one's own but as God's. The last chapter of the Gita spells this out for us, and adds a new, more personal note—one which in various forms came to dominate the relation between God and human beings in later Hindu religion. Even many Hindu says that Gita have all the answers to the problems and worries of the people. If someone is tensed he should read Gita and he will find the answer to his question which is making him tensed and worried.

RELIGIOUS SCRIPTURES

Four Vedas

In Hindu religion there are four Vedas, the Rig Veda, Sama Veda, Yajur Veda and Atharva Veda. The Vedas are the primary texts of Hinduism. They also had a vast influence on Buddhism, Jainism, and Sikhism. Customally the text of the Vedas was coetaneous with the universe. Scholars have determined that the Rig Veda, the oldest of the four Vedas, was composed about 1500 BC., and codified about 600 BC. It is unknown when it was at last committed to writing, but this probably was at some point after 300 BC. The Vedas contain hymns, conjurations, and rituals from ancient India. They are between the most ancient religious texts still in existence. Besides their spiritual value, they also give a unique view of everyday life in India four thousand years ago. The Vedas are also the most ancient wide texts in an Indo-European language, and as such are invaluable in the study of relative linguistics. Vedas in original are a large corpus of texts originating in Ancient India. They form the oldest layer of Sanskrit literature and the oldest sacred texts of Hinduism. As per the Hindu custom, the Vedas are not of human agency, being supposed to have been directly revealed, and thus are said to be the shruti (what is heard). At all the Hindu prayers, religious functions and other auspicious occasions these Vedic mantras are recited.

The class of Vedic texts is combined around the four canonical Samhitas or Vedas proper, of which three (trayi) are related to the carrying into action of yajna (sacrifice) in historical (Iron Age) Vedic religion:

- The Rigveda, containing hymns to be recited by the hotr or reciting priest;
- The Yajurveda, containing formulas to be recited by the adhvaryu or officiating priest;
- The Samaveda, containing formulas to be sung by the udgatr or chanting priest.
- The fourth is the Atharvaveda, a collection of magical spells and healing or apotropaic charms and some speculative hymns used by the Brahmin priest.

The Hindu Philosophies and sects that arose in the Indian subcontinent have taken differing positions on the Vedas. Schools of Indian philosophy which cite the Vedas as their scriptural authority are classified as orthodox (astika). Other customs, notably Buddhism and Jainism, though they are (vedanta) likewise concerned with liberation did not regard the Vedas as divine ordinances but rather human expositions of the sphere of higher spiritual knowledge, hence not sacrosanct. These groups are referred to by customal Hindu texts as "heterodox" or "non-orthodox" (nastika) schools. In addition to Buddhism and Jainism, Sikhism also does not accept the authority of the Vedas. The Yajurveda, Samaveda and Atharvaveda are independent aggregations of mantras and hymns intended as manuals for the Adhvaryu, Udgatr and Brahman priests respectively.

The fourth Veda is Atharvaveda. Its status has occasionally been ambiguous, probably due to its use in sorcery and healing. However, it comprises very old materials in early Vedic language. Manusmrti, which often speaks of the three Vedas, calling them trayam-brahma-sanatanam, "the triple eternal Veda". The Atharvaveda like the Rigveda, is a collection of original incantations, and other materials adopting relatively little from the Rigveda. It has no direct relation to the solemn Shrauta sacrifices, except for the fact that the for the most part silent Brahman priest observes the procedures and uses Atharvaveda mantras to 'heal' it when mistakes have been made. Its recitation also produces long life, cures diseases, or effects the ruin of enemies.

All the the four Vedas comprises the metrical Mantra or Samhita and the prose Brahmana part, giving discussions and directions for the detail of the ceremonies at which the Mantras were to be used and explanations of the legends connected with the Mantras and rituals. Both these portions are termed shruti (which custom says to have been heard but not composed or written down by men). Each of the four Vedas seems to have passed to numerous Shakhas or schools, giving rise to various recensions of the text. They each have an Index or Anukramanika, the main work of this kind being the general Index or Sarvanukramanika.

Rigveda

Some historians believe that the Rig Veda must have been composed more or less in the period 1450-1350 BC., in the Greater Punjab, before the onset of the Iron Age. The Rigveda Samhita is the oldest significant existent Indian text. It is a collection of 1,028 Vedic Sanskrit hymns and 10,600 verses in all, organized into ten books (Sanskrit: mandalas). The hymns are dedicated to Rigvedic deities.

The books of Vedas were composed by poets from various priestly groups over a period of some 500 years, which Avari dates as 1400 BC. to 900 BC., if not earlier. As per the Max Müller, based on internal evidence, the Rigveda was composed roughly between 1700–1100 BC. (early Vedic period) in the Punjab (Sapta Sindhu) region of the Indian subcontinent.

There are strong lingual and cultural laws of similarity between the Rigveda and the early Iranian Avesta, deriving from the Proto-Indo-Iranian times, often associated with the Andronovo culture; the earliest horse-drawn chariots were found at Andronovo sites in the Sintashta-Petrovka cultural area near the Ural mountains and date back to 2000 BC. Till this day these Vedas are similary valuable and authentic as they were at the time of their writing.

Yajurveda

The next veda is Yajur-Veda which comprises archaic prose mantras and also in part of verses borrowed and adapted from the Rig-Veda. Its motive was practical, in that each mantra must accompany an action in sacrifice but, unlike the Sama-Veda, it was compiled to apply to all sacrificial rites, not merely the Soma offering. There are two major recensions of this Veda known as the "Black" and "White" Yajur-Veda. The origin and meaning of these designations are not very clear. The White Yajur-Veda comprises only the verses and formulas (yajus) necessary for the sacrifice, while their discussion exist in a different work, the Shatapatha Brahmana. It differs widely from the Black Yajurveda, which incorporates such discussions in the work itself, often immediately following the verses. Of the Black Yajurveda four major recensions survive (Maitrayani, Katha, Kapisthala-Katha, Taittiriya), all showing by and large the same arrangement, but differing in a number of other respects, notably in the individual discussion of the rituals but also in matters of syntax and choice of words phonology, accent and grammatical forms.

Samaveda

The next to Yajur Veda is the Sama-Veda (Sanskrit samaveda) is the Veda of melodies or Knowledge of melodies. The name of this Veda is from the Sanskrit word saman which means a melody applied to metrical hymn or song of praise. It consists of 1549 stanzas, taken entirely from the Rig-Veda. Like the Rigvedic stanzas in the Yajurveda, the Samans have been changed and adapted for use in singing. Some of the Rig-Veda verses are repeated more than once. Including repetitions, there are a total of 1875 verses numbered in the Sama-Veda recension translated by Griffith. The Kauthuma/Ranayaniya and the Jaiminiya are the two major recensions which exist even today.

To serve as a songbook for the "singer" priests who took part in the liturgy, its motive was liturgical and practical. A priest who sings hymns from the Sama-Veda during a ritual is called an udgatr, a word derived from the Sanskrit root ud-gai (to chant). A similar word in English might be cantor. The hymns were to be sung As per the certain fixed melodies; hence the name of the collection. The styles of chanting are significant to the liturgical use of the verses.

Atharvaveda

The last of these vedas is Artharva-Veda and it is the Knowledge of the atharvans and angirasa. The Artharva-Veda or Atharvangirasa is the text belonging to the Atharvan and Angirasa poets. Apte defined an atharvan as a priest who worshipped fire and Soma. However, the etymology of Atharvan is unclear, but it is related to Avesta athravan; he denies any connection with fire priests. Atharvan was an ancient term for a certain Rishi even in the Rigveda. The Atharva-Veda Samhita has 760 hymns, and about 160 of the hymns are in common with the Rig-Veda. Most of the verses are metrical, but some sections are in prose. It was compiled around 900 BC., although some of its material may go back to the time of the Rig Veda, and though not in linguistic form some parts of the Atharva-Veda are older than the Rig-Veda.

Atharva-Veda has been preserved in two recensions, the Paippalada and Œaunaka. As per the Apte it had nine schools (shakhas). The Paippalada text, which exists in a Kashmir and an Orissa version, is longer than the Saunaka one; it is only partially printed in its two versions and remains largely in its original form.

The Atharvana-Veda has less connection with sacrifice unlike the other three Vedas. Its first part comprises chiefly of spells and incantations, concerned with protection against demons and disaster, spells for the healing of diseases, for long life and for various desires or objectives in life. Gavin Flood discusses the relatively late acceptance of the Atharva-Veda as follows:

"There were originally only three priests associated with the first three SaChitas, for the Brahman as overseer of the rites does not seem in the Rig Veda and is only incorporated later, thereby showing the acceptance of the Atharva Veda, which had been somewhat distinct from the other Samhitas and identified with the lower social strata, as being of equal standing with the other texts."

The second part of the text comprises speculative and philosophical hymns. In its third section, the Atharvaveda comprises Mantras used in marriage and death rituals, as well as those for kingship, female rivals and the Vratya (in Brahmana style prose).

Upanishads

After the Vedas the Upanishads were written. The Upanishads are a continuation of the Vedic philosophy, and were written between 800 and 400 B.C. They elaborate on how the soul (Atman) can be united with the ultimate truth (Brahman) through contemplation and mediation, as well as the doctrine of Karma– the cumulative effects of person's actions. The Upanishads are looked upon as part of the Vedas and as such form part of the Hindu scriptures. They form the core spiritual thought of Vedanta. The Upanishads are known as Vedânta ("the end/culmination of the Vedas"). The Upanishads do not belong to a particular period of Sanskrit literature. The oldest, such as the Brhadaranyaka, Chandogya Upanishads and Jaiminiya Upanisadbrahmana, date to the late Brahmana period (roughly around the mid first millennium BC., that is well before the Gita was composed), while the youngest were composed in the medieval or even the early modern period.

The scholars and researchers of the Vedic books consider the four Vedas as poetic liturgy, collectively called mantra or samhita, that is as adoration and supplication to the deities of Vedic religion, in parts melded with henotheist notions, and an overarching order (Rta) that transcended even the gods. The Brâhmanas are a collection of ritual discussions, detailing the meaning of the mantras, ritual actions, priestly functions as well as that of complete rituals. They are later than the Mantras. Vedanta, is chiefly composed of Âranyakas and Upanishads. The Aranyakas ("of the wilderness") are composed in Brahmana style and deal with the more secret Vedic Shrauta rituals. The Upanishads realized monist ideas, some of which are hinted at in earlier texts, and have maintained an significant influence on the rest of Hindu and Indian philosophy.

Shankra, the philosopher and commentator is thought to have composed commentaries on eleven Upanishads. These mukhya Upanishads are in general regarded as the oldest ones, spanning the late Vedic and the Mauryan periods. By the 17th century, there were a large number of Upanishads: The Muktika Upanishad (predates 1656) lists 108 Upanishads. The number of Upanishads translated into Persian by Dara Shikoh (d. 1659) is 50. There are also counts that give a total number of Upanishads in excess of 108: Max Müller (1879) is aware of 170, and there are other counts in excess of 200 or even 300. The category of Upanishads has remained somewhat permeable, with the later additions being highly sectarian, perhaps representing "one of the strategies used by sectarian movements to legitimate their own texts through granting them the nominal status of Œruti." The Upanishads hold information on basic Hindu beliefs, including belief in a world soul, a universal spirit, Brahman, and an individual soul, Atman (Smith 10).

In Sanskrit, the word Brahman has two genders (masculine, Brahmâ, the creator-god or Brahma, neuter, the Absolute). Custom sees a form of lesser gods as aspects of this one divine ground, Brahman (altogether different from Brahma). Brahman is the ultimate, both transcendent and immanent, the absolute infinite existence, the sum total of all that ever is, was, or ever shall be. Shankara's exegesis of the Upanishads describes Brahman not as God in the monotheistic sense; he ascribes to it no limiting characteristics, not even those of being and non-being. Thus, Shankara's philosophy is named advaita, "not two." Dvaita philosophy is a distinct interpretation. Founded by Madhvacharya, this school holds that Brahman is ultimately a personal God, Vishnu, or Krishna (*brahmano hi pratisthaham*, I am the Foundation of Brahman Bhagavad Gita 14.27). Vishishtadvaita, founded by Ramanujacharya is the third major school of Vedanta, and it has some aspects in common with the other two. The sages of the Upanishad try to solve these mysteries and seek knowledge of a Reality beyond ordinary knowing.

Philosophy of Upanishads

Because of their mystical nature and intense philosophical bent that does away with all ritual and completely embraces principals of One Brahman and the inner Atman (Self), the Upanishads have a universal feel that has led to their explication in numerous manners, giving birth to the three schools of Vedanta. The Upanishads are summed up in one phrase "Tat Tvam Asi" (That thou art) by the Advaita Vedanta. However, Vedic interpretation of this phrase varies. Vedantins believe that in the end, the ultimate, formless, inconceivable Brahman is the same as our soul, Atman. We only have to realize it through discrimination. The Upanishads also contain the first and most definitive explanations of Aum (om) as the divine word, the cosmic vibration that underlies all existence and comprises multiple trinities of being and principles colligated into its One Self.

List of Upanishads

The eleven principal (mukhya) Upanishads that were commented upon by Shankara, and that are accepted as shruti by most Hindus are as follows.

1. Ishavasyopanishad
2. Kenopanishad
3. Kathopanishad
4. Mandukyopanishad
5. Mundakopanishad
6. Prashnopanishad
7. Taittiriyopanshid
8. Aiteryopanishad
9. Brihadaranyopanishad
10. Chhandogyopanishad
11. Shwetashvataropanishad.

The Jaiminiya Upanishad brahmana that comprises the Kena Upanisad is as old as the Brhadaranyaka Upanisad. All these 15 Upanishads are the oldest ones, all of them dating to before the Common Era. From linguistic evidence, the oldest among them are the Brhadâramyaka, Chândogya Upanishads and the Jaiminîya UpanisadbrâhmaGa, belonging to the late

Vedic Sanskrit period; of nearly the same age are the Aitareya, Kausîtaki and Taittirîya Upanisads, while the remaining ones date to the transition from Vedic to Classical Sanskrit.

Canon by Vedic Shakha

The older Upanishads are related with Vedic Charanas (Shakhas or schools). The Aitareya Upanishad and the Kauúîtâki Upanishad with the Shakala shakha; the Chândogya Upanishad with the Kauthuma shakha, the Kena Upanishad, and the Jaiminiya Upanishad Brahmana, with the Jaiminiya shakha; the Kamha Upanishad with the Charaka-Katha shakha, the Taittirîya and Úvetâúvatara with the Taittiriya shakha; the MaitrâyaGi Upanishad with the Maitrayani shakha; the B[hadâraGyaka and Îsa Upanishads with the Vajasaneyi Madhyandina shakha, and the Mânûkya and Munaka Upanishads with the Shaunaka shakha. Alongwith it, parts of earlier texts, of Brahmanas or passages of the Vedas themselves, are sometimes regarded as Upanishads.

THE MUKTIKA UPANISHADS

The Muktika Upanishad comprises a list of the 108 canonical Upanishads, and lists itself as the final one. The first 10 are grouped as mukhya "principal". 21 are grouped as Sâmânya Vedânta "common Vedanta", 23 as Sannyâsa, 9 as Shâkta, 13 as Vaishnava, 14 as Shaiva and 17 as Yoga Upanishads.

Shakta Upanishads

The canonical Shakta Upanishads are sectarian tracts reflecting doctrinal and interpretative differences between the two principal sects of Srividya upasana (a major Tantric form of Shaktism). As a result, a number of surviving listings of "authentic" Shakta Upanisads are highly variable as to content, inevitably reflecting the sectarian bias of their compilers:

"Past efforts to construct lists of Shakta Upanisads have left us no closer to understanding either their 'location' in

Tantric custom or their place within the Vedic corpus. At stake for the Tantric is not the authority of sruti per se, which remains largely undisputed, but rather its correct interpretation. For non-Tantrics, [it is a text's] Tantric contents that brings into question its identity as an Upanishad. At issue is the text's classification as sruti and thus its inherent authority as Veda." The list excludes several notable and widely used Shakta Upanishads, comprising the Kaula Upanishad, the Úrîvidyâ Upanishad and the Œrichakra Upanishad.

The Smritis

In contrast to the Shruti literature, which comprises revelations, the Smriti literature is a product of human intellect. It comprises the works of various individuals who base their information and interpretations upon the Vedas. Smriti means that which is based upon memory. It is the literature produced out of human intellect. It is a sacred literature that is intellectual in origin and meant for the motive of human welfare. Strictly speaking all scriptures which are not shruti or divine in origin come under this classification.

However, standard classification comprises only those works that are based upon the knowledge contained in the Vedas. These are the law books known as Dharma shastras. They deal with various aspects of human life and social organization. They instruct how an individual should conduct himself or herself in society in the light of the caste to which the individual belongs. They define the rules and roles for various groups of individuals in the society. The topics range from such issues as the status, duties and responsibilities prescribed for the four chief castes, remedies against possible transgression of the prescribed laws and also remedies for divine retribution.

From the presently remaining Dharmashastras four are regarded to be very significant: They are the works of Manu, Yagjnavalkya, Sankha, and Parasara. Of these the first one known as Manusmriti is the most popular. Known as

Manavadharma shastra, or the scripture of human laws, Manusmriti was regarded in ancient Hindu society as the ultimate guide book for human conduct and social and religious behavior. It provided guidelines for the Hindus to conduct themselves in line with their social order and religious duties.

However, it is also said that these four works were supposed to provide guidance to people during the four great ages called the Maha Yugas: the Manu-smriti for the first great age called Sat Yug, the Yagnavalkya-smriti for the second great age called Treta Yug, the Sankha-smriti for the third great epoch called Dvapar Yug and the Parasara-smriti for the present and the last great epoch called Kali Yug. In recent times the Hindu law books have drawn widespread criticism from a number of quarters due to their preferential treatment of certain castes against the others and their narrow minded and one-sided approach to such sensitive subjects as the status of women and the process of creation.

Even after everything and having quite good knowledge we cannot deny the fact that the Law Books were particularly unkind and insensitive to the lower castes and women, it is however significant to remember that the dharma shastras do not enjoy the same status as the Vedas. They need not inevitably be accepted as final authority on any issue, unless your own sense of justice agrees with them. Unlike the Vedas they are neither eternal nor fallible since they are products of human intellect and social and political circumstances. They are not derived from the Divine directly. They are developed in a particular age, As per the the demands and general awareness of that age. Due to this they are prone to be defective and controversial. Hence in the event of any doubt or dispute regarding any information contained in these scriptures, one should check whether the data is line with the tenets of the Vedas and if it is not we can safely set it aside. The Vedas do not discriminate between man and woman. Nor do they suggest any caste discrimination. A Hindu is just Hindu in all forms.

NON-RELIGIOUS SCRIPTURES

Ramayana

In a broader context Ramayana is an ancient Sanskrit epic attributed to the poet Valmiki and an significant part of the Hindu canon (smrti). The name Ramayana is a tatpurush compound of Ram and ayan "going, advancing", translating to "the travels of Ram". The Ramayana consists of 24,000 verses in seven cantos and tells the story of Raam, whose wife Sita is abducted by the demon (Rakshas) king of Lanka, Ravan. Verses are written in thirty two syllable sex meter called Anustubh. In its current form, the Valmiki Ramayan is dated from 500 BC. to 100 BC., or about co-eval to early versions of the Mahabharat. As with most customal epics, it has since gone through a long process of interpolations and redactions and thus is impossible to date it accurately. The Ramayan is part of the Itihaas. Valmiki's version is the oldest written form and the most authentic. Customally the epic belongs to the Treta Yug, one of the four eons of Hindu chronology. Ram is said to have been born in the Treta Yug to King Dasharath. The Ramayan had an significant influence on later Sanskrit poetry, primarily through its establishment of the Slok meter. But, like its epic cousin Mahabharat, the Ramayan is not just an ordinary story. It comprises the teachings of ancient Hindu sages and presents them through allegory in narrative and the interspersion of the philosophical and the devotional.

The characters of Ram, Sita, Lakshman, Bharat, Hanuman and Ravana are all fundamental to the cultural consciousness of India. One of the most significant literary works on ancient India, the Ramayan has had a profound impact on art and culture in the Indian subcontinent and Southeast Asia. The story of Raam also inspired a large amount of latter-day literature in various languages, notable among which are the works of the sixteenth century Hindi poet Tulsidas, Tamil poet Kambar of the 13th century and the 14th century Kannada poet Narahari Kavi's Torave Ramayan.

The Ramayan became popular in Southeast Asia during the 8th century and demonstrated itself in text, temple architecture and performance. This is an epic poem of courage, magic and humour, containing 18 books and 24,000 verses divided into 500 songs. Set in India, Rama and his wife Sita have been banished from their kingdom of Kosala for fourteen years, due to a plot by the mother of one of Rama's four brothers to keep Rama from the throne. Rama's brother, Laksmana, accompanies the couple. King Rawana of Ceylon spies the beautiful Sita and creates a plan to abduct her. He sends one of his minions, magically disguised as a golden deer to entice Rama and Laksmana away from Sita. Rama goes after the deer, instructing Laksmana not to leave Sita. Rama brings down the golden deer with his bow and arrow.

The golden deer returns to its original shape and with its dying breath calls out "Help, help, help" in Rama's voice. Sita, hearing Rama's voice, entreats Laksmana to go and help Rama. When he refuses, she goads him into leaving. Laksmana draws a magic circle around Sita and tells her that she must stay inside it until he and Rama return. When Sita is alone, Rawana seem s, disguised as an ailing old man, who begs Sita for help. When Sita steps out of the magic circle to aid the old man, the old man changes into Rawana and abducts Sita, telling her that Rama is dead. He rises in the air with her and flies to his Kingdom. Jatayu, King of the Birds, (also known as Garuda) spies Rawana carrying off Sita and they battle in the air. Rawana delivers a fatal wound to Jatayu who falls to the ground, where he is discovered by Rama and Laksmana. Jatayu is near death and manages to tell Rama of his failure to rescue Sita.

Both Lord Rama and Laksmana travel onward and enlist the aid of the army of wanaras, a race of huge monkeys. Sugriwa, King of the wanaras, agrees to help Rama rescue Sita in return for Rama's support of Sugriwa's attempt to regain his rightful throne in the land of Guakiskenda. When Sugriwa meets his nemesis, Subali, Rama saves Sugriwa's life with a magic arrow which kills Subali. After Sugriwa is crowned King of Guakiskenda, the white monkey general, Hanuman, is sent to Alengka (Ceylon) to scout the defences and to deliver Rama's ring to Sita, so that she would know that Rama was alive. After a narrow escape from the stomach of Wikateksi, the enormous sea monster which guarded the approaches to Alengka, Hanuman kills Wikateksi and flies to the capital of Alengka, the kingdom of the giants. Luckily, there are a number of monkeys living among the giants, which provide cover for Hanuman, who reduces his size. He looks everywhere in the city for Sita. Finally Hanuman finds Rawana's palace and the women's quarters. Hanuman meets Sita in the garden and gives her Rama's ring, which she recognizes at once, and tells her that Rama is on his way to saving her.

In order to test the power of the city, Hanuman resumes his normal size, climbs to the top of a tall building and hurls a challenge to the awestruck crowd below. He begins to destroy the buildings around him by using an uprooted palm tree as a club. He is felled by an arrow shot by the crown prince of Alengka, Hindrajit. Hanuman is shackled in chains and sentenced to die by slow fire. Hanuman appeals to Agni, the god of fire, to save him. A wall of flame springs up between Hanuman and the watching crowd. With a burst of strength, Hanuman breaks his bonds, and swinging a glowing torch picked up from the fire, goes on a rampage which ends in the burning of a large part of the city. Assuring himself that Sita's pavilion is safe, Hanuman leaps into the air and flies back to Guakiskenda. After hearing of Hanuman's exploits, Rama adopts him as his own son.

The army then heads for Alengka, which they find surrounded by a boiling sea. By hurling huge boulders into the sea, the monkey soldiers build a causeway to the island. Rawana learns of the invasion and assembles his generals. Some of the generals resent Rawana's evil rule, but heretofore have lacked the courage to oppose him. Wibishana, Rawana's brother, as spokesman, points out that it was because Rawana abducted Sita that Alengka is now beset by enemy armies. He suggests that Rawana release Sita and avoid bloodshed and loss of life and property. Angered, Rawana strikes Wibishana, who then deserts to Rama's army. Rawana is tempted to murder Sita, but is thwarted by Trijata, Wibishana's beautiful daughter, who has grown to love Sita as a sister. Rawana turns to another brother, the giant Kumbhakarna, who although rejecting of Rawana's crimes and baseness, decides to help because they are of the same blood. After a number of guerilla attacks by the monkey soldiers, the two armies ultimately face each other.

Two opponent generals, Kumbakarna and Laksmana challenge each other. Kumbhakarna is killed by Laksmana's magic arrow. Other duels take place on the battlefield. Rama spots Rawana and pursues him, shooting showers of arrows, which seem to have no effect on Rawana other than to make him back off. Rawana backs in between two unusually formed rocks which snap together and hold him in an inescapable grip. These rocks are inhabited by the souls of two of his daughters, who Rawana had murdered, and who are at last able to avenge themselves on their father. Rawana's army surrenders and Rama gives the throne of Alengka to Wibisana. Rama and Sita are joyfully united. The fourteen years of exile being over, Rama, Sita and Laksmana return to Kosala, where they are welcomed by all.

However, rumors circulate about Sita's virtue. She offers to test her virtue by fire. She enters the ring of fire and emerges unscathed, her faithfulness confirmed. When the rumors persist, she leaves the palace for the spiritual life. The Ramayana story is especially significant to Hindus because it is possible for ordinary people to identify with the characters and situations. The heroes and heroines are emulated for their positive qualities of honesty, devotion, perseverance, fidelity, and bravery. Strongly apparent in this story is the portrayal of pure evil and those who have the courage to resist and overcome that evil. So the moral of the Ramanaya is that truth always wins over the evil.

Mahabharat

Just like Ramanaya, Mahabharata is another Sanskrit epics of ancient India, the other being the Ramayana. With more than 74,000 verses, long prose passages, and about 1.8 million words in total, the Mahabharata is one of the longest epic poems in the world. Including the Harivamsa, the Mahabharata has a total length of more than 90,000 verses. It is of immense significance to the culture of India and Nepal, and is a major text of Hinduism. Its discussion of human goals (artha or wealth, kama or pleasure, Dharma or duty/harmony, and moksha or liberation) takes place in a long-standing custom, attempting to explicate the kinship of the individual to society and the world (the nature of the 'Self') and the workings of karma. The title may be translated as the great tale of the Bharata Dynasty, as per the the Mahabharata's own testimony extended from a shorter version simply called Bharata of 24,000 verses The epic is part of the Hindu itihasa, literally "that which happened", which includes the Ramayana and the Puranas.

Customally, Hindus ascribe the Mahabharata to Vyasa. Because of its immense length, its philological study has a long history of attempts to unravel its historical growth and composition layers.

Its earliest layers date back to the late Vedic period (5 BC.) and it probably reached its final form in the early Gupta period (4 AD.). Mahabharat, (or Mahabharata as it is known in English), is the longest poem in the world, made up of 220,000 lines divided into 18 sections. It was written in Sanskrit, the ancient sacred language of India and it tells the story of a great battle that occurred about 3000 years back. It was on the banks of river Saraswati that saint Ved Vyas wrote Mahabharat, approximately in 900 BC. Lord Krishna preached 'Bhagvad Gita', the gospel of duty, to Arjun at the on set of the great battle of Mahabharat. Since then, this profound philosophy of the supremacy of duty has became the foundation of Hinduism, Indian culture and thought.

Dhritarashter and Pandu were born to Bhisham's brothers. Dhritarashter was born blind and though the elder, he had to forfeit his claim to the throne due to this physical defect. Pandu became king. Of the two brothers Dhritarashter married Gandhari, whereas Pandu, the younger had two wives, Kunti and Madri. Gandhari was so devoted to her husband that she bandaged her eyes, not to enjoy anything that she could not share with her royal husband, and thus remained voluntarily blind for life. She became the mother of the Kouravs, 100 in total, whereas Kunti got three sons and Madri two. One day while hunting, Pandu accidentally killed the wife of a sage, who got enraged and cursed Pandu that if ever he had intercourse with a woman, he would die instantly.

Pandu resigned his crown to become a hermit and went to the jungle with his two wives, Kunti and Madri. But one day, Pandu couldn't resist himself and had intercourse with Madri and thus died. Madri immolated herself and walked into her husband's funeral fire leaving behind her two sons Nakul and Sahadev in custody of Kunti who already had three sons Yudhishthir, Bheem and Arjun. On Pandu's death Dhritarashter became the king and the five sons of Pandu, known as the Pandavs grew up in the guardianship of Kunti. The five Pandav princes were educated along with Kourav boys under the supervision of Bhisham and the patronage of Dhritarashter. Drone, though a Brahmin was a very skilful and efficient teacher, who taught them the art of archery and the various techniques of warfare.

Yudhishthir, the eldest of the Pandavs, was so righteous that he gained the name Dharamputr. Bheem was a giant in physical strength. Arjun was handsome and the most skilful archer. Dharamputr was the beloved of the people and being the eldest among the 105 princes, was naturally, and by his right too, the heir to the throne. Duryodhan, the eldest of the Kouravs, however was jealous of the Pandavs and tried every means to destroy them. When Yudhishthir was proclaimed king, Duryodhan could not sit quiet and watch. Dhritarashter loved all the 105 princes alike, and there was no partiality in his mind between his own sons and the nephews, the Pandavs. The great blind royal father, came under the bad influence of Duryodhan and, though directly not an evil-doer, was in sympathy with his son's letdowns and sorrows.

Duryodhan's plan to kill the Pandavs cunningly giving poison to Bheem, burning down the lac-house etc., failed miserably. Bheem was strong enough to digest the poison. The Pandavs were warned in time by their uncle Vidur and so in the darkness of the night the five brothers along with their mother escaped into the jungle from the burning lac-house. After their miraculous escape from the lac-house, they did not return to the palace. They roamed about in the guise of Brahmins with their mother. Every one including the Kouravs believed them to be dead.

While wandering in the guise, they heard of the Swayamvara of Droupadi. The qualification to marry her lay in the extraordinary skill of archery in hitting a moving target. Arjun easily won. Everybody congratulated the winner, and discovered that it was Arjun. Thus the Pandavs were found out, He took his bride to their hut and called to his mother to come outside and see what he had brought. Instead of doing so, she answered back "My dear children, whatever it be, you share it among yourselves". Therefore, Droupadi became the common wife of all the five Pandavs. Krishna, who was also present, at the marriage ceremony became a great friend of the Pandavs from then onwards.

On Bhisham's advice, the kingdom was divided into two parts. Naturally the better half was taken away by the Kouravs. Still, the others built a wonderful city in their own half and called it Indraprastha. Duryodhan watching the increasing prosperity of the Pandavs and could contain himself no longer. He openly challenged Dharamputr for a game of dice, Sakuni, deceit in human form, was the uncle of the Kouravs. He played for them. Inevitably Dharamputr lost everything - his kingdom, his brothers and also his wife. Not satisfied with this gain, Duryodhan tried to insult Droupadi in public. By Lord Krishna's grace, nothing disastrous happened. Dhritarashter, fearing that this might bring unforeseen calamities begged Droupadi to take whatever she wanted. She asked for the freedom of her husbands. It was granted. Dhritarashter due to his excessive love for the eldest son was blind to what is right and what is wrong.

So again Duryodhan invited Dharamputr for another game of dice, and the bet was that the losers would live in the forest for 13 years without any claim to the kingdom, the last year however to be spent incognito. But if in the thirteenth year, they were detected, again a round of 13 years' exile; and this would go on forever. Dharamputr lost again. During the twelve years in the forests, the Pandavs visited a number of holy places. They had a number of interesting adventures at this time. One of them led to Hanuman's friendship and grace. Arjun is called Kapidhvaja as he keeps on his flag the emblem of Hanuman. Krishna visited them now and then. Arjun, at the advice of Vyasa, practiced penance, propitiated Siva and got from Him the mighty weapon, the Pasupatastra. He propitiated also the other gods Indra, Agni, Varuna and others and got from all of them very powerful weapons.

Thus the twelve years were not wasted but spent in securing the divine weapons, which would become useful later on. In the 13th year, hiding all their weapons in the hollow of a tree in a burial ground, all the Pandavs with Droupadi went to the palace of the king of the Viratas and stayed there as servants. Duryodhan was making frantic efforts to discover them. When he heard about the strange murder of Kichaka the brother-in-law of the king, he concluded that the Pandavs must be in the Virata country. So the Kouravs attacked the Viratas, with evident motive of carrying away its cattle-wealth. Of course the Pandavs took part in the battle, but when they were recognized as Pandavs the time limit of thirteen years had already passed.

Ḋharamputr was fond of peace, and was ever against any quarrel, much less war. So he sent Krishna as a messenger to Hastinapura to claim his kingdom back from Duryodhan. But Duryodhan had by this time come to regard Indraprastha as his own. He not only refused to give their kingdom back, but refused to give even 5 houses for the five brothers to live! War had to be declared. This is the great war fought at Kurukshetra to decide the right of claim. The hundred Kouravs, Bhisham, Drone, Asvathama, etc., were on one side and the Pandavs, Krishna, Drupada, etc., were on the other. Krishna did not in realfight. He was the charioteer of Arjun and hence He is called Parthasarathy. Krishna was very impartial. He gave his army to the Kouravs and himself offered to serve the Pandavs.

The Kourav and the Pandav armies arrayed themselves for the war. The Kouravs planned their attacks under the supervision of Bhisham, and under Bheem's management the Pandava army marched into formation. This is the point at which Arjun has second thoughts about fighting in the battle. Krishna gives Arjun good advise that brings back his war-spirit. This advice is known as: The Bhagvad-Gita. All the Kourav princes died in this battle, and Yudhishthir became king. He continued to reign until he felt that he had completed his life's work. Then he renounced the throne and set out for heaven with the other Pandavs and their wife, Droupadi. With them also went a dog which represented Dharma, the god of duty and moral law. After more adventures, the Pandavs were ultimately united in heaven. The whole story, which forms the chief theme of the Mahabharat, makes up only about a quarter of the poem. The Mahabharat comprises a number of other popular stories, including the tales of Nala and Damayanti, Savitri and Satyawan, Rama, and Shakuntala. The battle of Kurukshetra offers an opportunity to discuss military strategy, there is also a mention of a board game Chaturanga, from which the modern day Chess originated. But the underlying theme of the Mahabharat concerns moral duty and right conduct.

The long and complex dispute that divides the royal family of Bharat affords an opportunity to explain the duties and conduct expected of a king. It also shows the ideals of behaviour for subjects, soldiers, religious hermits, and people suffering misfortune. Sage Ved Vyasa is customally regarded as the author of the Mahabharat, but he is more likely to have been its compiler. The epic seems to be a collection of writings by several authors who lived at various times. The oldest parts are probably about 3,000 years old, while others can be traced to as late as AD 500.

The significance of Krishna as the chief god of this epic developed in Hindu thought between 200 BC and AD 200. As a result, the Mahabharat can be used to trace the spread and development of Vaishnavite thought in Hinduism. The god Vishnu became a very personal deity for his worshippers through his seem ance as Krishna, the adviser and friend of Prince Arjun in the Mahabharat. About 1,300 greatly varying manuscripts of the Mahabharat survive today. All of them show the poem in its later form because the earliest of them goes back only to the 1400's. The most famous addition to the Mahabharat is the Bhagvad-Gita. It occurs in the sixth book and is now the most widely recognized of Hinduism's sacred texts.

The Bhagavad Gita tells how Arjun, the third of the Pandav princes, has misgivings about whether he should be fighting his cousins, the Kouravs. Krishna, speaking with the authority of the god Vishnu, persuades him that his action is just, and then Arjun's military skill becomes a deciding factor in the ensuing Pandav victory. The teachings of the Bhagavad-Gita are fundamental to Hinduism. As already mentioned Gita is most sacred text of the Hindus and it comprises such verses and explanations which can bring a man out of his everyday worries.

The Narrative Context

Mahabharata is the story of the struggle for the kingdom of Bharata (roughly northern India), the world of the original audience for the poem. (Modern India is known by the same name.) The contending parties are cousins, the children of two royal brothers.

The elder of the two brothers, Dhritarashtra, has been born blind, so the younger one, Pandu, rules in his stead. Pandu dies, leaving five young sons – Yudhishthira, Bhima, and Arjuna from one wife, and Nakula and Sahadeva from another. Collectively, they are known as the Pandavas, 'descendants of Pandu'. Dhritarashtra, who in spite of his blindness has now become king, is the father of a hundred sons, known as the Kauravas, 'descendants of Kuru'. The eldest of the Kauravas is Duryodhana.

A stewing rivalry between the cousins, the Pandavas and Kauravas, over the legitimate succession endangers to boil into war.

In an attempt to avert this the blind Dhritarashtra divides the kingdom in two, one part to be ruled by Duryodhana, the other by Yudishthira. But this only postpones aggressions, and finally Duryodhana challenges the virtuous Yudhishthira to a game of dice.

Yudhishthira loses everything – not just his kingdom, but his brothers, himself, and their joint wife, Draupadi. The Kauravas savagely humiliate Draupadi, ensuring that the war, when it comes, will be a vengeful one.

In what is literally a last throw of the dice, Yudhishthira gambles again. This time the losers are to be exiled to the forest for twelve years and to spend a thirteenth year incognito. Only if these circumstances are met in full can they then lawfully return and reclaim their kingdom.

Yudhishthira loses again and the Pandavas go into exile. After a number of adventures and, in the Mahabharata as we have it, much religious teaching, the Pandavas return after thirteen years to claim what is theirs. Duryodhana, however, refuses to give it up. War can now no longer be avoided. Both Pandavs and Kouravs then assemble their allies.

Among them is Krishna, the king of Dvaraka, who has links with both parties. He hence gives his armies to fight on the Kaurava side, and goes himself to assist the Pandavas as Arjuna's charioteer. And this is where the Bhagavad Gita begins. The old blind king, Dhritarashtra, has asked his bard, Sanjaya, to report the events of the war to him, and the Gita constitutes part of his narrative.

The two armies are facing each other. Arjuna, the great warrior, the great archer, is in his chariot, driven by Krishna, and the battle is about to start. Suddenly Arjuna is overcome by apparently disabling moral scruples: how can it be right to kill his kinsmen? He avows his intention not to fight and sinks disconsolately into his chariot. This is totally unexpected and all the more shocking because of Arjuna's heroic martial status.

Real time, as is common enough in the epic, then comes to a halt while Krishna addresses the reluctant warrior. If the way Arjuna is portrayed in the Gita is unexpected in the context of the rest of the Mahabharata, the treatment of Krishna is astonishing.

More than an ally or even a teacher (although he is both those), he reveals himself as the universal God. Certainly he has previously demonstrated some miraculous powers, but this revelation is of a various order.

Indeed, so overwhelming is it that Arjuna finds it not only too much to bear but also apparently too much to remember. What does not fade, nevertheless, is the warrior's renewed determination to fight, inspired by what Krishna has shown and taught him. The Bhagavad Gita finishes here, at the moment in the epic when total war begins. After eighteen days of carnage, the Pandavas emerge victorious and Yudhishthira becomes king.

Later, in his equivocal hero mould, Krishna is killed in a hunting accident in the forest. The Pandava brothers hand on their hard-won kingdom and set off for the Himalayas in search of the king of the gods' heaven, but only Yudhishthira, the embodiment of Dharma, reaches it alive. The others, including Arjuna, the troubled warrior of the Gita, perish on the way.

The Puranas

According to the Hindu custom Puranas, part of Hindu Smriti, are religious scriptures that confer devotion and mythology. They are the richest collection of customal stories and teachings based on the spiritual philosophy of the Vedas and the Upanishads. These ancient books teach Hinduism in an easy and interesting way and provide information of all kinds. Purana means 'old' and were compiled by Sage Vyasa.

As per the Amara Simha, an ancient Sanskrit lexicographer, Purana must have five distinguishing topics - 1) Creation of Universe, 2) Its destruction and renovation, 3) The genealogy of gods and patriarchs, 4) The reigns of Manus and 5)The history of the solar and lunar races of kings.

Basically focusing on Vishnu, Shiva, Lord Brahma and Shakti there are eighteen major Puranas and some minor ones, known as Upa Puranas.

A large portion of each Purana deals with the incarnation of Lord Vishnu and his glorification. Apart from this, stories of Gods and Goddesses, hymns, an outline of ancient history, cosmology, rules of life and rituals, holy places, and instructions on spiritual knowledge are the significant contents of the Puranas. Out of the 18 puranas, six are Sattvic Puranas and glorify Vishnu; six are Rajasic and glorify Lord Brahma; six are Tamasic and they glorify Lord Shiva. Vishnu Purana, Naradiya Purana, Padma Purana, Garuda Purana, Varaha Purana, Bhagavata Purana are Sattvic Puranas. Brahmanda Purana, Brahmavaivarta Purana, Markandeya Purana, Bhavishya Purana, Vamana Purana, Brahma Purana are Rajasic Puranas. Matsya Purana, Kurma Purana, Linga Purana, Shiva Purana, Skanda Purana and Agni Purana are Tamasic Puranas. Puranas chiefly inculcate the teachings of Vedas and Upanishads in a simple manner through concrete instances, myths, stories, legends, lives of saints, kings and great men, allegories and chronicles of great historical events. They mainly tell about the stories of Hindu Gods and Goddesses.

Brahma Purana

The Brahma Purana contains two parts- Purva Bhaag and Uttar Bhaag. Purva Bhaag comprises tales of creation, description of Lord Rama and Lord Krishna. Uttar Bhaag comprises a detailed description of Purshottam Tirtha prominent among all the holy places.

Padma Purana

The Padma Purana contains five parts. In the first part, sage Pulastya explains the essence of religion to Bheeshma. The second part comprises a description of the earth. Third part comprises tales of creation as well as geographical description of India. Fourth part describes the life of Lord Rama. In the fifth part, essential knowledge of religion has been discussed in dialogue style between Lord Shiva and Parvati.

Vishnu Purana

The Vishnu Purana also comprises five parts. First part narrates about the creation of the universe, Pralay and churning of the sea. Second part comprises geographical description of earth divided into seven islands. Third part describes about the origin of Buddhism.

Fourth part comprises a description about the populating of the earth from the beginning. Fifth part is entirely devoted to the life and plays of Lord Krishna and his acts in Vrindavan.

Skanda Purana

The Skanda Purana is the largest Purana. It is mainly devoted to Kartikeya (Skanda), the son of Lord Shiva and Parvati. Besides, it comprises a lot of tales related to Lord Shiv and a number of holy places of pilgrimage devoted conspicuously to Shiv.

Shiv Mahapurana

The Shiv Mahapurana is also a huge compilation of tales devoted primarily to the life and plays of Lord Shiva. It is divided into seven Samhitas, which together contain more than twenty-four thousand stanzas.

Vamana Purana

The Vamana Purana is completely devoted to Vaman avtaar (incarnation) of Lord Vishnu narrated in dialogue style between the sage Pulastya and Narad.

Markandeya Purana

The Markandeya Purana commences with a question put forth by sage Jobjectiveini. In reply to this question, sage Markandeya narrates what constitutes the subject matter of this Purana.

Varaha Purana

The Varha Purana comprises the tale of rescue of the earth by 'Varaha' avtaar (boar incarnation) of Lord Vishnu.

Brahma Vaivat Purana

The Brahma Vaivat Purana comprises four parts. First part comprises the tale of creation. Second part comprises tales related to goddesses.

Third part comprises tales related to Lord Ganesh. In the fourth part, tales related to the life and plays of Lord Krishna have been given.

Agni Purana

The Agni Purana is devoted to Agni. It is presented in preaching style by Agni to sage Vashishta. It comprises the description of various incarnations of God, Lord Rama and Krishna as well as of the earth and stars.

Bhavishya Purana

The Bhavishya Purana comprises five Parvas (parts). The first part comprises description of creation. Second, third and fourth parts contain detailed description of Lord Shiva, Lord Vishnu and Surya respectively. In the fifth part, description of heaven has been given.

Kurma Purana

It is said that Lord Himself has narrated this Purana in Kurma (tortoise) incarnation to Narad.

Narad narrated it to Sutaji who in his term narrated it to an assembly of great sages.

Matsya Purana

The Tales of Lord's fish incarnation and preservation of Manu and the seeds of all life during Pralay by Matsya avtaar is the chief theme of this Purana.

Garuda Purana

In Garuda Purana, Lord Vishnu preaches his vehicle, Garuda about the subtleties of religion and life. Besides, trivial tales related to religion and moral, this Purana also contains description of diamond like jewels and the ways to identify best kind of jewels.

Brahmaand Purana

Brahamaand Puarana is the last of the eighteen Puranas. Presently it is available in various pieces and no connection seems to exist between them. Once, it had contained Aadhyatma Ramayana.

Shrimad Bhagwat Purana

Due to of its beautiful presentation style, Shrimad Bhagwat Purana has a high rank in Sanskrit literature.

It comprises tales related to various incarnations of Lord Vishnu and mainly deals with the life and plays of Lord Krishna.

Linga Purana

Preaching about the glory of Lord Shiva and Linga Puja is the chief objective of this Purana. In two parts, this Purana comprises tales related to the creation of the universe, origin of Linga, and of all the Vedas, Brahma, Vishnu etc. from this Linga.

Narad Purana

It is a Vaishnav Purana presented in a style of dialogue between Narad and Sanat kumar. This Purana comprises detailed description of major places of pilgrimage. In this way the whole Hindu religion its rules and laws, duties and ways of worshipping, do's and don't's all are well written in the books, its not just the word of mouth and told orally.

CHAPTER

3

The Yoga of the Despondency of Arjuna

The great Mahabharata war between the Pandavas and the Kauravas took place on the holy plain of Kurukshetra. After the failure of Lord Krishna's peace mission, when He himself went to Hastinapura as the emissary of the Pandavas, there was no other alternative for the Pandavas but to engage in war for their rightful share of the kingdom.

All the famous warriors from both sides had assembled on the battlefield. Tents and wagons, weapons and machines, chariots and animals covered the vast plain.

Lord Krishna arrived on the scene in a magnificent chariot yoked by white horses. He was to act as the charioteer of Arjuna, one of the Pandava princes.

The din of hundreds of conches, blaring forth suddenly, announced the commencement of the battle. Arjuna blew his conch "Devadatta", while Bhima, his brother, sounded the "Paundra". All the other great warriors blew their respective conches.

As the two armies were arrayed, ready for battle, Arjuna requested Krishna to place his chariot between them so that he might survey his opponents. He was bewildered by the scene before him, for he beheld on both sides, fathers and grandfathers, teachers and uncles, fathers-in-law, grandsons, relatives and comrades.

Confusion reigned in Arjuna's mind. Should he participate in this terrible carnage? Was it proper to destroy one's relatives for the sake of a kingdom and some pleasures? Would it not be much better for him to surrender everything in favour of his enemies and retire in peace?

As these thoughts rushed into his mind, a feeling of despondency overtook Arjuna. He had no enthusiasm to engage in this battle. Letting his bow slip from his hands, Arjuna could do nothing but turn to Lord Krishna for guidance and enlightenment.

Dhritaraashtra Uvaacha:

Dharmakshetre kurukshetre samavetaa yuyutsavah;

Maamakaah paandavaashchaiva kim akurvata sanjaya.

Dhritarashtra said:

1. What did the sons of Pandu and also my people do when they had assembled together, eager for battle on the holy plain of Kurukshetra, O Sanjaya?

Sanjaya Uvaacha:

Drishtwaa tu paandavaaneekam vyudham duryodhanastadaa;

Aachaaryam upasamgamya raajaa vachanam abraveet.

Sanjaya said:

2. Having seen the army of the Pandavas drawn up in battle array, King Duryodhana then approached his teacher (Drona) and spoke these words:

Pashyaitaam paanduputraanaam aachaarya mahateem chamoom;

Vyoodhaam drupadaputrena tava shishyena dheemataa.

3. "Behold, O teacher! this mighty army of the sons of Pandu, arrayed by the son of Drupada, thy wise disciple!

Atra shooraa maheshwaasaa bheemaarjunasamaa yudhi;

Yuyudhaano viraatashcha drupadashcha mahaarathah.

4. "Here are heroes, mighty archers, equal in battle to Bhima and Arjuna, Yuyudhana, Virata and Drupada, of the great car (mighty warriors),

Dhrishtaketush chekitaanah kaashiraajashcha veeryavaan;

Purujit kuntibhojashcha shaibyashcha narapungavah.

5. "Drishtaketu, Chekitana and the valiant king of Kasi, Purujit, and Kuntibhoja and Saibya, the best of men,

Yudhaamanyushcha vikraanta uttamaujaashcha veeryavaan;

Saubhadro draupadeyaashcha sarva eva mahaarathaah.

6. "The strong Yudhamanyu and the brave Uttamaujas, the son of Subhadra (Abhimanyu, the son of Arjuna), and the sons of Draupadi, all of great chariots (great heroes).

Asmaakam tu vishishtaa ye taan nibodha dwijottama;

Naayakaah mama sainyasya samjnaartham taan braveemi te.

7. "Know also, O best among the twice-born, the names of those who are the most distinguished amongst ourselves, the leaders of my army! These I name to thee for thy information.

Bhavaan bheeshmashcha karnashcha kripashcha samitinjayah;

Ashwatthaamaa vikarnashcha saumadattis tathaiva cha.

8. "Thyself and Bhishma, and Karna and Kripa, the victorious in war; Asvatthama, Vikarna, and Jayadratha, the son of Somadatta.

Anye cha bahavah shooraa madarthe tyaktajeevitaah;

Naanaashastrapraharanaah sarve yuddhavishaaradaah.

9. "And also many other heroes who have given up their lives for my sake, armed with various weapons and missiles, all well skilled in battle.

Ȧparyaaptam tad asmaakam balam bheeshmaabhirakshitam;

Paryaaptam twidam eteshaam balam bheemaabhirakshitam.

10. "This army of ours marshalled by Bhishma is insufficient, whereas their army, marshalled by Bhima, is sufficient.

Ayaneshu cha sarveshu yathaabhaagam avasthitaah;

Bheeshmam evaabhirakshantu bhavantah sarva eva hi.

11. "Therefore, do ye all, stationed in your respective positions in the several divisions of the army, protect Bhishma alone".

Tasya sanjanayan harsham kuruvriddhah pitaamahah;

Simhanaadam vinadyocchaih shankham dadhmau prataapavaan.

12. His glorious grandsire (Bhishma), the eldest of the Kauravas, in order to cheer Duryodhana, now roared like a lion and blew his conch.

Tatah shankhaashcha bheryashcha panavaanakagomukhaah;

Sahasaivaabhyahanyanta sa shabdastumulo'bhavat.

13. Then (following Bhishma), conches and kettle-drums, tabors, drums and cow-horns blared forth quite suddenly (from the side of the Kauravas); and the sound was tremendous.

Tatah shvetair hayair yukte mahati syandane sthitau;

Maadhavah paandavashchaiva divyau shankhau pradadhmatuh.

14. Then also, Madhava (Krishna), and the son of Pandu (Arjuna), seated in their magnificent chariot yoked with white horses, blew their divine conches.

Paanchajanyam hrisheekesho devadattam dhananjayah;

Paundram dadhmau mahaashankham bheemakarmaa vrikodarah.

15. Hrishikesa blew the "Panchajanya" and Arjuna blew the "Devadatta", and Bhima, the doer of terrible deeds, blew the great conch, "Paundra".

Anantavijayam raajaa kunteeputro yudhishthirah;

Nakulah sahadevashcha sughoshamanipushpakau.

16. Yudhisthira, the son of Kunti, blew the "Anantavijaya"; and Sahadeva and Nakula blew the "Manipushpaka" and "Sughosha" conches.

Kaashyashcha parameshwaasah shikhandee cha mahaarathah;

Dhrishtadyumno viraatashcha saatyakishchaaparaajitah.

17. The king of Kasi, an excellent archer, Sikhandi, the mighty car-warrior, Dhristadyumna and Virata and Satyaki, the unconquered,

Drupado draupadeyaashcha sarvashah prithiveepate;

Saubhadrashcha mahaabaahuh shankhaan dadhmuh prithak prithak.

18. Drupada and the sons of Draupadi, O Lord of the Earth, and the son of Subhadra, the mighty-armed, all blew their respective conches!

Sa ghosho dhaartaraashtraanaam hridayaani vyadaarayat;

Nabhashcha prithiveem chaiva tumulo vyanunaadayan.

19. The tumultuous sound rent the hearts of Dhritarashtra's party, making both heaven and earth resound.

Atha vyavasthitaan drishtwaa dhaartaraashtraan kapidhwajah;

Pravritte shastrasampaate dhanurudyamya paandavah.

Hrisheekesham tadaa vaakyamidamaaha maheepate;

20. Then, seeing all the people of Dhritarashtra's party standing arrayed and the discharge of weapons about to begin, Arjuna, the son of Pandu, whose ensign was that of a monkey, took up his bow and said the following to Krishna, O Lord of the Earth!

Arjuna Uvaacha:

Senayor ubhayormadhye ratham sthaapaya me'chyuta.

Yaavad etaan nireekshe'ham yoddhukaamaan avasthitaan;

Kair mayaa saha yoddhavyam asmin ranasamudyame.

Arjuna said:

21-22. In the middle of the two armies, place my chariot, O Krishna, so that I may behold those who stand here, desirous to fight, and know with whom I must fight when the battle begins.

Yotsyamaanaan avekshe'ham ya ete'tra samaagataah;

Dhaartaraashtrasya durbuddher yuddhe priyachikeershavah.

23. For I desire to observe those who are assembled here to fight, wishing to please in battle Duryodhana, the evil-minded. Sanjaya Uvaacha:

Evamukto hrisheekesho gudaakeshena bhaarata;

Senayor ubhayormadhye sthaapayitwaa rathottamam.

Sanjaya said:

24. Being thus addressed by Arjuna, Lord Krishna, having stationed that best of chariots, O Dhritarashtra, in the midst of the two armies,

Bheeshmadronapramukhatah sarveshaam cha maheekshitaam;

Uvaacha paartha pashyaitaan samavetaan kuroon iti.

25. In front of Bhishma and Drona and all the rulers of the earth, said: "O Arjuna, behold now all these Kurus gathered together!"

Tatraapashyat sthitaan paarthah pitrin atha pitaamahaan;

Aachaaryaan maatulaan bhraatrun putraan pautraan sakheemstathaa.

26. Then Arjuna beheld there stationed, grandfathers and fathers, teachers, maternal uncles, brothers, sons, grandsons and friends, too.

Shvashuraan suhridashchaiva senayorubhayorapi;

Taan sameekshya sa kaunteyah sarvaan bandhoon avasthitaan.

Kripayaa parayaa'vishto visheedannidam abraveet;

27. (He saw) fathers-in-law and friends also in both armies. The son of Kunti – Arjuna – seeing all these kinsmen standing arrayed, spoke thus sorrowfully, filled with deep pity.

Arjuna Uvaacha:

Drishtwemam swajanam krishna yuyutsum samupasthitam.

Arjuna said:

28. Seeing these, my kinsmen, O Krishna, arrayed, eager to fight,

Seedanti mama gaatraani mukham cha parishushyati;

Vepathushcha shareere me romaharshashcha jaayate.

29. My limbs fail and my mouth is parched up, my body quivers and my hairs stand on end!

Gaandeevam sramsate hastaat twak chaiva paridahyate;

Na cha shaknomyavasthaatum bhramateeva cha me manah.

30. The (bow) "Gandiva" slips from my hand and my skin burns all over; I am unable even to stand, my mind is reeling, as it were.

Nimittaani cha pashyaami vipareetaani keshava;

Na cha shreyo'nupashyaami hatwaa swajanam aahave.

31. And I see adverse omens, O Kesava! I do not see any good in killing my kinsmen in battle.

Na kaangkshe vijayam krishna na cha raajyam sukhaani cha;

Kim no raajyena govinda kim bhogair jeevitena vaa.

32. For I desire neither victory, O Krishna, nor pleasures nor kingdoms! Of what avail is a dominion to us, O Krishna, or pleasures or even life?

Yeshaam arthe kaangkshitam no raajyam bhogaah sukhaani cha;

Ta ime'vasthitaa yuddhe praanaamstyaktwaa dhanaani cha.

33. Those for whose sake we desire kingdoms, enjoyments and pleasures, stand here in battle, having renounced life and wealth.

Aachaaryaah pitarah putraastathaiva cha pitaamahaah;

Maatulaah shwashuraah pautraah shyaalaah sambandhinas tathaa.

34. Teachers, fathers, sons and also grandfathers, grandsons, fathers-in-law, maternal uncles, brothers-in-law and relatives, —

Etaan na hantum icchaami ghnato'pi madhusoodana;

Api trailokya raajyasya hetoh kim nu maheekrite.

35. These I do not wish to kill, though they kill me,OKrishna, even for the sake of dominion over the three worlds, leave alone killing them for the sake of the earth!

Nihatya dhaartaraashtraan nah kaa preetih syaaj janaardana;

Paapam evaashrayed asmaan hatwaitaan aatataayinah.

36. By killing these sons of Dhritarashtra, what pleasure can be ours, O Janardana? Only sin will accrue by killing these felons.

Tasmaan naarhaa vayam hantum dhaartaraashtraan swabaandhavaan;

Swajanam hi katham hatwaa sukhinah syaama maadhava.

37. Therefore, we should not kill the sons of Dhritarashtra, our relatives; for, how can we be happy by killing our own people, O Madhava (Krishna)?

Yadyapyete na pashyanti lobhopahatachetasah;

Kulakshayakritam dosham mitradrohe cha paatakam.

38. Though they, with intelligence overpowered by greed, see no evil in the destruction of families, and no sin in hostility to friends,

Katham na jneyam asmaabhih paapaad asmaan nivartitum;

Kulakshayakritam dosham prapashyadbhir janaardana.

39. Why should not we, who clearly see evil in the destruction of a family, learn to turn away from this sin, O Janardana (Krishna)?

COMMENT: Ignorance of the law is no excuse and wanton sinful conduct is a crime unworthy of knowledgeable people.

Kulakshaye pranashyanti kuladharmaah sanaatanaah;

Dharme nashte kulam kritsnam adharmo'bhibhavatyuta.

40. In the destruction of a family, the immemorial religious rites of that family perish; on the destruction of spirituality, impiety overcomes the whole family.

COMMENT: Dharma pertains to the duties and ceremonies practised by the family in accordance with scriptural injunctions.

Adharmaabhibhavaat krishna pradushyanti kulastriyah;

Streeshu dushtaasu vaarshneya jaayate varnasankarah.

41. By prevalence of impiety, O Krishna, the women of the family become corrupt and, women becoming corrupted, O Varsneya (descendant of Vrishni), there arises intermingling of castes!

Sankaro narakaayaiva kulaghnaanaam kulasya cha;

Patanti pitaro hyeshaam luptapindodakakriyaah.

42. Confusion of castes leads to hell the slayers of the family, for their forefathers fall, deprived of the offerings of rice-ball and water.

Doshair etaih kulaghnaanaam varnasankarakaarakaih;

Utsaadyante jaatidharmaah kuladharmaashcha shaashwataah.

43. By these evil deeds of the destroyers of the family, which cause confusion of castes, the eternal religious rites of the caste and the family are destroyed.

Utsannakuladharmaanaam manushyaanaam janaardana;

Narake'niyatam vaaso bhavateetyanushushruma.

44. We have heard, O Janardana, that inevitable is the dwelling for an unknown period in hell for those men in whose families the religious practices have been destroyed!

Aho bata mahat paapam kartum vyavasitaa vayam;

Yadraajya sukhalobhena hantum swajanam udyataah.

45. Alas! We are involved in a great sin in that we are prepared to kill our kinsmen through greed for the pleasures of a kingdom.

Yadi maam aprateekaaram ashastram shastrapaanayah;

Dhaartaraashtraa rane hanyus tanme kshemataram bhavet.

46. If the sons of Dhritarashtra, with weapons in hand, should slay me in battle, unresisting and unarmed, that would be better for me.

Sanjaya Uvaacha:

Evamuktwaa'rjunah sankhye rathopastha upaavishat;

Visrijya sasharam chaapam shokasamvignamaanasah.

Sanjaya said:

47. Having thus spoken in the midst of the battlefield, Arjuna, casting away his bow and arrow, sat down on the seat of the chariot with his mind overwhelmed with sorrow.

Hari Om Tat Sat

Iti Srimad Bhagavadgeetaasoopanishatsu Brahmavidyaayaam

Yogashaastre Sri Krishnaarjunasamvaade

Arjunavishaadayogo Naama Prathamo'dhyaayah.

Thus in the Upanishads of the glorious Bhagavad Gita, the science of the Eternal, the scripture of Yoga, the dialogue between Sri Krishna and Arjuna, ends the first discourse entitled: "The Yoga Of the Despondency of Arjuna"

THE YOGA OF ACTION

In order to remove Moha or attachment, which was the sole cause of Arjuna's delusion, Sri Krishna taught him the imperishable nature of the Atman, the realisation of which would grant him the freedom of the Eternal.Adoubt therefore arises in Arjuna's mind as to the necessity of engaging in action even after one has attained this state.

Sri Krishna clears this doubt by telling him that although one has realised oneness with the Eternal, one has to perform action through the force of Prakriti or Nature. He emphasises that perfection is attained not by ceasing to engage in action but by doing all actions as a divine offering, imbued with a spirit of non-attachment and sacrifice.

The man of God-vision, Sri Krishna explains to Arjuna, need not engage in action, as he has attained everything that has to be attained. He can be ever absorbed in the calm and immutable Self. But to perform action for the good of the world and for the education of the masses is no doubt superior. Therefore, action is necessary not only for one who has attained perfection but also for one who is striving for perfection. Sri Krishna quotes the example of Janaka, the great sage-king of India, who continued to rule his kingdom even after attaining God-realisation.

Prakriti or Nature is made up of the three qualities – Rajas, Tamas and Sattwa. The Atman is beyond these three qualities and their functions. Only when knowledge of this fact dawns in man does he attain perfection.

The Lord tells Arjuna that each one should do his duty according to his nature, and that doing duty that is suited to one's nature in the right spirit of detachment will lead to perfection.

Arjuna raises the question as to why man commits such actions that cloud his mind and drag him downwards, by force, as it were. Sri Krishna answers that it is desire that impels man to lose his discrimination and understanding, and thus commit wrong actions. Desire is the root cause of all evil actions. If desire is removed, then the divine power manifests in its full glory and one enjoys peace, bliss, light and freedom.

Arjuna Uvaacha:

Jyaayasee chet karmanaste mataa buddhir janaardana;

Tat kim karmani ghore maam niyojayasi keshava.

Arjuna said:

1. If it be thought by Thee that knowledge is superior to action, O Krishna, why then, O Kesava, dost Thou ask me to engage in this terrible action?

Vyaamishreneva vaakyena buddhim mohayaseeva me;

Tadekam vada nishchitya yena shreyo'ham aapnuyaam.

2. With these apparently perplexing words Thou confusest, as it were, my understanding; therefore, tell me that one way for certain by which I may attain bliss.

Sri Bhagavaan Uvaacha:

Loke'smin dwividhaa nishthaa puraa proktaa mayaanagha;

Jnaanayogena saankhyaanaam karmayogena yoginaam.

The Blessed Lord said:

3. In this world there is a twofold path, as I said before, O sinless one,—the path of knowledge of the Sankhyas and the path of action of the Yogis!

Na karmanaam anaarambhaan naishkarmyam purusho'shnute;

Na cha sannyasanaad eva siddhim samadhigacchati.

4. Not by the non-performance of actions does man reach actionlessness, nor by mere renunciation does he attain to perfection.

COMMENT: Even if a man abandons action, his mind may be active. One cannot reach perfection or freedom from action or knowledge of the Self, merely by renouncing action. He must possess knowledge of the Self.

Na hi kashchit kshanamapi jaatu tishthatyakarmakrit;

Kaaryate hyavashah karma sarvah prakritijair gunaih.

5. Verily none can ever remain for even a moment without performing action; for, everyone is made to act helplessly indeed by the qualities born of Nature.

COMMENT: The ignorant man is driven to action helplessly by the actions of the Gunas—Rajas, Tamas and Sattwa.

Karmendriyaani samyamya ya aaste manasaa smaran;

Indriyaarthaan vimoodhaatmaa mithyaachaarah sa uchyate.

6. He who, restraining the organs of action, sits thinking of the sense-objects in mind, he, of deluded understanding, is called a hypocrite.

Yastwindriyaani manasaa niyamyaarabhate'rjuna;

Karmendriyaih karmayogam asaktah sa vishishyate.

7. But whosoever, controlling the senses by the mind, O Arjuna, engages himself in Karma Yoga with the organs of action, without attachment, he excels!

Niyatam kuru karma twam karma jyaayo hyakarmanah;

Shareerayaatraapi cha te na prasiddhyed akarmanah.

8. Do thou perform thy bounden duty, for action is superior to inaction and even the maintenance of the body would not be possible for thee by inaction.

Yajnaarthaat karmano'nyatra loko'yam karmabandhanah;

Tadartham karma kaunteya muktasangah samaachara.

9. The world is bound by actions other than those performed for the sake of sacrifice; do thou, therefore, O son of Kunti, perform action for that sake (for sacrifice) alone, free from attachment!

COMMENT: If anyone does actions for the sake of the Lord, he is not bound. His heart is purified by performing actions for the sake of the Lord. Where this spirit of unselfishness does not govern the action, such actions bind one to worldliness, however good or glorious they may be.

Sahayajnaah prajaah srishtwaa purovaacha prajaapatih;

Anena prasavishyadhwam esha vo'stvishtakaamadhuk.

10. The Creator, having in the beginning of creation created mankind together with sacrifice, said: "By this shall ye propagate; let this be the milch cow of your desires (the cow which yields the desired objects)".

Devaan bhaavayataanena te devaa bhaavayantu vah;

Parasparam bhaavayantah shreyah param avaapsyatha.

11. With this do ye nourish the gods, and may the gods

nourish you; thus nourishing one another, ye shall attain to the highest good.

Ishtaan bhogaan hi vo devaa daasyante yajnabhaavitaah;

Tair dattaan apradaayaibhyo yo bhungkte stena eva sah.

12. The gods, nourished by the sacrifice, will give you the desired objects. So, he who enjoys the objects given by the gods without offering (in return) to them, is verily a thief.

Yajnashishtaashinah santo muchyante sarva kilbishaih;

Bhunjate te twagham paapaa ye pachantyaatma kaaranaat.

13. The righteous, who eat of the remnants of the sacrifice, are freed from all sins; but those sinful ones who cook food (only) for their own sake, verily eat sin.

Annaad bhavanti bhootaani parjanyaad anna sambhavah;

Yajnaad bhavati parjanyo yajnah karma samudbhavah.

14. From food come forth beings, and from rain food is produced; from sacrifice arises rain, and sacrifice is born of action.

Karma brahmodbhavam viddhi brahmaakshara samudbhavam;

Tasmaat sarvagatam brahma nityam yajne pratishthitam.

15. Know thou that action comes from Brahma, and Brahma proceeds from the Imperishable. Therefore, the all-pervading (Brahma) ever rests in sacrifice.

Evam pravartitam chakram naanuvartayateeha yah;

Aghaayur indriyaaraamo mogham paartha sa jeevati.

16. He who does not follow the wheel thus set revolving, who is of sinful life, rejoicing in the senses, he lives in vain, O Arjuna!

COMMENT: He who does not follow the wheel by studying the Vedas and performing the sacrifices prescribed therein, but who indulges only in sensual pleasures, lives in vain. He wastes his life.

Yastwaatmaratir eva syaad aatmatriptashcha maanavah;

Aatmanyeva cha santushtas tasya kaaryam na vidyate.

17. But for that man who rejoices only in the Self, who is satisfied in the Self, who is content in the Self alone, verily there is nothing to do.

Naiva tasya kritenaartho naakriteneha kashchana;

Na chaasya sarvabhooteshu kashchidartha vyapaashrayah.

18. For him there is no interest whatsoever in what is done or what is not done; nor does he depend on any being for any object.

COMMENT: The sage who rejoices in his own Self does not gain anything by doing any action. To him no real purpose is served by engaging in any action. No evil can touch him as a result of inaction. He does not lose anything by being inactive.

Tasmaad asaktah satatam kaaryam karma samaachara;

Asakto hyaacharan karma param aapnoti poorushah.

19. Therefore, without attachment, do thou always perform action which should be done; for, by performing action without attachment man reaches the Supreme.

Karmanaiva hi samsiddhim aasthitaa janakaadayah;

Lokasangraham evaapi sampashyan kartum arhasi.

20. Janaka and others attained perfection verily by action only; even with a view to the protection of the masses thou shouldst perform action.

Yadyad aacharati shreshthas tattadevetaro janah;

Sa yat pramaanam kurute lokas tad anuvartate.

21. Whatsoever a great man does, that other men also do; whatever he sets up as the standard, that the world follows.

Na me paarthaasti kartavyam trishu lokeshu kinchana;

Naanavaaptam avaaptavyam varta eva cha karmani.

22. There is nothing in the three worlds, O Arjuna, that should be done by Me, nor is there anything unattained that should be attained; yet I engage Myself in action!

Yadi hyaham na varteyam jaatu karmanyatandritah;

Mama vartmaanuvartante manushyaah paartha sarvashah.

23. For, should I not ever engage Myself in action, unwearied, men would in every way follow My path, O Arjuna!

Utseedeyur ime lokaa na kuryaam karma ched aham;

Sankarasya cha kartaa syaam upahanyaam imaah prajaah.

24. These worlds would perish if I did not perform action; I should be the author of confusion of castes and destruction of these beings.

Saktaah karmanyavidwaamso yathaa kurvanti bhaarata;

Kuryaad vidwaam stathaa saktash chikeershur lokasangraham.

25. As the ignorant men act from attachment to action, O Bharata (Arjuna), so should the wise act without attachment, wishing the welfare of the world!

Na buddhibhedam janayed ajnaanaam karmasanginaam;

Joshayet sarva karmaani vidwaan yuktah samaacharan.

26. Let no wise man unsettle the minds of ignorant people who are attached to action; he should engage them in all actions, himself fulfilling them with devotion.

Prakriteh kriyamaanaani gunaih karmaani sarvashah;

Ahamkaaravimoodhaatmaa kartaaham iti manyate.

27. All actions are wrought in all cases by the qualities of Nature only. He whose mind is deluded by egoism thinks: "I am the doer".

COMMENT: Prakriti or Nature is that state in which the three Gunas exist in a state of equilibrium. When this equilibrium is disturbed, creation begins and the body, senses and mind are formed. The man who is deluded by egoism identifies the Self with the body, mind, the life-force and the senses, and ascribes to the Self all the attributes of the body and the senses. In reality the Gunas of nature perform all actions.

Tattwavittu mahaabaaho gunakarma vibhaagayoh;

Gunaa guneshu vartanta iti matwaa na sajjate.

28. But he who knows the truth, Omighty-armed Arjuna, about the divisions of the qualities and their functions, knowing that the Gunas as senses move amidst the Gunas as the sense-objects, is not attached.

Prakriter gunasammoodhaah sajjante gunakarmasu;

Taan akritsnavido mandaan kritsnavin na vichaalayet.

29. Those deluded by the qualities of Nature are attached to the functions of the qualities. A man of perfect knowledge should not unsettle the foolish one of imperfect knowledge.

Mayi sarvaani karmaani sannyasyaadhyaatma chetasaa;

Niraasheer nirmamo bhootwaa yudhyaswa vigatajwarah.

30. Renouncing all actions in Me, with the mind centred in the Self, free from hope and egoism, and from (mental) fever, do thou fight.

COMMENT: Surrender all actions to Me with the thought: "I perform all actions for the sake of the Lord only."

Ye me matam idam nityam anutishthanti maanavaah;

Shraddhaavanto'nasooyanto muchyante te'pi karmabhih.

31. Those men who constantly practise this teaching of Mine with faith and without cavilling, they too are freed from actions.

Ye twetad abhyasooyanto naanutishthanti me matam;

Sarvajnaanavimoodhaam staan viddhi nashtaan achetasah.

32. But those who carp at My teaching and do not practise it, deluded in all knowledge and devoid of discrimination, know them to be doomed to destruction.

Sadrisham cheshtate swasyaah prakriter jnaanavaan api;

Prakritim yaanti bhootaani nigrahah kim karishyati.

33. Even a wise man acts in accordance with his own nature; beings will follow nature; what can restraint do?

COMMENT: Only the ignorant man comes under the sway of his natural propensities. The seeker after Truth who is endowed with the 'Four Means' and who constantly practises meditation, can easily control Nature if he rises above the sway of the pairs of opposites, like love and hate, etc.

Indriyasyendriyasyaarthe raagadweshau vyavasthitau;

Tayor na vasham aagacchet tau hyasya paripanthinau.

34. Attachment and aversion for the objects of the senses abide in the senses; let none come under their sway, for they are his foes.

Shreyaan swadharmo vigunah paradharmaat swanushthitaat;

Swadharme nidhanam shreyah paradharmo bhayaavahah.

35. Better is one's own duty, though devoid of merit, than the duty of another well discharged. Better is death in one's own duty; the duty of another is fraught with fear.

Arjuna Uvaacha:

Atha kena prayukto'yam paapam charati poorushah;

Anicchann api vaarshneya balaad iva niyojitah.

Ȧrjuna said:

36. But impelled by what does man commit sin, though against his wishes, O Varshneya (Krishna), constrained, as it were, by force?

Sri Bhagavaan Uvaacha:

Kaama esha krodha esha rajoguna samudbhavah;

Mahaashano mahaapaapmaa viddhyenam iha vairinam.

The Blessed Lord said:

37. It is desire, it is anger born of the quality of Rajas, all-sinful and all-devouring; know this as the foe here (in this world).

Dhoomenaavriyate vahnir yathaadarsho malena cha;

Yatholbenaavrito garbhas tathaa tenedam aavritam.

38. As fire is enveloped by smoke, as amirror by dust, and as an embryo by the amnion, so is this enveloped by that.

Aavritam jnaanam etena jnaanino nityavairinaa;

Kaamaroopena kaunteya dushpoorenaanalena cha.

39. O Arjuna, wisdom is enveloped by this constant enemy of the wise in the form of desire, which is unappeasable as fire!

Indriyaani mano buddhir asyaadhishthaanam uchyate;

Etair vimohayatyesha jnaanam aavritya dehinam.

40. The senses, mind and intellect are said to be its seat; through these it deludes the embodied by veiling his wisdom.

Tasmaat twam indriyaanyaadau niyamya bharatarshabha;

Paapmaanam prajahi hyenam jnaana vijnaana naashanam.

41. Therefore, O best of the Bharatas (Arjuna), controlling the senses first, do thou kill this sinful thing (desire), the destroyer of knowledge and realisation!

Indriyaani paraanyaahur indriyebhyah param manah;

Manasastu paraa buddhir yo buddheh paratastu sah.

42. They say that the senses are superior (to the body); superior to the senses is the mind; superior to the mind is the intellect; and one who is superior even to the intellect is He—the Self.

Evam buddheh param buddhwaa samstabhyaatmaanam aatmanaa;

Jahi shatrum mahaabaaho kaamaroopam duraasadam.

43. Thus, knowing Him who is superior to the intellect and restraining the self by the Self, slay thou, O mighty-armed Arjuna, the enemy in the form of desire, hard to conquer!

COMMENT: Restrain the lower self by the higher Self. Subdue the lower mind by the higher mind. It is difficult to conquer desire because it is of a highly complex and incomprehensible nature. But a man of discrimination and dispassion, who does constant and intense Sadhana, can conquer it quite easily.

Hari Om Tat Sat

Iti Srimad Bhagavadgeetaasoopanishatsu Brahmavidyaayaam

Yogashaastre Sri Krishnaarjunasamvaade

Karmayogo Naama Tritiyo'dhyaayah

Thus in the Upanishads of the glorious Bhagavad Gita, the science of the Eternal, the scripture of Yoga, the dialogue between Sri Krishna and Arjuna, ends the third discourse entitled: "The Yoga of Action"

THE YOGA OF WISDOM : SUMMARY

Lord Krishna declares that He is born from age to age, in order to raise man and take him to the Supreme. Whenever there is a prevalence of unrighteousness and the world is ruled by the forces of darkness, the Lord manifests Himself to destroy these adverse forces and to establish peace, order and harmony. Hence we see the appearance of the great saviours of the world.

What is the secret of Yogic action? This the Lord proceeds to explain to Arjuna. Even though one is not engaged in action, but if the mind is active with the idea of doership and egoism, then it is action in inaction. On the other hand, though engaged physically in intense action, if the idea of agency is absent, if one feels that Prakriti does everything, it is inaction in action. The liberated man is free from attachment and is always calm and serene though engaged in ceaseless action. He is unaffected by the pairs of opposites like joy and grief, success and failure.

One who has true union with the Lord is not subject to rebirth. He attains immortality. Such a union can only be achieved when one is free from attachment, fear and anger, being thoroughly purified by right knowledge. The Lord accepts the devotion of all, whatever path they may use to approach Him.

Various kinds of sacrifices are performed by those engaged in the path to God. Through the practice of these sacrifices the mind is purified and led Godward. Here also there must be the spirit of non-attachment to the fruits of actions.

Divine wisdom, according to Sri Krishna, should be sought at the feet of a liberated Guru, one who has realised the Truth. The aspirant should approach such a sage in a spirit of humility and devotion. God Himself manifests in the heart of the Guru and instructs the disciple. Having understood the Truth from the Guru by direct intuitive experience the aspirant is no longer deluded by ignorance.

The liberated aspirant directly beholds the Self in all beings and all beings in the Self. He cognises through internal experience or intuition that all beings, from the Creator down to a blade of grass, exist in his own Self and also in God.

Arjuna is given the most heartening assurance that divine wisdom liberates even the most sinful. When knowledge of the Self dawns, all actions with their results are burnt by the fire of that knowledge, just as fuel is burnt by fire. When there is no idea of egoism, when there is no desire for the fruits of one's actions, actions are no actions. They lose their potency.

In order to attain divine wisdom one must have supreme faith and devotion. Faith is therefore the most important qualification for a spiritual aspirant. The doubting mind is always led astray from the right path. Faith ultimately confers divine knowledge, which removes ignorance once and for all.

Mere intellectual knowledge does not lead to liberation. It cannot grant one supreme peace and freedom.When one has achieved complete self-mastery and self-control, when one has intense faith and devotion, then true knowledge dawns within and one attains liberation and freedom from all weaknesses and sins.

The Lord concludes by emphasising that the soul that doubts goes to destruction. Without faith in oneself, in the scriptures and in the words of the preceptor, one cannot make any headway on the spiritual path. It is doubt that prevents one from engaging in spiritual Sadhana and realising the highest knowledge and bliss. By following the instructions of the Guru and through sincere service, one's doubts are rent asunder and divine knowledge manifests itself within. Spiritual progress then goes on at a rapid pace.

Sri Bhagavaan Uvaacha:

Imam vivaswate yogam proktavaan aham avyayam;

Vivaswaan manave praaha manur ikshwaakave'braveet.

The Blessed Lord said:

1. I taught this imperishable Yoga to Vivasvan; he told it to Manu; Manu proclaimed it to Ikshvaku.

Evam paramparaa praaptam imam raajarshayo viduh;

Sa kaaleneha mahataa yogo nashtah parantapa.

2. This, handed down thus in regular succession, the royal sages knew. This Yoga, by a long lapse of time, has been lost here, O Parantapa (burner of foes)!

COMMENT: The royal sages were kings who at the same time possessed divine knowledge. They learnt this Yoga.

Sa evaayam mayaa te'dya yogah proktah puraatanah;

Ḃhakto'si me sakhaa cheti rahasyam hyetad uttamam.

3. That same ancient Yoga has been today taught to thee by Me, for, thou art My devotee and friend; it is the supreme secret.

COMMENT: This ancient Yoga consists of profound and subtle teachings. Hence it is the supreme secret which the Lord reveals to Arjuna.

Arjuna Uvaacha:

Aparam bhavato janma param janma vivaswatah;

Katham etadvijaaneeyaam twam aadau proktavaan iti.

Arjuna said:

4. Later on was Thy birth, and prior to it was the birth of Vivasvan (the Sun); how am I to understand that Thou didst teach this Yoga in the beginning?

Sri Bhagavaan Uvaacha:

Bahooni me vyateetaani janmaani tava chaarjuna;

Taanyaham veda sarvaani na twam vettha parantapa.

The Blessed Lord said:

5. Many births of Mine have passed, as well as of thine, O Arjuna! I know them all but thou knowest not, O Parantapa!

Ajo'pi sannavyayaatmaa bhootaanaam eeshwaro'pi san;

Prakritim swaam adhishthaaya sambhavaamyaatmamaayayaa.

6. Though I am unborn and of imperishable nature, and though I am the Lord of all beings, yet, ruling over My own Nature, I am born by My own Maya.

Yadaa yadaa hi dharmasya glaanir bhavati bhaarata;

Abhyutthaanam adharmasya tadaatmaanam srijaamyaham.

7. Whenever there is a decline of righteousness, O Arjuna, and rise of unrighteousness, then I manifest Myself!

COMMENT: That which elevates a man and helps him to reach the goal of life and attain knowledge is Dharma (righteousness); that which drags him into worldliness is unrighteousness. That which helps a man to attain liberation is Dharma; that which makes him irreligious is Adharma or unrighteousness.

Paritraanaaya saadhoonaam vinaashaaya cha dushkritaam;

Dharma samsthaapanaarthaaya sambhavaami yuge yuge.

8. For the protection of the good, for the destruction of the wicked, and for the establishment of righteousness, I am born in every age.

Janma karma cha me divyam evam yo vetti tattwatah;

Tyaktwa deham punarjanma naiti maameti so'rjuna.

9. He who thus knows in true light My divine birth and action, after having abandoned the body is not born again; he comes to Me, O Arjuna!

Veetaraagabhayakrodhaa manmayaa maam upaashritaah;

Bahavo jnaana tapasaa pootaa madbhaavam aagataah.

10. Freed from attachment, fear and anger, absorbed in Me, taking refuge in Me, purified by the fire of knowledge, many have attained to My Being.

Ye yathaa maam prapadyante taamstathaiva bhajaamyaham;

Mama vartmaanuvartante manushyaah paartha sarvashah.

11. In whatever way men approach Me, even so do I reward them; My path do men tread in all ways, O Arjuna!

Kaangkshantah karmanaam siddhim yajanta iha devataah;

Kshipram hi maanushe loke siddhir bhavati karmajaa.

12. Those who long for success in action in this world sacrifice to the gods, because success is quickly attained by men through action.

Ċhaaturvarnyam mayaa srishtam gunakarma vibhaagashah;

Tasya kartaaram api maam viddhyakartaaram avyayam.

13. The fourfold caste has been created by Me according to the differentiation of Guna and Karma; though I am the author thereof, know Me as the non-doer and immutable.

COMMENT: The four castes are Brahmana, Kshatriya, Vaisya and Sudra. This division is according to the Guna and Karma. *Guna is quality. Karma is the kind of work. Both Guna and Karma determine the caste of a man.* In front of god, Cast is not determined by the birth of a person.

Na maam karmaani limpanti na me karmaphale sprihaa;

Iti maam yo'bhijaanaati karmabhir na sa badhyate.

14. Actions do not taint Me, nor have I a desire for the fruits of actions. He who knows Me thus is not bound by actions.

Evam jnaatwaa kritam karma poorvair api mumukshubhih;

Kuru karmaiva tasmaat twam poorvaih poorvataram kritam.

15. Having known this, the ancient seekers after freedom also performed actions; therefore, do thou perform actions as did the ancients in days of yore.

Kim karma kim akarmeti kavayo'pyatra mohitaah;

Tat te karma pravakshyaami yajjnaatwaa mokshyase'shubhaat.

16. What is action? What is inaction? As to this even the wise are confused. Therefore, I shall teach thee such action (the nature of action and inaction), by knowing which thou shalt be liberated from the evil (of Samsara, the world of birth and death).

Karmano hyapi boddhavyam boddhavyam cha vikarmanah;

Akarmanashcha boddhavyam gahanaa karmano gatih.

17. For, verily the true nature of action (enjoined by the scriptures) should be known, also (that) of forbidden (or unlawful) action, and of inaction; hard to understand is the nature (path) of action.

Karmanyakarma yah pashyed akarmani cha karma yah;

Sa buddhimaan manushyeshu sa yuktah kritsnakarmakrit.

18. He who seeth inaction in action and action in inaction, he is wise among men; he is a Yogi and performer of all actions.

COMMENT: It is the idea of agency, the idea of "I am the doer" that binds man to worldliness. If this idea vanishes, action is no action at all. It does not bind one to worldliness. This is inaction in action. But if a man sits quietly, thinking of actions and that he is their doer, he is ever doing actions. This is referred to as action in inaction.

Yasya sarve samaarambhaah kaamasankalpa varjitaah;

Jnaanaagni dagdhakarmaanam tam aahuh panditam budhaah.

19. He whose undertakings are all devoid of desires and (selfish) purposes, and whose actions have been burnt by the fire of knowledge,—him the wise call a sage.

Tyaktwaa karmaphalaasangam nityatripto niraashrayah;

Karmanyabhipravritto'pi naiva kinchit karoti sah.

20. Having abandoned attachment to the fruit of the action, ever content, depending on nothing, he does not do anything though engaged in activity.

Ṅiraasheer yatachittaatmaa tyaktasarvaparigrahah;

Shaareeram kevalam karma kurvannaapnoti kilbisham.

21. Without hope and with the mind and the self controlled, having abandoned all greed, doing mere bodily action, he incurs no sin.

Yadricchaalaabhasantushto dwandwaateeto vimatsarah;

Samah siddhaavasiddhau cha kritwaapi na nibadhyate.

22. Content with what comes to him without effort, free from the pairs of opposites and envy, even-minded in success and failure, though acting, he is not bound.

Gatasangasya muktasya jnaanaavasthitachetasah;

Yajnaayaacharatah karma samagram pravileeyate.

23. To one who is devoid of attachment, who is liberated, whose mind is established in knowledge, who works for the sake of sacrifice (for the sake of God), the whole action is dissolved.

Brahmaarpanam brahmahavirbrahmaagnau brahmanaa hutam;

Brahmaiva tena gantavyam brahmakarmasamaadhinaa.

24. Brahman is the oblation; Brahman is the melted butter (ghee); by Brahman is the oblation poured into the fire of Brahman; Brahman verily shall be reached by him who always sees Brahman in action.

COMMENT: This is wisdom-sacrifice, wherein the idea of Brahman is substituted for the ideas of the instrument and other accessories of action, the idea of action itself and its results.

By having such an idea the whole action melts away.

Daivam evaapare yajnam yoginah paryupaasate;

Brahmaagnaavapare yajnam yajnenaivopajuhwati.

25. Some Yogis perform sacrifice to the gods alone, while

others (who have realised the Self) offer the Self as sacrifice by the Self in the fire of Brahman alone.

Shrotraadeeneendriyaanyanye samyamaagnishu juhwati;

Shabdaadeen vishayaananya indriyaagnishu juhwati.

26. Some again offer hearing and other senses as sacrifice in the fire of restraint; others offer sound and various objects of the senses as sacrifice in the fire of the senses.

Sarvaaneendriya karmaani praanakarmaani chaapare;

Aatmasamyamayogaagnau juhwati jnaanadeepite.

27. Others again sacrifice all the functions of the senses and those of the breath (vital energy or Prana) in the fire of the Yoga of self-restraint kindled by knowledge.

Dravyayajnaas tapoyajnaa yogayajnaastathaapare;

Swaadhyaayajnaana yajnaashcha yatayah samshitavrataah.

28. Some again offer wealth, austerity and Yoga as sacrifice, while the ascetics of self-restraint and rigid vows offer study of scriptures and knowledge as sacrifice.

Apaane juhwati praanam praane'paanam tathaa'pare;

Praanaapaana gatee ruddhwaa praanaayaamaparaayanaah.

29. Others offer as sacrifice the outgoing breath in the incoming, and the incoming in the outgoing, restraining the courses of the outgoing and the incoming breaths, solely absorbed in the restraint of the breath.

COMMENT: Some Yogis practise inhalation, some practise exhalation, and some retention of breath. This is Pranayama.

Apare niyataahaaraah praanaan praaneshu juhwati;

Sarve'pyete yajnavido yajnakshapita kalmashaah.

30. Others who regulate their diet offer life-breaths in life-breaths; all these are knowers of sacrifice, whose sins are all destroyed by sacrifice.

Yajnashishtaamritabhujo yaanti brahma sanaatanam;

Naayam loko'styayajnasya kuto'nyah kurusattama.

31. Those who eat the remnants of the sacrifice, which are like nectar, go to the eternal Brahman. This world is not for the man who does not perform sacrifice; how then can he have the other, O Arjuna?

COMMENT: They go to the eternal Brahman after attaining knowledge of the Self through purification of the mind by performing the above sacrifices. He who does not perform any of these is not fit even for this miserable world. How then can he hope to get a better world than this?

Evam bahuvidhaa yajnaa vitataa brahmano mukhe;

Karmajaan viddhi taan sarvaan evam jnaatwaa vimokshyase.

32. Thus, various kinds of sacrifices are spread out before Brahman (literally at the mouth or face of Brahman). Know them all as born of action, and knowing thus, thou shalt be liberated.

Shreyaan dravyamayaadyajnaaj jnaanayajnah parantapa;

Sarvam karmaakhilam paartha jnaane parisamaapyate.

33. Superior is wisdom-sacrifice to sacrifice with objects, O Parantapa! All actions in their entirety, O Arjuna, culminate in knowledge!

Tadviddhi pranipaatena pariprashnena sevayaa;

Upadekshyanti te jnaanam jnaaninas tattwadarshinah.

34. Know that by long prostration, by question and by service, the wise who have realised the Truth will instruct thee in (that) knowledge.

Yajjnaatwaa na punarmoham evam yaasyasi paandava;

Yena bhootaanyasheshena drakshyasyaatmanyatho mayi.

35. Knowing that, thou shalt not, O Arjuna, again become deluded like this; and by that thou shalt see all beings in thy Self and also in Me!

Api chedasi paapebhyah sarvebhyah paapakrittamah;

Sarvam jnaanaplavenaiva vrijinam santarishyasi.

36. Even if thou art the most sinful of all sinners, yet thou shalt verily cross all sins by the raft of knowledge.

COMMENT: One can overcome sin through Self-knowledge.

Yathaidhaamsi samiddho'gnir bhasmasaat kurute'rjuna;

Jnaanaagnih sarvakarmaani bhasmasaat kurute tathaa.

37. As the blazing fire reduces fuel to ashes, O Arjuna, so does the fire of knowledge reduce all actions to ashes!

Na hi jnaanena sadrisham pavitram iha vidyate;

Tat swayam yogasamsiddhah kaalenaatmani vindati.

38. Verily there is no purifier in this world like knowledge. He who is perfected in Yoga finds it in the Self in time.

Shraddhaavaan labhate jnaanam tatparah samyatendriyah;

Jnaanam labdhvaa paraam shaantim achirenaadhigacchati.

39. The man who is full of faith, who is devoted to it, and who has subdued all the senses, obtains (this) knowledge; and, having obtained the knowledge, he goes at once to the supreme peace.

Ajnashchaashraddhadhaanashcha samshayaatmaa vinashyati;

Naayam loko'sti na paro na sukham samshayaatmanah.

40. The ignorant, the faithless, the doubting self proceeds to destruction; there is neither this world nor the other nor happiness for the doubting.

Yogasannyasta karmaanam jnaanasamcchinnasamshayam;

Aatmavantam na karmaani nibadhnanti dhananjaya.

41. He who has renounced actions by Yoga, whose doubts are rent asunder by knowledge, and who is self-possessed,—actions do not bind him, O Arjuna!

Tasmaad ajnaanasambhootam hritstham jnaanaasinaatmanah;

Cchittwainam samshayam yogam aatishthottishtha bhaarata.

42. Therefore, with the sword of knowledge (of the Self) cut asunder the doubt of the self born of ignorance, residing in thy heart, and take refuge in Yoga; arise, O Arjuna!

Hari Om Tat Sat

Iti Srimad Bhagavadgeetaasoopanishatsu Brahmavidyaayaam

Yogashaastre Sri Krishnaarjunasamvaade

Jnaanavibhaagayogo Naama Chaturtho'dhyaayah

Thus in the Upanishads of the glorious Bhagavad Gita, the science of the Eternal, the scripture of Yoga, the dialogue between Sri Krishna and Arjuna, ends the fourth discourse entitled: "The Yoga of Wisdom"

CHAPTER

4

The Mahabharata

The *Mahabharata* (Devanagari), is one of the two major Sanskrit epics of ancient India, the other being the *Rmyaga*. With more than 74,000 verses, plus long prose passages, or some 1.8 million words in total, it is one of the longest epic poems in the world. Taken together with the Harivamsa, the *Mahabharata* has a total length of more than 90,000 verses.

It is also of immense religious and philosophical importance in India, in particular for including the Bhagavad Gita, an important text of Hinduism.

The title may be translated as "Great India", or "the great tale of the Bharata Dynasty", according to the *Mahabharata*'s own testimony extended from a shorter version simply called *Bhrata* of 24,000 verses The epic is part of the Hindu *itihsa*s, literally "that which happened", along with the *Ramayana* and the *Purgas*.

Traditionally, the *Mahabharata* is ascribed to Vyasa. Due to its immense length, its philological study has a long history of attempting to unravel its historical growth and composition layers. In its final form, it was completed by the first century, with its central core *Bharata* (consisting of 24,000 verses) dating back to the 6th century BCE, and some parts possibly dating back as far as the 8th century BCE. The events depicted in the *Mahabharata* are thought to have taken place around the 12th century BCE.

Influence: With its philosophical depth and sheer magnitude, a consummate embodiment of the ethos of not only India but of Hinduism and Vedic tradition, the

Mahabharata's scope and grandeur is best summarized by one quotation from the beginning of its first *parva* (section): "What is found here, may be found elsewhere. What is not found here, will not be found elsewhere." This quotation rightly sums up Mahabharata, within which one finds myriads of relationships, stories and events.

In its scope, the *Mahabharata* is more than simply a story of kings and princes, sages and wisemen, demons and gods; its author, Vyasa, says that one of its aims is elucidating the four goals of life: kama (pleasure), artha (wealth), dharma (duty) and Moksha (liberation). The story culminates in Moksha, believed by Hindus to be the ultimate goal of human beings. Karma and dharma play an integral role in the *Mahabharata*.

The *Mahabharata* includes large amounts of Hindu mythology, cosmological stories of the gods and goddesses, and philosophical parables aimed at students of Hindu philosophy. Among the principal works and stories that are a part of the *Mahabharata* are the following (often considered isolated as works in their own right):

- Bhagavad Gita (Krishna instructs and teaches Arjuna. Anusasanaparva.)
- Damayanti (or Nala and Damayanti, a love story. Aranyakaparva.)
- Krishnavatara (the story of Krishna, the *Krishna Lila*, which is woven through many chapters of the story)
- Rama (an abbreviated version of the Ramayana. Aranyakaparva.)
- Rishyasringa (also written as Rshyashrnga, the horned boy and rishi. Aranyakaparva.)
- Vishnu sahasranama (the most famous hymn to Vishnu, which describes His 1000 names; Anushasanaparva.)

Textual History and Organization: It is undisputed that the full length of the *Mahabharata* has accreted over a long period. The *Mahabharata* itself (1.1.61) distinguishes a core portion of 24,000 verses, the *Bharata* proper, as opposed to additional "secondary" material, while the Ashvalayana Grhyasutra (3.4.4) makes a similar distinction. According to the *Adi-parva* of the *Mahabharata* (shlokas 81, 101-102), the text was originally 8,800 verses when it was composed by Krishna Dwaipayana Vyasa and was known as the *Jaya* ("*Victory*"), which later became 24,000 verses in the *Bharata* recited by Vaisampayana, and finally over 90,000 verses in the*Mahabharata* recited by Ugrasravas.

Not unlike the field of Homeric studies, research on the *Mahabharata* has put an enormous effort into recognizing and dating various layers within the text. Oldenberg (1922) stipulated that the supposed original poem once carried an immense "tragic force", but dismissed the full text as a "horrible chaos".

The earliest known references to the *Mahabharata* and its core *Bharata* date back to the 6th-5th century BCE, in the Ashtadhyayi (sutra 6.2.38) of Pgini (c. 520-460 BCE), and in the *Ashvalayana Grhyasutra* (3.4.4), while various characters from the epic are also mentioned in earlier Vedic literature. This indicates that the core 24,000 verses, known as the *Bharata*, as well as an early version of the extended *Mahabharata*, were composed by the 6th-5th century BCE, with parts of *Jaya*'s original 8,800 verses possibly dating back as far as the 9th-8th century BC.

However, the earliest testimony of the existence of the full text of the *Mahabharata* is by the Greek Sophist Dion Chrysostom (c. 40-105), who mentions that "the Indians possess an Iliad of 100,000 verses". The later copper-plate inscription of the Maharaja Sharvanatha (533-534) from Khoh (Satna District, Madhya Pradesh) also describes the *Mahabharata* as a "collection of 100,000 verses" (*shatasahasri samhita*). The redaction of this large body of text was carried out after formal principles, emphasizing the numbers 18 and 12.

The addition of the latest parts may be dated by the absence of the *Anushasana-parva* from *MS Spitzer*, the oldest surviving

Sanskrit philosophical manuscript dated to the first century, that contains among other things a list of the books in the *Mahabharata*. From this evidence, it is likely that the redaction into 18 books took place in the first century. An alternative division into 20 parvas appears to have co-existed for some time. The division into 100 sub-parvas (mentioned in Mbh. 1.2.70) is older, and most parvas are named after one of their constituent sub-parvas. The Harivamsa consists of the final two of the 100 sub-parvas, and was considered an appendix (*khila*) to the *Mahabharata* proper by the redactors of the 18 parvas.

According to Mbh. 1.1.50, there were three versions of the epic, beginning with *Manu* (1.1.27), *Astika* (1.3, sub-parva 5) or *Vasu* (1.57), respectively. These versions probably correspond to the addition of one and then another 'frame' settings of dialogues. The *Vasu* version corresponds to the oldest, without frame settings, beginning with the account of the birth of Vyasa. The Astika version adds the Sarpasattra and Ashvamedha material from Brahmanical literature, and introduces the name *Mahabharata* and identifies Vyasa as the work's author. The redactors of these additions were probably Pancharatrin scholars who according to Oberlies (1998) likely retained control over the text until its final redaction. Mention of the Hunas in the *Bhishma-parva* however appears to imply that this parva may have been edited around the 4th century.

Historicity: The historicity of the Mahabharata war is unclear. The epic's setting certainly has a historical precedent in Vedic India, where the Kuru kingdom was the centre of political power in the late 2nd and early 1st millennia BCE.

Ancient Indian scholars have calculated chronologies for the *Mahabharata* war, the 5th century mathematician Aryabhatta arriving at an approximate date for the Kurukshetra battle of 3137 BCE. The Aihole inscription of Pulakesin II (7th century CE) dates the Kurukshetra War to 3102 BCE. Vriddha-Garga, Varahamihira and Kalhana dated the War to 653 years after 3102 BCE.

Contentious and disputable attempts to date the events of the *Mahabharata* with the help of archaeoastronomy have claimed dates in the 6th millennium BCE..

According to Varahamihira, Yudhisthira lived 2526 years before the beginning of the Saka era (Brhatsamhita 13.3).

According to the Puranas, there is a time gap of 1015 or 1500 years between Parikshit's birth during the *Mahabharata* war and the coronation of king Mahapadma Nanda (ca. 364-382 BCE). Between Mahapadma Nanda and the last Andhra king Pulomavi, the Puranas count 836 or 829 years. Vayu Purana has the Saptarsi in Magha when Yudhisthira lived, in Purvasadha when Nanda lived and in Satabhisaj at the end of Andhra rule. This could correspond to a difference of 1000 (or more) years between Pariksit (seven generations after Pratipa) and Nanda, and 400 (or more) years between Nanda and the end of Andhra rule.

The Brhadaranyaka Upanisad has eight generations between Pariksit and Yaska. Pargiter remarked that the Great Bear (the rksas or the Saptarsi) "was situated equally with regard to the lunar constellation Pusya while Pratipa was king." The Puranas list a number of kings between the Mahabharata War and Mahapadma Nanda which indicates that 1451 or 1503 years could have passed between them. Pargiter has argued that there were 26 kings between Adhisimakrishna and Mahapadma Nanda.

Synopsis: The epic employs the story within a story structure popular in many Indian religious and secular works. It is recited to the King Janamejaya by Vaisampayana, a disciple of Vyasa.

The core story of the work is that of a dynastic struggle for the throne of Hastinapura, the kingdom ruled by the Kuru clan. The two collateral branches of the family that participate in the struggle are the Kauravas, the elder branch of the family, and the Pandavas, the younger branch.

The struggle culminates leading to the Great battle of

Kurukshetra, and the Pandavas are ultimately victorious. The *Mahabharata* itself ends with the death of Krishna, and the subsequent end of his dynasty, and ascent of the Pandava brothers to Heaven.

It also marks the beginning of the Hindu age of Kali (Kali Yuga), the fourth and final age of mankind, where the great values and noble ideas have crumbled, and man is speedily heading toward the complete dissolution of right action, morality and virtue. Some of the most noble and revered figures in the *Mahabharata* end up fighting on the side of the Kauravas, due to conflicts of their dharma, or duty. For example, Bhishma had vowed to always protect the king of Hastinapura, whoever he may be. Thus, he was required to fight on the side of evil knowing that his Pandavas would end up victorious only with his death.

Authorship: The epic is traditionally ascribed to Maha Rishi Veda Vyasa, who is one of the major dynastic characters within the epic. The first section of the *Mahabharata* states that it was Ganesha who, at the behest of Vyasa, fixed the text in manuscript form. Lord Ganesha is said to have agreed, but only on condition that Vyasa never pause in his recitation. Vyasa then put a counter-condition that Ganesha understand whatever he recited, before writing it down. In this way Vyasa could get some respite from continuously speaking by saying a verse which was difficult to understand. This situation also serves as a popular variation on the stories of how Ganesha's right tusk was broken (a traditional part of Ganesha imagery). This version attributes it to the fact that, in the rush of writing, the great elephant-headed divinity's pen failed, and he snapped off his tusk as a replacement in order that the transcription not be interrupted.

Bhishma: Janamejaya's ancestor Shantanu, the king of Hastinapura has a short-lived marriage with the goddess Ganga and has a heroic son, Devavrata (later to be called Bhishma). Devavrata, a young man already with a reputation as a fearsome warrior, is the heir apparent to the throne.

Many years later, when the king goes hunting, he spots Satyavati, the daughter of a fisherman, and wants to marry her. Eager to secure his daughter's and her children's future happiness, the fisherman refuses to consent to the marriage unless Shantanu promises to make the future son of Satyavati the king upon his death, instead of Devavrata. To solve the king's dilemma, Devavrata agrees to that. Finding that the fisherman, though convinced of Devavrata's commitment, is not sure about the prince's children honouring the promise, Devavrata makes a severe vow of lifelong celibacy to guarantee his father's promise. Hearing such a vow, unheard of amongst warriors, the heavens bestow Devavrata with the name Bhishma, 'the person of the terrible oath'.

When King Shantanu is on his deathbed, his concern for his children and the stability of the kingdom delays his death. To ease the king's pains Bhishma promises to stay alive until the kingdom is safe and secure. Again, an awesome promise as all kingdoms are under constant threat. This promise was to cost him dearly, giving him a long life with constant tribulations and battles. Later, though seriously wounded, Bhishma could not give up his soul until the final battle resulted in the rule of the righteous Pandavas.

The Pandavas: Unfortunately Satyavati's sons die young and her grandson Pandu ascends the throne as his elder brother Dhrtarashtra is blind. Pandu whilst out hunting deer, is however cursed by a sage (whom he accidentally kills while he is having sex with his wife, mistaking their moans of pleasure to be the sounds of a deer) that he can never engage in sexual act with any woman. He retires to the forest along with his two wives. Kunti, using a boon granted by another sage whom Kunti, tended and cared for with great dilligence to summon the gods Dharma, Vayu, and Indra, his elder queen Kunti gives birth to three sons Yudhishthira, Bhima, and Arjuna through their respective "fathers".

The sons of course inherit the primary character of their respective father. Kunti shares her boon with her "sister" queen

Madri, who bears the twins Nakula and Sahadeva through the Ashwini twins. However Pandu and Madri cannot resist temptation, indulge in sex and die in the forest and Kunti returns to Hastinapura with her sons. The rivalry between the Pandavas and the Kauravas starts from childhood itself. Dhrtarashtra's sons, the Kauravas, led by the eldest Duryodhana, detest their cousins the Pandavas. However, they were the favourite of their teacher Drona and (the Pandavas) grow up to be exceptional. Each one of the Pandavas is said to have one exceptional strength or virtue-Yudhisthira is the most virtuous, Arjuna the bravest warrior, Bhima the strongest, Nakula the most handsome and Sahadeva wise and able to predict the future.

When the princes of Hastinapura come of age, a tournament is held to display their strength and skill. When Arjuna was hailed as a master of archery, a young man challenges him for a duel. He declares his name is Karna, and he is the son of a charioteer. When asked to prove that he is of royal birth, which is the criterion for joining the tournament, Duryodhana, spotting a potential ally, jumps over to his side and gives his kingdom of Anga. Karna is forever grateful for this act. Because of this, he becomes Duryodhana's closest friend and plays a crucial role in the war.

The House of Wax: Meanwhile Duryodhana plots to get rid of the Pandavas and tries to kill the Pandavas secretly by burning their palace which is made of lac. However, the Pandavas are warned by their uncle, Vidura who sends them a miner to dig a tunnel. Therefore, when Duryodhana's servants set the house on flames, they will be able to escape in safety. After escaping from the tragedy, the Pandavas arrive in a forest and rest. Bhima and Arjuna want to confront the Kauravas, but Kunti and Yudhisthira decide against it. Bheeshma goes to the river Ganga to perform the last rites of the Pandavas. Vidura then informs him that the Pandavas are alive and to keep the secret to himself.

City of Ekchakra: The Pandavas stay in the city of Ekchara in the guise of Brahmans. Kunti and Bhima then learn of a cruel and terrible rakshasa named Bakasura who has made a deal with the villagers that if he receives 1 villager a month to eat, he will not harm the villagers. Bhima sets out to eliminate this rakshasa. A great fight arises and Bhima with his might kills him. In order to avoid being caught by the villagers, the Pandavas leave the City of Ekchakra and move on.

Draupadi: In course of this exile the Pandavas are informed of a "competition" called a swayamvar taking place with the prize being the hand of the Panchal princess and the daughter of King Drupad, Draupadi. The Pandavas enter the competition in disguise as Brahmans, the task being to string a mighty steel bow and shoot with a steel arrow the eye of a rotating fish on the ceiling while concentrating on the reflection underneath. No king manages to come close to do so. They fail to even pick up the bow! Karna, the only one who picks up the bow, is about to try is halted by Draupadi by the excuse that he is the son of a charioteer and may not participate.

Arjuna becomes successful and manages to complete the task. When he returns with his bride, Arjuna goes to his mother to show her his prize, exclaiming, "Mother, I have brought you a present!". Kunti, not noticing the princess, tells Arjuna that whatever he has won must be shared with his brothers. To ensure that their mother never utters a falsehood even by mistake, the brothers take her as a common wife. All of the Pandavas love Draupadi dearly. In some interpretations, Draupadi alternates months or years with each brother. At this juncture they also meet Krishna who would become their lifelong ally and guide.

Indraprasth: Duryodhana and Shakuni are furious when they learn that the Pandava brothers are alive and that King Dhritrashtra has sent Vidur to call them back to Hastinapura. Karna, as usual, is ready to fight them, but Shakuni realizes that with King Drupad and Krishna on the side of the Pandavas it would be difficult to defeat them. Dhritrashtra consoles

Duryodhana and assures him that his rights as the Heir Apparent to the throne of Hastinapura will be fully protected.

In Kampilya, King Drupad and Shri Krishna advise Yudhisthira to fight for his right to the throne of Hastinapura. Just then Vidur arrives and tells the Pandava brothers that they have been invited back to Hastinapura along with their bride. The Pandavas and Draupadi return to Hastinapura. Dhritrashtra conceals his disappointment and orders everyone to welcome them. Determined to establish peace between the Kauravas and the Pandavas, Bhishma suggests giving half the Kingdom to Yudhisthira.

Dhritrashtra agrees to this suggestion. Krishna and Balram, also give their consent and it is decided that Yudhisthira's coronation as King of Indraprasth be held in Hastinapura. This land given to them again becomes another unjustice to the Pandavas as it neither has any agricultural soil neither any buildings nor people. Krishna consolidates the Pandavas saying that Indraprasth is not a waste but instead a Land of Action. Taking the advice of Krishna, the Pandavas make Indraprasth a beautiful town where justice is always met and the inhabitants are happy.

The Rajsuya Yagna: Shortly after this, Arjuna and Subhadra (Krishna's sister) get married and return to Indraprastha to be welcomed by Draupadi. Here, Yudhisthira seeks Sri Krishna's advice on performing the Rajsuya Yagna which will make him the emperor of India. Krishna advises him that Jarasandha who has imprisoned 86 kings must be killed as he may interfere in the ceremony. Hence Yuddhisthira decides to send Krishna, Bhima and Arjuna to challenge Jarasandh for combat. Jarasandh chooses to fight with Bhima. Bhima and Jarasandh were so equally matched in strength that they fought for nearly fourteen days without rest. When Jarasandha finally showed signs of exhaustion, Krishna prompted Bhima to make an end of him. After Jarasandha had been destroyed, Jarasandha's son was crowned King of Magadha. The Rajsuya Yagna is celebrated and Yudhisthira is recognized as an Emperor.

The House of Illusion: Duryodhana is unhappy about the prosperity of the Pandavas, Shakuni consoles him and later loses in a game of dice to Yudhisthira. Duryodhana walks around Yudhisthira's 'Maya Mahal" ("The House of Illusion") and falls into one of the pools. Draupadi calls him the "blind son of a blind father." Duryodhana, Karna and Shakuni plan to avenge Draupadi for her taunting remarks.

Duryodhana's Game: Duryodhana, who now has a friend in the peerless warrior Karna becomes aware of Yudhisthira becoming the emperor. This proves too much for Duryodhana who feels death would be better than watching one's foes prosper. His maternal uncle Shakuni, convinced that however brave his nephew may be, he was no match for his cousins, decides to use a ruse to destroy the Pandavas. He forces Dhrtarashtra to invite the Pandavas for a game of dice in which he wins everything from Yudhisthira, including himself, his brothers and Draupadi through the use of a trick. The jubilant Kauravas insult them in their helpless state and even try to disrobe Draupadi in front of the entire court. Her honour is saved by the grace of Krishna. When the elders intervene and Dhrtarashtra has to restore everything to the Pandavas, Shakuni forces another game of dice which he again wins. The Pandavas are required to go into exile for 13 years, and on the 13th year they must remain hidden. If discovered by the Kauravas, they will be forced into exile for another 12 years.

The Years in Exile: The Pandavas having lost the game of dice go on exile for 12 years and a year of hiding. During the period of exile, they visit many religious places and are often visited by Krishna. Draupadi who has been insulted by Dushasana (Duryodhana's brother), takes a vow never to tie up her hair until she had blood from Dushasana's thigh to wash her hair with. This constantly reminds her husbands of how war was inevitable. Krishna advises Arjuna that since war was inevitable, he should enter heaven to seek the divine weapons held by Gods and that he who is favoured by Lord Indra would be able to do so.

Through the prayer of Lord Indra, Arjuna gains access to heaven from where he obtains the divine weapons and also learns how to use them. Finally, Lord Indra advises Arjuna to learn the art of dance as it would come to his aid in the 13th year of hiding. It is during this time that the Pandavas get to face a demon called Hidumba. Bhima kills him and marries his sister, Hidumbi. With her, he begets a son called Ghatothkacha.

The Battle at Kurukshetra: When the Pandavas return from their exile after many hardships, they request for a peace treaty with the Kauravas to gain Indraprastha back. However, Duryodhana disagrees and argues that since the Pandavas where "caught" in their year of hiding, they must go into another 13 years of exile before they can have Indraprastha. The Pandavas on Krishna's advice again ask for a peace treaty asking for at least five villages for the five brothers, from the Kauravas' vast kingdom. Duryodhana refuses to give in. Krishna intervenes to mediate peace but is unsuccessful. War becomes inevitable.

The two sides summon vast armies to their help and line up at Kurukshetra for a war. The Kingdoms of Dwaraka, Kasi, Kekaya, Magadha, Matsya, Chedi, Pandya and the Yadus of Mathura and some other clans like the Parama Kambojas from Transoxiana were allied with the Pandavas; the allies of the Kauravas comprised the kings of Pragjyotisha, Anga, Kekaya (Kekaya brothers who were enemies of the Kekeya brothers on the Pandava side), Sindhudesa (including Sindhus, Sauviras and Sivis), Mahishmati, Avanti in Madhyadesa, Madras, Gandharas, Bahlikas, Kambojas (with Yavanas, Sakas, Tusharas etc.) and many others. Prior to war being declared, Krishna's brother, Balarama, had left to go on pilgrimage, thus he does not take part in the battle itself.

Arjuna, seeing himself facing grandsire Bhishma and his teacher Drona on Duryodhana's side due to their vow to serve the state of Hastinapura is heartbroken and at the idea of killing them he fails to lift his Gandiva bow. Krishna who has chosen to drive Arjuna's chariot wakes him up to his call of duty in the famous Bhagavad Gita section of the epic. Though initially sticking to chivalrous notions of warfare, the Kauravas and Pandavas soon descended into dishonourable warfare. At the end of the 14 days slaughter only the Pandavas and Krishna survive with a few old warriors from the Kaurava side.

The end of the Pandavas: Beholding the carnage, the noble mother of the Kauravas, Gandhari who had lost all her sons, curses Krishna to be a witness to a similar annihilation of his family, for though divine and capable of stopping the war, he had not done so. Krishna who had incarnated precisely to destroy the wicked kings accepts the curse, which bears fruit 36 years later. He then departs from the world and the Pandavas who had ruled righteously all along, now tired, decide to renounce everything. Clad in skins and rags they retire to the Himalayas and ascend the peaks towards heaven in their bodily form. Legend reveals that a mangy, stray dog travels along with them. One by one the Pandavas and Draupadi fall on their way.

As each one stumbles, Yudhishtra gives the rest the reason for their fall (Draupadi was partial to Arjuna, Nakula and Sahadeva were vain and proud of their looks, Bhima and Arjuna were proud of their strength and archery skills, respectively). Only the virtuous Yudhisthra who had tried everything to prevent the carnage and the dog remain. The dog reveals himself to be the god Dharma, who reveals the nature of the test and assures Yudhishtra that his fallen siblings and wife are in heaven. Yudhistra alone transcends to heaven in his bodily form for being just and humble.

Arjuna's grandson Parikshita rules after them and dies bitten by a snake. His furious son, Janamejaya, decides to perform a snake sacrifice (sarpasattra) in order to destroy the snakes. It is at this sacrifice that the tale of his ancestors is narrated to him.

CHAPTER

5

Vedas and Upanishads

Although they did use some writing with pictographic symbols at Mohenjo-daro, they were not extensive nor alphabetic nor have they been deciphered yet, and the Indo-European Sanskrit which did develop in India is probably quite different. Nevertheless the Harappan civilization of the Indus Valley in what is now Pakistan did borrow many ideas from Mesopotamia and is considered the third civilization to develop. Two seals of the Mohenjo-daro type were discovered at Elam and Mesopotamia, and a cuneiform inscription was unearthed at Mohenjo-daro.

The pastoral villages that spread out east of Elam through Iran and Baluchistan prepared the way for the cities that were to develop around the Indus River, particularly at Harappa and Mohenjo-daro. By about 3000 BC they were building mud-brick houses; burials in the houses included funereal objects; and pottery had fine designs and the potters' marks. After 2500 BC farmers moved out into the alluvial plain of the Indus River valley and achieved full-sized villages using copper and bronze pins, knives, and axes; figurines of women and cattle indicate probable religious attitudes.

The urban phase began about 2300 BC and lasted for about six hundred years with elaborate cities like Mohenjo-daro (called locally Mound of the Dead), which was excavated in the 1920s. This city and others not yet excavated had about 40,000 inhabitants congregated in well built houses with private showers and toilets that drained into municipal sewer lines. Suffering from occasional flooding by the Indus, Mohenjo-daro was rebuilt seven times. The largest structures were the elevated granary and the great bath or swimming pool which was 12 by 7 meters. Around the pool were dressing rooms and private baths.

The people of the Harappan culture did not seem to be very warlike, although they hunted wild game and domesticated cattle, sheep, and goats. Wheat and barley were the main food supplemented by peas, sesame, and other vegetables and fruits, beef, mutton, pork, eggs, fish, and milk. Compared to other ancient civilizations, the houses were of nearly equal size, indicating a more egalitarian social structure. The potter's wheel and carts were used; children played with miniature toy carts. Cotton, perhaps first used here, and wool were made into clothing. A bronze figurine was found of an expressive dancing girl with her hand on her hip, naked except for jewellery. The numerous figurines of the Mother Goddess indicate a likely source for what later became the Shakti worship of the feminine power in India. A male god in a yoga posture, depicted with three faces and two horns, has been identified with Shiva, another important figure in later Indian religion. Phallic lingams, also associated with Shiva, have been found. A civilization that endured dangerous flooding for six hundred years very likely had a strong religion to help hold people together. With no written histories the decline of this civilization is subject to much speculation. The traditional theory is that the Aryans invaded from the northwest. Although this is likely, the decline of Harappan culture was quite gradual and indicates problems beyond foreign conquest. One theory is deforestation, because of all the wood needed for the kilns to make the bricks used to keep out the flood waters that gradually brought about salinization of the soil, as it had to Sumer over centuries, so that the Harappan culture had greatly declined by 1900 BC.

However, a more comprehensive explanation comes from an analysis of the consequences of the extensive herds of cattle that indicate overgrazing and a general degradation of the ecosystem, including salinization of water supplies. This led farmers to move on to greener pastures, leaving behind abandoned villages and depopulated cities. Even though fodder was probably grown to feed the cattle, this would not have been enough; and the overgrazing by the bullocks and milk cows could have caused the surrounding land to deteriorate. By 1500 BC the Harappan civilization had faded away into a culture that was spreading throughout India with new ideas from the west.

The traditional theory, well documented by the ancient hymns of the *Vedas,* is that a people calling themselves Aryans conquered the native peoples of India and destroyed their forts. Because of language similarities these Aryans are associated particularly with the Iranians and even further back with the origins of the Indo-European language group. The general consensus seems to be that this culture must have begun somewhere in the Russian steppes and Central Asia about 2000 BC, though some have put their origin in Lithuania because of similarity to that language. The branch of these speakers, who came to India under the name Aryans, which means "noble ones," is the Indo-Iranian group. In fact "Iran" derives from the Persian cognate of the word for Aryan. Other branches spread into Greece and western Asia as Hittites, Kassites, and Mitanni. A rock inscription found at Boghaz Koi dated about 1400 BC, commemorating a treaty between the Mitanni and Hittites, invokes the Aryan gods Indra, Varuna, Mitra, and the twins Nasatya (Asvins).

The ancient writings of the Persian *Avesta* and the Hindu *Vedas* share many gods and beliefs. Eventually they must have split, causing later authors to demonize the divinities of their adversaries. In early Hindu writings the *asuras* were respected gods, but later they became the demons most hated, while Ahura Mazda became the chief god of the Zoroastrians. (Persian often uses an h where Sanskrit uses an s, such as *haoma* for *soma.*) On the other hand the Hindu term for divinities, devas, was used by Zoroastrians to describe the devils from which even our English word is derived. Some scholars have concluded that the ancient Hindus did not want to admit that they came from Iran, and therefore the origin of the Aryans is never mentioned in the ancient texts, although they frankly boast of their conquest over the indigenous Dasas or Dasyus in India.

The word *Veda* means knowledge, and the *Vedas* are considered the most sacred scripture of Hinduism referred to as *sruti,* meaning what was heard by or revealed to the *rishis* or seers. The most holy hymns and mantras put together into four collections called the *Rig, Sama, Yajur,* and *Atharva Vedas* are difficult to date, because they were passed on orally for about a thousand years before they were written down. More recent categories of *Vedas* include the *Brahmanas* or manuals for ritual and prayer, the *Aranyakas* or forest texts for religious hermits, and the *Upanishads* or mystical discourses.

RIG VEDA

The hymns of the *Rig Veda* are considered the oldest and most important of the *Vedas,* having been composed between 1500 BC and the time of the great Bharata war about 900 BC.

More than a thousand hymns are organized into ten mandalas or circles of which the second through the seventh are the oldest and the tenth is the most recent. The Hindu tradition is that even the *Vedas* were gradually reduced from much more extensive and ancient divine revelations but were perverted in the recent dark age of *Kaliyuga*. As the only writings from this ancient period of India, they are considered the best source of knowledge we have; but the ethical doctrines seem to have improved from the ancient hymns to the mystical *Upanishads*.

Essentially the *Rig Veda* is dominated by hymns praising the Aryan gods for giving them victories and wealth plundered from the local Dasas through warfare. The Aryans apparently used their advances in weaponry and skill in fighting to conquer the agricultural and tribal peoples of the fading Harappan culture. Numerous hymns refer to the use of horses and chariots with spokes which must have given their warriors a tremendous advantage. Spears, bows, arrows, and iron weapons are also mentioned. As a nomadic and pastoral culture glorifying war, they established a new social structure of patriarchal families dominated by warriors and, eventually with the power of the *Vedas* themselves, by priests also.

The *Rig Veda* does mention assemblies, but these were probably of the warrior elite, which may have had some controlling influence on the kings and the tribal priest called a *purohita*. The gods worshiped resemble the Indo-European gods and were headed by the powerful Indra, who is often credited with destroying ninety forts. Also popular was Agni, the fire-god considered a messenger of the gods.

Varuna and Mitra, the gods of the night and day sky, have been identified with the Greek Uranos and the Persian Mithras respectively. Dyaus, who is not mentioned nearly as often, has been correlated with the Greek Zeus. Surya the sun-god is referred to as the eye of Varuna and the son of Dyaus and rides through the sky on his chariot led by his twin sons, the Asvins who represent his rays; Ushas the dawn is his wife or daughter. Maruts are storm-gods shaped by Rudra, who may have been one of the few indigenous deities adopted by the Aryans. Like the Iranian *Avesta*, the *Rig Veda* refers to the thirty-three gods. Generally the hymns of the *Rig Veda* praise the gods and ask them for worldly benefits such as wealth, health, long life, protection, and victory over the Dasa peoples.

He, self-reliant, mighty and triumphant, brought low the dear head of the wicked Dasas.

Indra the Vritra-slayer, Fort-destroyer, scattered the Dasa hosts who dwelt in darkness.

For men hath he created earth and waters, and ever helped the prayer of him who worships.

To him in might the Gods have ever yielded, to Indra in the tumult of battle.

When in his arms they laid the bolt, he slaughtered the Dasyus and cast down their forts of iron.

They call upon Brihaspati or Brahmanaspati, who has been related to a Hittite thunder-god, to avenge the sinner and protect them from the deceitful and wicked man. The Aryans did have a concept of eternal law called *rita*, which the immortal Agni in serving the gods is said to never break (*Rig Veda* III:3:1).

In *Rig Veda* III:34:9 Indra killed the Dasyus and "gave protection to the Aryan colour." Not only did the Aryans shamelessly pray for booty in war, but they based their militarily won supremacy on the lightness of their skin colour compared to the dark colors of the native Dasyus. They arrogantly proclaimed, "Let those who have no weapons suffer sorrow." (*Rig Veda* IV:5:14.)

Renowned is he when conquering and when slaying:
'tis he who wins cattle in the combat.

When Indra hardens his indignation all that is fixed and all that moves fear him.

Indra has won all kine, all gold, all horses, -
Maghavan, he who breaks forts in pieces;

Indra is praised for killing thousands of the abject tribes of Dasas with his arrow and taking great vengeance with "murdering weapons." (*Rig Veda* IV:28:3-4) One hymn mentions sending thirty thousand Dasas "to slumber" and another hymn sixty thousand slain. A hymn dedicated to the weapons of war (*Rig Veda* VI:75) refers to a warrior "armed with mail," using a bow to win cattle and subdue all regions, "upstanding in the car the skillful charioteer guides his strong horses on whithersoe'er he will." The arrows had iron mouths and shafts "with venom smeared" that "not one be left alive." Hymn VII:83 begins, "Looking to you and your alliance, O ye men, armed with broad axes they went forward, fain for spoil. Ye smote and slew his Dasa and his Aryan enemies."

Only occasionally did the authors of these hymns look to their own sins.

> *Free us from sins committed by our fathers, from those wherein we have ourselves offended.*
>
> *O king, loose, like a thief who feeds the cattle, as from the cord a calf, set free Vasishtha.*
>
> *Not our own will betrayed us, but seduction, thoughtlessness, Varuna! wine, dice or anger.*
>
> *The old is near to lead astray the younger: even sleep removes not all evil-doing.*

A hymn to the frogs compares the repetitions of the priests around the soma bowl to the croaking of the frogs around a pond after the rains come. (*Rig Veda* VII:103)

The basic belief of the prayers and sacrifices is that they will help them to gain their desires and overcome their enemies, as in *Rig Veda* VIII:31:15: "The man who, sacrificing, strives to win the heart of deities will conquer those who worship not." Some awareness of a higher law seems to be dawning in the eighth book in hymn 75: "The holy law hath quelled even mighty men of war. Break ye not off our friendship, come and set me free." However, the enemies are now identified with the Asuras and still are intimidated by greater weapons: "Weaponless are the Asuras, the godless: scatter them with thy wheel, impetuous hero." (*Rig Veda* VIII:85:9)

Many of the hymns refer to the intoxicating soma juice, which is squeezed from the mysterious soma plant and drank.

All of the hymns of the ninth book of the *Rig Veda* are dedicated to the purifying soma, which is even credited with making them feel immortal, probably because of its psychedelic influence. The first hymn in this book refers to the "iron-fashioned home" of the Aryans.

In the first book of the *Rig Veda* the worshipers recognize Agni as the guard of eternal law (I:1:8) and Mitra and Varuna as lovers and cherishers of law who gained their mighty power through law (I:2:8). In the 24th hymn they pray to Varuna, the wise Asura, to loosen the bonds of their sins. However, the prayers for riches continue, and Indra is thanked for winning wealth in horses, cattle, and gold by his chariot. Agni helps to slay the many in war by the hands of the few, "preserving our wealthy patrons with thy succors, and ourselves." (*Rig Veda* I:31:6, 42) Indra helped win the Aryan victory:

> *He, much invoked, hath slain Dasyus and Simyus, after his wont, and laid them low with arrows.*
>
> *The mighty thunderer with his fair-complexioned friends won the land, the sunlight, and the waters.*

Control of the waters was essential for agricultural wealth. Indra is praised for crushing the godless races and breaking down their forts. (*Rig Veda* I:174)

In the tenth and last book of the *Rig Veda* some new themes are explored, but the Dasyus are still condemned for being "riteless, void of sense, inhuman, keeping alien laws," and Indra still urges the heroes to slay the enemies; his "hand is prompt to rend and burn, O hero thunder-armed: as thou with thy companions didst destroy the whole of Sushna's brood." (*Rig Veda* X:22)

One unusual hymn is on the subject of gambling with dice. The speaker regrets alienating his wife, wandering homeless in constant fear and debt, envying others' well-ordered homes. He finally warns the listener not to play with dice but recommends cultivating his land. (*Rig Veda* X:34) Hymn 50 of this most recent last book urges Indra to win riches with valour "in the war for water on their fields." Now the prayer is that "we Gods may quell our Asura foemen." (*Rig Veda* X:53:4) A wedding ceremony is indicated in a hymn of Surya's bridal, the daughter of the sun. (*Rig Veda* X:85)

The first indication of the caste system is outlined in the hymn to Purusha, the embodied human spirit, who is one-fourth creature and three-fourths eternal life in heaven.

The Brahmin was his mouth, of both his arms was the Rajanya made.

His thighs became the Vaisya, from his feet the Sudra was produced.

The Brahmin caste was to be the priests and teachers; the Rajanya represents the king, head of the warrior or Kshatriya caste; Vaishyas are the merchants, craftsmen, and farmers; and the Sudras are the workers. In hymn 109 the *brahmachari* or student is mentioned as engaged in duty as a member of God's own body.

The hymn to liberality is a breath of fresh air:

The riches of the liberal never waste away, while he who will not give finds none to comfort him.

The man with food in store who, when the needy comes in miserable case begging for bread to eat,

Hardens his heart against him - even when of old he did him service - find not one to comfort him.

Yet later we realize that the priests are asking for liberality to support their own services, for the "plowing makes the food that feeds us," and thus a speaking (or paid) Brahmin is better than a silent one.

The power of speech is honored in two hymns.

Where, like men cleansing corn-flour in a cribble, the wise in spirit have created language,

Friends see and recognize the marks of friendship: their speech retains the blessed sign imprinted.

In hymn 125 of the tenth mandala Vak or speech claims to have penetrated earth and heaven, holding together all existence. A philosophical hymn of creation is found in *Rig Veda* X:129. Beginning from non-being when nothing existed, not even water nor death, that One breathless breathed by itself. At first this All was concealed by darkness and formless chaos, but by heat *(tapas)* that One came into existence. Thus arose desire, the primal seed and germ of Spirit.

Sages searching in their hearts discovered kinship with the non-existent. A ray of light extended across the darkness, but what was known above or below? Creative fertility was there with energy and action, but who really knows where this creation came from? For the gods came after the world's creation. Who could know the source of this creation and how it was produced? The one seeing it in the highest heaven only knows, or maybe it does not.

THE GEOGRAPHY OF THE RIGVEDA

The internal chronology of the Rigveda being firmly established, the next step in our historical analysis of the Rigveda is the establishment of the geography of the text.

The geography of the Rigveda has been the most misrepresented aspect of the text in the hands of the scholars: the geographical information in the Rigveda, to put it in a nutshell, more or less pertains to the area from Uttar Pradesh in the east to Afghanistan in the west, the easternmost river mentioned in the text being the Ganga, and the westernmost being the western tributaries of the Indus.

This geographical information is treated in a simplistic manner by the scholars, and the result is a completely distorted picture of Rigvedic geography:

1. Firstly, taking the, Rigveda as one monolithic unit, the information is interpreted to mean that the area of the Rigveda extended from western Uttar Pradesh to Afghanistan.

   It is further assumed that the habitat of the Vedic Aryans, during the period of composition of the

Rigveda, was the central part of this area: the Saptasindhu or Punjab, the Land of the Five Rivers bounded on the east by the Saraswati and on the west by the Indus. Their eastern horizon was western Uttar Pradesh and their western horizon was Afghanistan.

The consensus on this point is so general that even in our *own* earlier book dealing with the Aryan invasion theory, where we have *not* yet analysed the Rigveda in detail, we have automatically assumed the Punjab to be the habitat of the Vedic Aryans during the period of the Rigveda.

However, as we shall see in the course of our analysis, the habitat of the Vedic Aryans during the period was considerably to the *east* of the Punjab.

2. Secondly, after taking the Punjab to be the habitat of the Rigvedic Aryans, the matter is not left at that. A further slant is introduced into the interpretation of the geographical data in the Rigveda: it is automatically assumed, on the basis of an extraneous theory based on a misinterpretation of linguistic data, and without any basis within the Rigvedic data itself, that a movement from west to east is to be discerned in the Rigveda.

   Thus, western places within the horizon of the Rigveda are treated as places old and familiar to the Vedic Aryans, being their "early habitats"; while eastern places within the horizon of the Rigveda are treated as new and unfamiliar places with which the Vedic Aryans are "becoming acquainted".

   The same goes for places *outside* the horizon of the Rigveda (i.e. places *not* named in the Rigveda): places to the west of Afghanistan, not named in the Rigveda, are treated as places which have been "forgotten" by the Vedic Aryans; while places to the east of western Uttar Pradesh, not named in the Rigveda, are treated as places "still unknown" to the Vedic Aryans.

3. Thirdly, and as a direct corollary to the above, it is automatically assumed that there was a movement of place-names as well from west to east.

   There are three rivers named in the Rigveda to which this applies: the Saraswati, Gomati and Sarayu. The Saraswati in the Rigveda is the river to the *east* of the Punjab (flowing through Haryana) and the Gomati and Sarayu in the Rigveda are rivers to the west of the Punjab (western tributaries of the Indus). This is the general consensus, and it is confirmed by an examination of the references in the Rigveda.

   But a Saraswati (Haraxvaiti) and a Sarayu (Haroiiu) are also found in Afghanistan; and a Gomati and a Sarayu are found in northeastern Uttar Pradesh. Clearly, there has been a transfer of name, in the case of these three river-names, from one river to another.

   The logical procedure would be to suspend judgement, till further evidence is forthcoming, as to the locations of the rivers which originally bore these three names. A second, and slightly less logical, procedure, would be to automatically assume that the Rigvedic rivers originally bore all the three names, since the oldest recorded occurrence of the three names is in the Rigveda. However, a west-to-east movement is assumed in respect of all three names, and consequently, the westernmost rivers bearing the three names are taken to be the original bearers of those names.

4. Thus far, the distortion in interpretation and presentation of the geographical data in the Rigveda is still relatively mild. It is in fact too mild for some extremist scholars who would like to present a more definitive picture of a west-to-east movement into India.

Some of these scholars attempt to connect stray words in the Rigveda, *often words not even having any geographical context*, with places far to the west of the horizon of the Rigveda: an extreme example of this is the attempt to suggest that a root word *rip*-in the Rigveda indicates a subdued memory of the Rhipaean mountains: the Urals.

Some scholars, not satisfied with the idea that the Vedic Aryans *came* from the west, attempt to show that they were *still* in the west even during the period of composition of the Rigveda: the Saptasindhu, it is suggested by some, refers to seven rivers in Central Asia, and the Saraswati in the Rigveda is *not* the river of Haryana, but the river of Afghanistan.

There is even an extreme lunatic fringe which would like to suggest that the Ganga and Yamuna of the Rigveda are rivers in Afghanistan. A political "scholar", Rajesh Kochhar, as part of a concerted campaign to show that the events in the Ramayana took place in Afghanistan, transfers the entire locale of the epic to Afghanistan: "Ravana's Lanka can be a small island in the midst of river Indus... by Vindhyas is meant Baluch hills, and by sea the Lower Indus." He does this under cover of examining the geography of the Rigveda, in his book, *The Vedic People: Their History and Geography* (Orient Longman, New Delhi, 1999), where he decides that in the Ramayana (which he examines for the geography of the Rigveda), Saraswati is identified with Helmand and Ganga and Yamuna as its tributaries in the hilly areas of Afghanistan. He makes this revolutionary discovery on the basis of a verse in the Valmiki Ramayana (2.65.6) where "Yamuna is described as surrounded by mountains".

This is the level to which "scholarship" can stoop, stumble and fall. In this book, we will examine the geography of the Rigveda, *not* on the basis of interpretations of verses from the Valmiki Ramayana or the Hanuman Calisa, but on the basis of the actual geographical data within the hymns and verses of the Rigveda itself, under the following heads:

I. The Rigvedic Rivers.

II. The Evidence of River-names.

III. The Evidence of Place-names.

IV. The Evidence of Animal-names.

THE RIGVEDIC RIVERS

The rivers named in the Rigveda can be classified into five geographical categories:

1. *The Northwestern Rivers (i.e. western tributaries of the Indus, flowing through Afghanistan and the north):*
   Trstama (Gilgit)
   Susartu
   Anitabha
   Rasa
   Sveti
   Kubha (Kabul)
   Krumu (Kurrum)
   Gomati (Gomal)
   Sarayu (Siritoi)
   Mehatnu
   Svetyavarai
   Prayiyu (Bara)
   Vayiyu
   Suvastu (Swat)
   Gauri (Panjkora)
   Kusava (Kunar)
2. *The Indus and its minor eastern tributaries:*
   Sindhu (Indus)
   Susoma (Sohan)
   Arjikiya (Haro)
3. *The Central Rivers (i.e. rivers of the Punjab):*
   Vitasta (Jhelum)
   Asikni (Chenab)
   Parusni (Ravi)
   Vipas (Beas)
   Suturi (Satlaj)
   Marudvrdha (Maruvardhvan)

4. *The East-central Rivers (i.e. rivers of Haryana):*
   Saraswati
   DRSadvatI/Hariyupiya/Yavyavati
   Apaya
5. *The Eastern Rivers:*
   Asmanvati (Assan, a tributary of the Yamuna)
   Yamuna/Amsumati
   Ganga/Jahnnvi

A few words of clarification will be necessary in the case of the identities of some of these rivers:

1. *Hariyupiya/Yavyavati*: Hariyupiya is another name of the Drsadvati: the river is known as Raupya in the Mahabharata, and the name is clearly a derivative of Hariyupiya.

   The Yavyavati is named in the same hymn and context as the Hariyupiya, and almost all the scholars agree that both the names refers to the same river.

   It is also possible that Yavyavati may be another name of the Yamuna. M.L. Bhargava, in his study of Rigvedic Geography, incidentally (i.e. without making such an identification) makes the following remarks: "The old beds of the ancient Drsadvati and the Yamuna... ran very close to each other... the two rivers appear to have come close at a place about three miles southwest of Chacharauli town, but diverged again immediately after... the Yamuna... then again ran southwestwards almost parallel to the Drsadvati, the two again coming about two miles close to each other near old Srughna......"

   The battle described on the Hariyupiya-Yavyavati may therefore have taken place in the area between these rivers.

   However, pending further evidence (of this identity of Yavyavati with the Yamuna), we must assume, with the scholars, that the Yavyavati is the same as the Hariyupiya.

2. *Jahnnvi*: Jahnnvi, which is clearly another name of the Ganga, is named in two hymns; and in both of them, it is translated by the scholars as something other than the name of a river: Griffith translates it as "Jahnu's children" (I.116.19) and "the house of Jahnu" (III.58.6).

The evidence, however, admits of only one interpretation:

a. Jahnnvi is clearly the earlier Rigvedic form of the later word Jahnavi: the former word is not found after the Rigveda, and the latter word is not found in the Rigveda.

   The word clearly belongs to a class of words in the Rigveda which underwent a particular phonetic change in the course of time: *Jahnavi* in the Rigveda becomes *Jahnavi after* the Rigveda; *Brahmana* becomes *Brahmana* in the Rigveda itself (both words are found in the Rigveda while only the latter is found after the Rigveda); and the word *Pavaka* has already become *Pavaka* in the course of compilation of the Rigveda (only the latter form is found in the Rigveda, but according to B.K. Ghosh, "the evidence of the metres... clearly proves that the actual pronunciation of the word *Pavaka* must have been *Pavaka* in the Rigvedic age").

b. The word Jahnavi (and therefore also the word Jahnavi which has no independent existence, and for which there is no alternative source of information since it is found only twice in the Rigveda and nowhere outside it) literally means "daughter of Jahnu", and not "Jahnu's children" or "the house of Jahnu".

   And the word Jahnavi (and therefore also Jahnavi as well) has only one connotation in the entire length and breadth of Sanskrit literature: it is a name of the Ganga.

c. One of the two references to the Jahnavi in the Rigveda provides a strong clue to the identity of this word: JahndvI (I. 116.19) is associated with the *Simsumara* (I.116.18) or the Gangetic dolphin. The dolphin is not referred to anywhere else in the Rigveda.

The Mandala-wise distribution of the names of the rivers in the Rigveda is as follows:

Early Mandala I

Saraswati: I.3.10-12.

Middle Mandala I

Saraswati: I.89.3.

Sindhu: I.83.1.

General and Late Mandala I

Gauri: I.164.4.

Rasa: I. 112.12.

Sindhu: I.44.12; 122.6; 126.1; 186.5

(plus the references to the Sindhu in the refrain of the Kutsas in the last verses of I.94-96, 98, 100-103, 105-115).

Saraswati: I.13.9; 142.9; 164.49, 52; 188.8

Jahnavi: I.116.19.

Mandala II

Saraswati: II.1.11; 3.8; 30.8; 32.8; 41.16-18.

Mandala III

Vipas: III.33.1.

Sutudri: III.33.1.

Saraswati: III.4.8; 23.4; 54.13.

Drsadvati: III.23.4,

Apaya: III.23.4.

Jahnavi: III.58.6.

Mandala IV

Sarayu: IV.30.18.

Kusava: IV.18.8.

Sindhu: IV.30.12; 54.6; 55.3.

Parusni: IV.22.2.

Vipas: IV.30.11.

Rasa: IV.43.6.

Mandala V

Sarayu: V.53.9.

Kubha: V.53.9.

Krumu: V.53.9.

Anitabha: V.53.9.

Rasa: V.41.15; 53.9.

Sindhu: V.53.9.

Parusni: V.52.9.

Saraswati: V.5.8; 42.12; 43.11; 46.2,

Yamuna: V.52.17.

Mandala VI

Saraswati: VI.49.7; 50.12. 52.6; 61.1-7, 10-11, 13-14

Hariyupiya: VI.27.5.

Yavyavati: VI.27.6.

Ganga: VI.45.31.

Mandala VII

Asikni: VII.5.3.

Parusni: VII.18.8, 9.

Saraswati: VII.2.8; 9.5; 35.11; 36.6; 39.5; 40.3; 95.1-2, 4-6; 96.1, 3-6.

Yamuna: VII.18.19.

Mandala VIII

Gomati: VIII.24.30.

Svetyavarai: VIII.26.18.

Suvastu: VIII.19.37.

Prayiyu: VIII.19.37.

Vayiyu: VIII.19.37.

Sindhu: VIII.12.3; 20.24, 25; 25.14; 26.18, 72.7.

Arjikiya: VIII.7.29; 64.11.

Susoma: VIII.7.29; 64.11.

Asikni: VIII.20.25.

Parusni: VIII.75.15.

Saraswati: VIII.21.17, 18; 38.10; 54.4

Amsumati: VIII.96.13.

Rasa: VIII.72.13.

Mandala IX

Sindhu: IX.97.58.

Arjikiya: IX.65.23.

Saraswati: IX.5.8; 67.32; 81.4.

Rasa: IX.41.6.

Mandala X

Sarayu: X.64.9.

Gomati: X.75.6.

Mehatnu: X.75.6.

Kubha: X.75.6.

Krumu: X.75.6.

Sveti: X.75.6.

Rasa: X.75.6; 108.1, 2; 121.4.

Susartu: X.75.6.

Trstama: X.75.6.

Sindhu: X.64.9; 65.13; 66.11; 75.1, 3-4, 6-9.

Arjikiya: X.75.5.

Susoma: X.75.5.

Vitasta: X.75.5.

Marudvrdha: X.75.5.

Asikni: X.75.5.

Parusni: X.75.5.

Sutudri: X.75.5.

Saraswati: X.17.7-9; 30.12; 64.9; 65.1,13; 66.5; 75.5; 110.8; 131.5; 141.5; 184.2

Asmanvati: X.53.8.

Yamuna: X.75.5.

Ganga: X.75.5.

THE EVIDENCE OF RIVER NAMES

The names of the rivers in the Rigveda have always formed the basis for any analysis of Rigvedic geography.

Let us examine the geographical picture presented by these river-names when the Mandalas are arranged in their chronological order (click on the link).

As the Chinese put it, one picture is worth a thousand words. The graph gives us the entire geographical picture in a nutshell: (click on the link)

1. In the pre-Rigvedic period and the early part of the Early Period (Mandala VI), the Vedic Aryans were inhabitants of an area to the east of the Saraswati.
2. In the course of the Early Period (Mandalas III and VII), and the early part of the Middle Period (Mandala IV and the middle upa-mandalas), there was a steady expansion westwards.
3. Though there was an expansion westwards, the basic area of the Vedic Aryans was still restricted to the east in the Middle Period (Mandala II), and even in the early parts of the Late Period: Mandala V knows the western rivers from the Kubha (Kabul) in the north to the Sarayu (Siritoi) in the south, but its base is still in the east. Saraswati is still the most important river in the Mandala: it is referred to by the eponymous Rsi Atri (V.42.12; 43.11) who also refers to the Rasa (V.41.15).

All the other references to the western rivers (Sarayu, Kubha, Krumu, Anitabha, Rasa, Sindhu) occur in a single verse (V.53.9) by a single Rsi Syavasva, obviously a very mobile Rsi who also refers elsewhere to the Parusni (V.52.9) and even the Yamuna (V.52.17).

4. In the later part of the Late Period (Mandalas VIII, IX, X, and the general and late upa-mandalas) the Vedic Aryans were spread out over the entire geographical horizon of the Rigveda.

Let us examine the evidence of the river-names in greater detail under the following heads:

A. The Westward Expansion in the Bharata Period.

B. The Evidence of Some Key Rivers.

The Westward Expansion in the Bharata Period: The graph of the rivers clearly shows that there was a *westward* expansion of the Vedic Aryans from the time of Sudas onwards.

In the Early period, right from pre-Rigvedic times to the time of Sudas, the Vedic Aryans were settled in the area to the *east* of the Punjab: Mandala VI knows of no river to the west of the Saraswati.

However, in the Mandalas and upa-mandalas following Mandala VI, we find a steady movement westwards:

a. Mandala III refers to the *first two* rivers of the Punjab *from the east*: the Sutudri and the Vipas.

b. Mandala VII refers to the next two rivers of the Punjab *from the east*: the Parusni and Asikni.

c. The middle upa-mandalas of Mandala I contain the first reference to the Indus, but none to the rivers *west* of the Indus.

d. Mandala IV contains the first references to rivers *west* of the Indus.

If the case for the westward expansion is strong enough even merely from the evidence of the *names* of the rivers, it becomes unimpeachable when we examine the *context* in which these names appear in the hymns:

1. The Sutudri and Vipas are not referred to in a casual vein. They are referred to in a special context: hymn III.33 is a special ode to these two rivers by Vishvamitra in commemoration of a historical movement of the warrior bands of the Bharatas led by Sudas and himself, across the billowing waters of these rivers.

   What is important is that this hymn is characterized *by the Western scholars themselves* as a historical hymn commemorating the migratory movement of the Vedic Aryans across the Punjab.,

   But the Western scholars depict it as a movement from the west to the east: Griffith calls the hymn "a relic of the traditions of the Aryans regarding their progress eastward in the land of the Five Rivers".

   However, an examination of the facts leaves no doubt that the direction of this historical movement was *from the east to the west*: the very distribution of the river-names in the Rigveda, as apparent from our graph of the rivers, makes this clear.

   But there is more specific evidence within the hymns to show that this movement was from the east to the west:

   Sudas is a descendant of Divodasa (VII.18.25), Divodasa is a descendant of Srnjaya (VI.47.22 and Griffith's footnotes to it) and Srnjaya is a descendant of Devavata (IV.15.4): Sudas is therefore clearly a remote descendant of Devavata.

   Devavata established the sacrificial fire on the banks of the Apaya between the Saraswati and the Drsadvati (III.23.3-4) The Saraswati is to the *east* of the Vipas and Sutudri, and the Apaya and Drsadvati are *even further east*. No ancestor of Sudas is associated with any river to the west of the Saraswati.

   The historical movement of the Vedic Aryans across the Sutudri and the Vipas, at the time of Sudas, can only be a *westward* movement.

2. The Parusni and Asikni, also, are not referred to in a casual vein: they also are referred to in a special context. The context is a major battle fought on the Parusni by the Bharatas under Sudas and Vasishtha (who replaced Vishvamitra as the priest of Sudas).

   The direction of the movement is crystal clear in this case as well: Sudas with his *earlier* priest Vishvamitra is associated with the Sutudri and Vipas, and with his *later* priest Vasishtha is associated with the Parusni which is to the west of the two other rivers. But there is more specific evidence in Mandala VII about the direction of movement in this battle, which is the subject of various references throughout the Mandala:

   a. The battle is fought on the Parusni and the enemies of Sudas (who is referred to here as the Puru) are described in VII.5.3 as the people of the Asikni. The Asikni is to the west of the Parusni hence it is clear that the enemies of Sudas are fighting from the *west* of the Parusni while Sudas is fighting from the *east*.

      Curiously, Griffith mistranslates the name of the river Asikni as "dark-hued", thereby killing two birds with one stone: the people of the Asikni become "the dark-hued races", thereby wiping out the sense of direction inherent in the reference, while at the same time introducing the racial motif

   b. In VII.83.1, two of the tribes fighting against Sudas, the Prthus and the Parsus, are described as marching *eastwards* (*praca*) towards him.

      Griffith again mistranslates the names of the tribes as "armed with broad axes" and the word praca as "forward".

   c. VII.6.5 refers indirectly to this battle by talking of the defeat of the tribes of Nahus (i.e. the tribes of the Anus and Druhyus who fought against Sudas) as follows: "Far, far away hath Agni chased the

Dasyus, and, in the east, *hath turned the godless westward"*. Sudas is therefore clearly pressing forward from the east.

3. The first references to the Indus are in the middle upa-mandalas (I.83.1) and in Mandala IV (IV.30.12; 54.6; 55.3). There is, perhaps, a westward movement indicated even in the very identity of the composers of the hymns which contain these references: I.83 is composed by Gautama Rahugana *who does not refer to any river west of the Indus*, while the references in Mandala IV are by his *descendants*, the Vamadeva Gautamas, who also refer to two rivers to the west of the Indus (IV.18.8; 30.18).

   Thus, we have a clear picture of the westward movement of the Vedic Aryans from their homeland in the east of the Saraswati to the area to the west of the Indus, towards the end of the Early Period of the Rigveda: IV.30.18 refers to what is clearly the westermnost point in this movement, a battle fought in southern Afghanistan "on yonder side of Sarayu".

The Evidence of Some Key Rivers: The key rivers in the Rigveda are:

a. The Indus to the west of the Five Rivers of the Punjab.
b. The Saraswati to the east of the Five Rivers of the Punjab.
c. The Ganga and Yamuna, the easternmost rivers named in the Rigveda.

The evidence of these key rivers is extremely significant:

1. *The Indus and the Saraswati:* The word Sindhu in the Rigveda primarily means "river" or even "sea"; it is only secondarily a name of the Indus river: thus Saptasindhava can mean "seven rivers" but not "seven Induses".

   The relative insignificance of the Indus in the Rigveda is demonstrated by the fact that *the Indus is not mentioned even once in the three oldest Mandalas of the Rigveda.*

Since the word Sindhu, in its meaning of "river", occurs frequently throughout the Rigveda, scholars are able to juggle with the word, often mistranslating the word Sindhu as "the Indus" even when it means "river".

However, *even this sophistry is not possible in the case of the three oldest Mandalas (VI, III and VII)*: the word Sindhu, except in eight verses, occurs only in the plural, and can be translated only as "rivers".

In seven of the eight references, in which the word occurs in the singular, it clearly refers to some other "river" which is specified within the context of the reference itself:

a. III.33.3, 5; 53.9: Vipas.
b. VII.18.5: Parusni.
c. VII.33.3: Yamuna.
d. VII.36.6; 95.1: Saraswati.

In the eighth reference (VII.87.6) the word means "sea": the verse talks of the sun setting in the sea.

In sharp contrast, the Saraswati is referred to many times in the three oldest Mandalas. In fact, there are three whole hymns dedicated to it in these Mandalas: VI.61; VII.95, 96.

All in all, the Saraswati is referred to in nine Mandalas out of ten in the Rigveda (i.e. in all except Mandala IV, which represents the westernmost thrust in the westward movement of the Vedic Aryans).

The Indus is referred to in only six Mandalas (I, IV, V, VIII, IX, X); and in three of these (V, IX, X), the references to the Saraswati far outnumber the references to the Indus.

It is only in the *latest* parts of the Rigveda that the Indus overshadows the Saraswati:

a. In Mandala VIII, the references to the Indus outnumber the references to the Saraswati (by six verses to four).
b. In the general and late upa-mandalas of Mandala I, the

Indus, but not the Saraswati, is enumerated with other deities in the refrain of the Kutsas which forms the last verse of nineteen out of their twenty-one hymns.

c. In Mandala X, although there are more references to the Saraswati, it is the Indus, and not the Saraswati, which is the main river lauded in the *nadIstuti* (X.75), the hynm in Praise of the Rivers.

The Saraswati is so important in the *whole* of the Rigveda that it is worshipped as one of the Three Great Goddesses in the Apri-suktas of all the ten families of composers (being named in nine of them and implied in the tenth). The Indus finds no place in these Apri-suktas.

The contrast between the overwhelming importance of the Saraswati and the relative unimportance of the Indus is so striking, and so incongruous with the theory of an Aryan invasion from the northwest, that many scholars resort to desperate explanations to account for it: Griffith, in his footnote to VI.61.2, suggests that perhaps "Saraswati is also another name of Sindhu or the Indus".

2. *The Eastern Rivers*: The Ganga and the Yamuna are the two easternmost rivers named in the Rigveda. One or the other of these two rivers (either by these names, or by their other names, Jahnavi and Amsumati respectively) is named in seven of the ten Mandalas of the Rigveda, *including the three oldest Mandalas* (VI, III and VII).

By contrast, the Indus and its western tributaries, as we saw, are named in only six Mandalas, which do *not* include the three oldest Mandalas of the Rigveda.

But even more significant than these bare statistics is the particular nature of the four references to the Ganga, the easternmost river of them all:

a. The *nadIstuti* begins its enumeration of the rivers with the Ganga and moves westwards.

Whether this circumstance in itself is a significant one

or not is debatable; but while many scholars, without necessarily having arrived at any specific ideas about Rigvedic chronology or geography, find it important, certain others seek to deflect its importance, and even to dismiss the importance of the Ganga itself in the Rigveda:

Griffith, in his footnote to X.75.5, takes pains to suggest that "the poet addresses first the most distant rivers. *Ganga*: the Ganges is mentioned, indirectly, in only one other verse of the *Rigveda*, and even there, the word is said by some to be the name of a woman. See VI.45.31."

b. The reference in VI.45.31 is definitely significant: the composer compares the height of a patron's generosity to the height of the wide bushes on the banks of the Ganga.

   This makes it clear that even in the oldest Mandala in the Rigveda, the Ganga is a familiar geographical landmark, whose features conjure up images which are very much a part of traditional idiomatic expression.

c. The reference in III.58.6. is infinitely more significant. Griffith translates the verse as follows: "Ancient your home, auspicious is your friendship: Heroes, your wealth is with the house of Jahnu."

   Here, not only does Griffith mistranslate Jahnavi as "the house of Jahnu", he compounds it with a further misinterpretation of the grammatical form:

   Jahnavyam is clearly "on (the banks of) the Jahnavi" on the lines of similar translations by Griffith himself in respect of other rivers: *Parusnyam* (V.52.9: on the banks of the Parusni), *Yamunayam* (V.52.17: on the banks of the Yamuna), *Drsadvatyam... Apayayam Sarasvatyam* (III.23.4: on the banks of the Drsadvati, Apaya and Saraswati).

   The correct translation of III.58.6, addressed to the Asvins, is: "Your ancient home, your auspicious friendship, O Heroes, your wealth is on (the banks of the Jahnavi." What is noteworthy is that the phrase *Puranamokah* "ancient home" is used in the second oldest Mandala in the Rigveda, in reference to the banks of the Ganga.

d. The reference in I.116.19 associates the Jahnavi with Bharadvaja, Divodasa and the Gangetic dolphin (all of whom are referred to in the earlier verse I.116.18). It is clear, therefore, that the river is specially associated with the oldest period of the Rigveda, the period of Mandala VI (which is also the only place, outside the *nadistuti*, where the Ganga is referred to by that name).

The evidence of the rivers in the Rigveda is therefore unanimous in identifying the area to the east of the Saraswati as the original homeland of the Vedic Aryans.

SAMA VEDA

The *Sama Veda* contains the melodies or music for the chants used from the *Rig Veda* for the sacrifices; almost all of its written verses are traceable to the *Rig Veda,* mostly the eighth and ninth books and most to Indra, Agni, or Soma.

These are considered the origin of Indian music and probably stimulated great artistry to make the sacrifices worthwhile to their patrons who supported the priests. The *Sama Veda* helped to train the musicians and functioned as a hymnal for the religious rites. The animal sacrifices did not use the *Śama* chants, but they were used extensively in agricultural rites and in the soma rituals for which the plant with inebriating and hallucinogenic qualities was imported from the mountains to the heartland of India.

By this time the priests were specializing in different parts of the sacrifices as professional musicians and singers increased. The singing was like the strophe, antistrophe, and epode of the Greek chorus and used the seven tones of the European scale. By the tenth century BC the Aryans had invaded most of northern India, and once again trade resumed with Babylon and others in the near east. As the sacrifices became more complex, the priestly class used them to enhance their role in the society. Many considered this musical portion the most important of the *Vedas*.

YAJUR VEDA

Though also following many of the hymns of the *Rig Veda*, the *Yajur Veda* deviates more from the original text in its collection of the ritual formulas for the priests to use in the sacrifices, which is what *yaja* means. It explains how to construct the altars for new and full-moon sacrifices and other ceremonies.

The *Yajur Veda* has two collections or *samhitas* called White and Black, the latter being more obscure in its meanings. By this time (10th century BC and after) the Aryan conquest has proceeded from the northwest and Punjab to cover northern India, especially the Ganges valley. The caste system was in place, and as the warriors settled down to ruling over an agricultural society, the role of the priests and their ceremonies gained influence and justified the Aryan ways to the native workers, who labored for the farmers, merchants, craftsmen, who in turn were governed by their kings and priests. Land and wealth were accumulated in the hands of a few ruling families, and with food scarce the indigenous people were enslaved or had to sell their labour cheap to the ruling classes.

By instituting more elaborate sacrifices for their wealthy patrons, the priests could grow both in numbers and wealth as well. The famous horse sacrifice was not celebrated often but was used by a king to show his lordship over potential adversaries, who were invited to acknowledge this overlordship in the ritual. The parts of the horse symbolize different aspects of the universe so that tremendous power is invoked. The complicated and obscure rituals were presided over by the priests - the three symbols of the lotus leaf, the frog (for rain), and the golden man (for the sun) representing the Aryan dominance over the land and waters of India and the natural powers that sustain agriculture.

The soma sacrifice was the most important and could last up to twelve years. Since the soma plant was imported from distant mountains, it had to be purchased. A ritual drama re-enacted this business and aggressive Aryan history by showing the buyer snatching back the calf, which was paid for the soma plant, after the transaction occurs. The soma plant was then placed in a cart and welcomed as an honored guest and king at the sacrifice. Animals were slain and cut up in the rites before their meat was eaten. After various offerings and other ceremonies the soma juice is poured and toasted to different gods, and finally the text lists the sacrificial fees, usually goats, cows, gold, clothes, and food.

Coronation ceremonies supported the inauguration of kings. The priests tried to keep themselves above the warrior caste though by praising soma as king of the Brahmins. Waters were drawn from various rivers to sprinkle on the king and indicate the area of his kingdom, and he strode in each direction to signify his sovereignty. The king was anointed by the royal priest, giving some water to his son, the designated prince, and ritually enacting a raid against a kinsman's cattle, once again affirming their history of conquest. The booty was taken and divided into three parts for the priest, those who drank, and the original owner. A ritual dice game was played, which the king was allowed to win. The king then rode out in his chariot and was publicly worshiped as a divine ruler.

Agricultural rites were common and regular, and chariot races were no doubt popular at some of the festivals. The Purusha (person) sacrifice symbolized human sacrifice, which may refer back to the time when a hunting and pastoral people did not allow their enemies to live because of the shortage of food. However, in an agricultural society more labour was needed and could produce surplus food. The Purusha sacrifice recognized 184 professional crafts and guilds.

Finally the highest sacrifice was considered to be the Sarvamedha in which the sacrificer offered all of his possessions as the fee at the end of the ceremony. The *Yajur Veda* is actually the *Isha Upanishad,* expressing the mystical view that the supreme spirit pervades everything. This society was highly patriarchal, and the status of women declined, especially as men often married non-Aryan women. Women did not attend public assemblies and could not inherit property on their own. Polyandry was discouraged, but polygamy, adultery, and prostitution were generally accepted except during certain rituals. A sacrificer was not allowed to seek a prostitute on the first day of the sacrificial fire, nor the wife of another on the second day, nor his own wife on the third day.

The priests placed themselves at the top of the caste system as they supervised a religion most of the people could not understand without them. After the *Atharva Veda* was accepted, each sacrifice required at least four priests, one on each side of the fire using the *Rig, Sama, Yajur,* and *Atharva Vedas,* plus their assistants. After the wars of conquest were completed and the warrior caste settled down to rule, the priests were needed to sustain social stability. Yet in these times the caste system was much more flexible, as it is indicated that one should not ask about the caste of a learned man. The Brahmins, as the priest caste was called, had three obligations or debts to pay back in life: they paid back the seers by studying the *Vedas,* the gods by offering sacrifices, and their fathers by raising a family. Like their European ancestors, the Aryan warriors considered themselves above laboring for food and so organized society that food would be provided for them. One ethical duty later found in the epics was that of taking care of refugees, probably because as marauding raiders they had often been refugees themselves. The priests assured their livelihood by making sure that penance through religious ritual was a prime social value.

ATHARVA VEDA

The latest and fourth *Veda* is in a different category. For a long time many referred to only three *Vedas,* by which complete ceremonies could be conducted with the *Rig hotr* reciting, the *Sama udgatri* singing, and the *Yajur adhvaryu* performing the ritual. Even later the *Atharvan* Brahmin's part was often performed unaccompanied by the other three priests. Also much of it draws from the customs and beliefs of pre-Aryan or pre-Vedic India. The *Atharva Veda* is much longer than the *Sama* and *Yajur* and only about a sixth of it is from the *Rig Veda.*

The *Atharva Veda* is primarily magical spells and incantations. The line between prayer and magic and between white and black magic is usually drawn by ethical considerations. The *bheshajani* are for healing and cures using herbs to treat fever, leprosy, jaundice, dropsy, and other diseases. The Aryans looked down on doctors and medicine, probably because the natives were more skilled in these than they. Other more positive spells were for successful childbirth, romance, fecundity, virility, etc.

The negative or bewitching spells were called *abhichara* and attempted to cause diseases or harm to enemies; often they were aimed at serpents and demons.

The sorcery is ascribed to one of the authors, Angiras, whose name is related to Agni (Latin *ignis),* the divine messenger and possibly a distant cognate of the Greek word for messenger, angel. Another author, Atharvan, derives from the old Iranian root, *atar,* meaning fire. The third author, Bhrigu, was the name of a tribe which opposed Sudas in the battle of ten kings in the *Rig Veda,* and his name has also been related to a Greek word for fire. The fourth author is Brahmin, the name which was given to the *Atharvan* priest, which eventually became so sacred that it was used as a name not only for the priestly caste but even for God the Creator.

In addition to physicians the Vedic Aryans also held in contempt *Atharvan* astrologers as well as magic, but from this came not only astrology but also the beginning of Ayurvedic medicine. Like most ancient peoples, they also believed that the main cause of disease was evil spirits, possession, or what we would call psychological factors.

The magical elements, particularly the *abhicara*, and the subjects of healing, herbs, and cooking, which were mostly in the woman's domain, made the *Atharva Veda* obnoxious to many Vedic priests. However, these rituals were very popular, and the Brahmin priest's share of the fees soon became equal to the other three priests' combined. Eventually this shamanic tradition had to be incorporated into the Vedic religion, especially later when it faced the new challenges of Jainism and Buddhism.

The Brahmin caste became even stronger, and their wealth can be seen by the belief that the cow by right belonged exclusively to them. Taxes were collected probably by the warrior Kshatriya caste from the Vaisya artisans, farmers, and merchants. The Sudra workers were too poor to be taxed, and the Brahmins were exempt. One verse (*Atharva Veda* 3:29:3) describes heaven as "where a tax is not paid by a weak man for a stronger." Marriage ceremonies are included. Here is a brief example:

I am he; you are she.

I am song; you are verse.

I am heaven; you are earth.

Let us two dwell together here;

let us generate children.

According to the *Atharva Veda* (5:17:8-9), a Brahmin could take a wife from the husband of any other caste simply by seizing her hand. Book 18 contains only funeral verses. There are coronation rites for kings, though the prayer is that the people will choose the king, usually already selected by heredity or the council. Philosophy and abstraction are creeping in, as there are two hymns to the deity of time, and *kama* (love, desire, pleasure) is praised as "the first seed of the mind" that generated heaven. (*Atharva Veda* 19:52)

Let us conclude this section on the *Atharva Veda* with some selections from its beautiful hymn to the Earth as a sample of the more positive expression of the *Vedas*:

High Truth, unyielding Order, Consecration,

Ardor and Prayer and Holy Ritual uphold the Earth, may she, the ruling Mistress of what has been and what will come to be, for us spread wide a limitless domain.

Untrammeled in the midst of men, the Earth, adorned with heights and gentle slopes and plains, bears plants and herbs of various healing powers.

May she spread wide for us, afford us joy!

On whom are ocean, river, and all waters, on whom have sprung up food and plowman's crops, on whom moves all that breathes and stirs abroad-

Earth, may she grant to us the long first draught!

To Earth belong the four directions of space.

On her grows food; on her the plowman toils.

She carries likewise all that breathes and stirs.

Earth, may she grant us cattle and food in plenty!

On whom the men of olden days roamed far, on whom the conquering Gods smote the demons, the home of cattle, horses, and of birds, may Earth vouchsafe to us good fortune and glory!

Bearer of all things, hoard of treasures rare, sustaining mother, Earth the golden-breasted who bears the Sacred Universal Fire, whose spouse is Indra - may she grant us wealth!

Limitless Earth, whom the Gods, never sleeping, protect forever with unflagging care, may she exude for us the well-loved honey, shed upon us her splendor copiously!

Earth, who of yore was Water in the oceans, discerned by the Sages' secret powers, whose immortal heart, enwrapped in Truth, abides aloft in the highest firmament, may she procure for us splendor and power, according to her highest royal state!

On whom the flowing Waters, ever the same, course without cease or failure night and day, may she yield milk, this Earth of many streams, and shed on us her splendor copiously!

May Earth, whose measurements the Asvins marked, over whose breadth the foot of Vishnu strode, whom Indra, Lord of power, freed from foes, stream milk for me, as a mother for her son!

Your hills, O Earth, your snow-clad mountain peaks, your forests, may they show us kindliness!

Brown, black, red, multifarious in hue and solid is this vast Earth, guarded by Indra.

Invincible, unconquered, and unharmed,

I have on her established my abode.

Impart to us those vitalizing forces that come, O Earth, from deep within your body, your central point, your navel, purify us wholly.

The Earth is mother; I am son of Earth.

The Rain-giver is my father; may he shower on us blessings!

The Earth on which they circumscribe the altar, on which a band of workmen prepare the oblation, on which the tall bright sacrificial posts are fixed before the start of the oblation - may Earth, herself increasing, grant us increase!

That man, O Earth, who wills us harm, who fights us, who by his thoughts or deadly arms opposes, deliver him to us, forestalling action.

All creatures, born from you, move round upon you.

You carry all that has two legs, three, or four.

To you, O Earth, belong the five human races, those mortals upon whom the rising sun sheds the immortal splendor of his rays.

May the creatures of earth, united together, let flow for me the honey of speech!

Grant to me this boon, O Earth.

Mother of plants and begetter of all things, firm far-flung Earth, sustained by Heavenly Law, kindly and pleasant is she. May we ever dwell on her bosom, passing to and fro!...

Do not thrust us aside from in front or behind, from above or below! Be gracious, O Earth.

Let us not encounter robbers on our path.

Restrain the deadly weapons!

As wide a vista of you as my eye may scan, O Earth, with the kindly help of Sun, so widely may my sight be never dimmed in all the long parade of years to come!

Whether, when I repose on you, O Earth,

I turn upon my Right *side or my left, or whether, extended flat upon my back,*

I meet your pressure from head to foot, be gentle, Earth! You are the couch of all!

Whatever I dig up of you, O Earth, may you of that have quick replenishment!

O purifying One, may my thrust never reach Right *into your vital points, your heart!*

Your circling seasons, nights succeeding days, your summer, O Earth, your splashing rains, your autumn, your winter and frosty season yielding to spring—may each and all produce for us their milk!...

From your numberless tracks by which mankind may travel, your roads on which move both chariots and wagons your paths which are used by the good and the bad, may we choose a way free from foes and robbers!

May you grant us the blessing of all that is wholesome!

She carries in her lap the foolish and also the wise.

She bears the death of the wicked as well as the good.

She lives in friendly collaboration with the boar, offering herself as sanctuary to the wild pig....

Peaceful and fragrant, gracious to the touch, may Earth, swollen with milk, her breasts overflowing, grant me her blessing together with her milk!

The Maker of the world sought her with oblations when she was shrouded in the depth of the ocean.

A vessel of gladness, long cherished in secret, the earth was revealed to mankind for their joy.

Primeval Mother, disperser of men, you, far-flung Earth, fulfill all our desires.

Whatever you lack, may the Lord of creatures, the First-born of Right, supply to you fully!

May your dwellings, O Earth, free from sickness and wasting, flourish for us! Through a long life, watchful, may we always offer to you our tribute!

O Earth, O Mother, dispose my lot in gracious fashion that I be at ease.

In harmony with all the powers of Heaven set me, O Poet, in grace and good fortune!

Brahmanas

Between about 900 and 700 BC the *Brahmanas* were written in prose as sacerdotal commentaries on the four *Vedas* to guide the practices of the sacrifices and give explanations often mythical and fanciful for these customs. However, their limited focus of justifying the priestly actions in the sacrifices restricted the themes of these first attempts at imaginative literature. Nevertheless they do give us information about the social customs of this period and serve as a transition from the *Vedas* to the *Aranyakas* and the mystical *Upanishads*.

The caste system based on colour *(varna)* was now established, though not as rigidly as it became later. The essential difference was between the light-skinned Aryans, who made up the top three castes of the priestly Brahmins, warrior Kshatriyas, and artisan Vaishyas, and the dark-skinned Dasas, who were the servant Sudras. Sudras, like women, could not own property, and only rarely did they rise above service positions. The Vaishyas were the basis of the economic system of trade, crafts, and farming. The Vaishyas were considered inferior by the Brahmins and Kshatriyas, and a female was generally not allowed to marry below her caste, though it was common for a male to do so. Even a Brahmin's daughter was not supposed to marry a Kshatriya.

The rivalry for prestige and power was between the Brahmins and the Kshatriyas or *rajanyas*. Brahmins often held debates on Brahman and other religious issues. Janaka, a *rajanya* gained knowledge and defeated some Brahmins in discussion. So some Brahmins suggested a symposium on Brahman to prove who was superior, but since Brahmins were expected to be superior on these issues, Yajnavalkya prudently replied, "We are Brahmins; he is a *rajanya*. If we win, whom shall we say that we have defeated? But if he defeats us, they will say a *rajanya* has defeated Brahmins; so let us not convene this symposium." Kings were consecrated by Vedic rites and ruled with the help of the assembly *(sabha)* that met in a hall to administer justice; women were excluded. Ordeals were used, such as making a suspected thief touch a hot ax to see if his hand burned, which might be the origin of the saying, "being caught red-handed." Politics and legislation took place in a larger council *(samiti)*. Taxes were collected to support these institutions and the army. Each village was administered by a Gramani, a Vaisya who functioned like a mayor with civil rather than military authority. The Gramani and the royal charioteer *(Suta)* were considered the kingmakers. This latter privileged position was not merely the driver of the king but also his chief advisor and perhaps storyteller as well. The royal priest or *Purohito* was also supposed to advise the king in peace and protect him in war. The season of dew after the monsoons ended was considered the time for "sacking cities," as ambitious kings came into conflict with each other in wars.

In addition to the discussions of sacerdotal matters, the *Brahmanas* do contain some stories meant to explain or rationalize their religious practices. Some of these are quite imaginative, though the usual pattern is for the hero to discover a rite to perform or a chant to intone which miraculously solves whatever problem is pressing to give a happy ending.

Wendy O'Flaherty has translated some stories from the *Jaiminiya Brahmana*, illustrating how they dealt with the fears of death, God, the father, wives, and demonic women; many of these stories are sexually explicit, indicating that these people were not afraid of discussing their sexuality. However, since the usual way of handling these fears was to use a sacrificial ritual, the solutions probably had only limited social and psychological value.

The most famous of these stories, and the best in my opinion, is the tale of Bhrigu's journey in the other world. Bhrigu was the son of Varuna and devoted to learning, and he thought that he was better than the other Brahmins and even better than the gods and his own father. So Varuna decided to teach him something by stopping his life breaths, causing Bhrigu to enter the world beyond, where he saw someone cut another man to pieces and eat him, a second man eating another who was screaming, a third eating a man who was silently screaming, another world where two women were guarding a treasure, a fifth where a stream of blood was guarded by a naked black man with a club and a stream of butter provided all the desires of golden men in golden bowls, and a sixth world where flowed five rivers of blue and white lotuses and flowing honey with wonderful music, celestial nymphs dancing and singing, and a fragrant odor. When Bhrigu returned, his father Varuna explained to him that the first man represented people who in ignorance destroy trees, which in turn eat them; the second are those who cook animals that cry out and in the other world are eaten by them in return; the third are those who ignorantly cook rice and barley, which scream silently and also eat them in return; the two women are Faith and non-Faith; the river of blood represents those who squeeze the blood out of a Brahmin, and the naked black man guarding is Anger; but the true sacrificers are the golden men, who get the river of butter and the paradise of the five rivers.

To me this myth is a clear warning against the harmful actions of deforestation and meat-eating, and even the eating of living vegetables is to be done in silent respect. It shows an intuitive understanding of the principle of karma or the consequences of action as well as the growing importance of the concept of faith in addition to the usual theme of the sacrifice.

The power of the word is increasing, as the sacrifices were glorified and given power even over the Vedic gods. *Japa* or the practice of chanting a *mantram* like *Aum* practiced ascetically with the sacrifices was believed to produce all one's desires. At the same time knowledge was beginning to be valued. In one exchange mind says that speech merely imitates it, but speech emphasizes the importance of expression and communication; however, Prajapati decides that mind is more important even than the word. This new god, Prajapati, is said to have given birth to both the gods and the demons. The ethical principle of truth appears as the gods are described as being truthful and the demons as being false. However, realizing the ways of the world, many complain that the demons grew strong and rich, just as cattle like salty soil; but by performing the sacrifice the gods attained the whole truth and triumph, as, analogically I might add, people will eventually realize that cattle as well as salt ruins the land.

Prajapati not only was the first to sacrifice but was considered the sacrifice itself. He practiced *tapas* to create by the heat of his own effort, and this heat was also related to cosmic fire and light as well as the warmth of the body and breath. Another concept of energy associated with the breath was *prana;* it also was identified with goodness, as the texts imply that as the life force it cannot be impure or bad. Prajapati not only created but entered into things as form and name, giving them order. Eventually Prajapati would be replaced by Brahman, who was identified with truth and would become the Creator God in the trinity that would include Vishnu, a sun-god who becomes the Preserver, and Shiva, who is derived from the indigenous Rudra, the Destroyer. With all the mental activity going on analysing the rites and their explanation, abstractions were increasing in the religion.

A judgment after death using a scale to weigh good against evil is described in the *Satapatha Brahmana*, an idea which may have been transported from Egypt by merchants. This text recommends that the one who knows this will balance one's deeds in this world so that in the next the good deeds will rise, not the evil ones. Belief in repeated lives through reincarnation is indicated in several passages in the *Brahmanas*. A beef-eater is punished by being born into a strange and sinful creature. As knowledge rivaled the value of ritual, this new problem of how to escape from an endless cycle of rebirth presented itself.

EARLY UPANISHADS

The term *Upanishad* means literally "those who sit near" and implies listening closely to the secret doctrines of a spiritual teacher. Although there are over two hundred *Upanishads*, only fifteen are mentioned by the philosophic commentator Shankara (788-820 CE). These fifteen and the *Maitri* are considered Vedic and the principal *Upanishads*; the rest were written later and are related to the Puranic worship of Shiva, Shakti, and Vishnu. The oldest and longest of the *Upanishads* are the *Brihad-Aranyaka* and the *Chandogya* from about the seventh century BC.

The *Brihad-Aranyaka* has three *Aranyaka* chapters followed by six *Upanishad* chapters. The first chapter of the *Brihad-Aranyaka* Upanishad describes the world as represented by the horse-sacrifice. The primordial battle between the gods and the devils accounts for the evil found in the senses, mind, and speech, but by striking off the evil the divinities were carried beyond death. The priest chants for profound aspiration, one of the most famous verses from the *Upanishads*:

From the unreal lead me to the real!
From darkness lead me to light!
From death lead me to immortality!

The primary message of the *Upanishads* is that this can be done by meditating with the awareness that one's soul *(atman)* is one with all things. Thus whoever knows that one is Brahman (God) becomes this all; even the gods cannot prevent this, since that one becomes their soul *(atman)*. Therefore whoever worships another divinity, thinking it is other than oneself, does not know.

Out of God *(Brahman)* came the Brahmin caste of priests and teachers and the Kshatriyas to rule, development through the Vaishyas and the Sudras. However, a principle was created as justice *(dharma)*, than which nothing is higher, so that a weak person may control one stronger, as if by a king. They say that those who speak the truth speak justice and vice versa, because they are the same. By meditating on the soul *(atman)* alone, one does not perish and can create whatever one wants. Whatever suffering occurs remains with the creatures; only the good goes to the soul, because evil does not go to the gods. The soul is identified with the real, the immortal, and the life-breath *(prana)*, which is veiled by name and form (individuality). By restraining the senses and the mind, one may rest in the space within the heart and become a great Brahmin and like a king may move around within one's body as one pleases. The world of name and form is real, but the soul is the truth or reality of the real. Immortality cannot be obtained through wealth, and all persons and things in the world are dear not for love of them (husband, wife, sons, wealth, gods, etc.); but for the love of the soul, all these are dear. The soul is the overlord of all things, as the spokes of the wheel are held together by the hub.

The principle of action *(karma)* is explained as "one becomes good by good action, bad by bad action." How can one get beyond the duality of seeing, smelling, hearing, speaking to, thinking of, and understanding another? Can one see the seer, smell the smeller, hear the hearer, think the thinker, and understand the understander? It is the soul which is in all things; everything else is wretched. By passing beyond hunger and thirst, sorrow and delusion, old age and death, by overcoming desire for sons, wealth, and worlds, let a Brahmin become disgusted with learning and live as a child; disgusted with that, let one become an ascetic until one transcends both the non-ascetic and the ascetic states. Thus is indicated a spiritual path of learning and discipline that ultimately transcends even learning and discipline in the soul, the inner controller, the immortal, the one dwelling in the mind, whom the mind does not know, who controls the mind from within.

The one departing this world without knowing the imperishable is pitiable, but the one knowing it is a Brahmin. The following refrain is repeated often:

That soul is not this, not that.

It is incomprehensible, for it is not comprehended.

It is indestructible, for it is never destroyed.

It is unattached, for it does not attach itself.

It is unfettered; it does not suffer; it is not injured.

The soul is considered intelligent, dear, true, endless, blissful, and stable. As a king prepares a chariot or ship when going on a journey, one should prepare one's soul with the mystic doctrines of the *Upanishads*. The knowledge that is the light in the heart enables one to transcend this world and death while appearing asleep. The evils that are obtained with a body at birth are left behind upon departing at death. One dreams by projecting from oneself, not by sensing actual objects. In sleep the immortal may leave one's nest and go wherever one pleases. In addition to being free from desire the ethical admonition of being without crookedness or sin is also indicated. At death the soul goes out first, then the life, and finally the breaths go out.

The soul is made of everything; as one acts, one becomes. The doer of good becomes good; the doer of evil becomes evil.

As is one's desire, such is one's resolve; as is the resolve, such is the action, which one attains for oneself. When one's mind is attached, the inner self goes into the action. Obtaining the consequences of one's actions, whatever one does in this world comes again from the other world to this world of action *(karma)*.

By releasing the desires in one's heart, one may be liberated in immortality, reaching *Brahman* (God). One is the creator of all, one with the world. Whoever knows this becomes immortal, but others go only to sorrow. The knowing is sought through the spiritual practices of repeating the *Vedas*, sacrifices, offerings, penance, and fasting. Eventually one sees everything, as the soul overcomes both the thoughts of having done wrong and having done right. The evil does not burn one; rather one burns the evil. In the soul's being the world-all is known. The student should practice self-restraint, giving, and compassion.

The *Chandogya Upanishad* belongs to the *Sama Veda* and is the last eight chapters of the ten-chapter *Chandogya Brahmana*. The first two chapters of the *Brahmana* discuss sacrifices and other forms of worship. As part of the *Sama Veda*, which is the chants, the *Chandogya Upanishad* emphasizes the importance of chanting the sacred *Aum*.

The chanting of *Aum* is associated with the life breath *(prana)*, which is so powerful that when the devils struck it, they fell to pieces. The religious life recommended in the *Chandogya Upanishad* has three parts.

The first is sacrifice, study of the *Vedas*, and giving alms; the second is austerity; and the third is studying the sacred knowledge while living in the house of a teacher. One liberal giver, who had many rest-houses built and provided with food, said, "Everywhere people will be eating of my food."

The soul in the heart is identified with *Brahman* (God), and it is the same as the light which shines higher than in heaven. Knowing and reverencing the sacrificial fire is believed to repel evil-doing from oneself. To the one who knows the soul, evil action does not adhere, just as water does not adhere to the leaf of the lotus flower. To know the soul as divine is called the "Loveliness-uniter" because all lovely things come to such.

The doctrine of reincarnation is clearly implied in the *Chandogya Upanishad* as it declares that those whose conduct is pleasant here will enter a pleasant womb of a Brahmin, Kshatriya, or Vaisya; but those of stinking conduct will enter a stinking womb of a dog, swine, or outcast. Thus reincarnation is explained as an ethical consequence of one's actions *(karma)*.

At death the voice goes into the mind, the mind into the breath, the breath into heat, and heat into the highest divinity, the finest essence of truth and soul. Speaking to Svetaketu, the teacher explains that a tree may be struck at the root, the middle, or the top, but it will continue to live if pervaded by the living soul. Yet if the life leaves one branch of it, it dries up; and if it leaves the whole of it, the whole dries up. Then the teacher explains how the soul is the essence of life and does not die, concluding with the repeated refrain that his student thus ought to identify with the soul.

Truly, indeed, when the living soul leaves it,
This body dies; the living soul does not die.
That which is the subtle essence
This whole world has for its soul.
That is reality (truth). That is the soul.
That you are, Svetaketu.

Then the teacher placed salt in water and asked his student to taste different parts of the water. Just so is Being hidden in all of reality, but it is not always perceived. Just as the thief burns his hand on the hot ax when tested, the one who did not steal and is true does not burn his hand, so the whole world has that truth in its soul.

Speech is to be valued, because it makes known right and wrong, true and false, good and bad, pleasant and unpleasant. Mind is revered, because it enables one to do sacred works.

Will is valued, because heaven and earth and all things were formed by being willed. Thought is important, because it is better not to be thoughtless. Meditation is revered, because one attains greatness by meditating. Understanding is valued, because by it we can understand everything. Strength maintains everything. Food, water, heat, and space each have their values. Finally also memory, hope, and life *(prana)* are to be revered.

Those, who take delight in the soul, have intercourse with it and find pleasure and bliss in it and freedom; but those, who do not, have perishable worlds and no freedom. The seer does not find death nor sickness nor any distress but sees the all and obtains the all entirely. The soul is free of evil, ageless, deathless, sorrowless, hungerless, and thirstless. For those, who go from here having found the soul here, there is freedom in all worlds. No evil can go into the Brahma-world.

The chaste life of the student of sacred knowledge is the essence of austerity, fasting, and the hermit life, for in that way one finds the reality of the soul. The soul must be searched out and understood. The *Chandogya Upanishad* concludes with the advice that one should learn the *Veda* from the family of a teacher while working for the teacher, then study in one's own home producing sons and pupils, concentrate one's senses upon the soul, be harmless toward all living things except in the sacrifices (The religion has not yet purified itself of animal sacrifices.), so that one may attain the Brahma-world and not return here again. The implication is that one may become free of the cycle of reincarnation.

The *Taittiriya* and *Aitareya Upanishads* were associated with *Aranyakas* of the same name. In the *Taittiriya Upanishad* once again *Aum* is emphasized, as is peace of soul. Prayers often end with *Aum* and the chanting of peace *(shanti)* three times. This may be preceded by the noble sentiment, "May we never hate."17 One teacher says truth is first, another austerity, and a third claims that study and teaching of the *Veda* is first, because it includes austerity and discipline.

The highest goal is to know *Brahman,* for that is truth, knowledge, infinite and found hidden in the heart of being and in the highest heaven, where one may abide with the eternal and intelligent Spirit *(Brahman).* Words turn away from it, and the mind is baffled by the delight of the eternal; the one who knows this shall not fear anything now or hereafter. Creation becomes a thing of bliss, for who could labour to draw in breath or have the strength to breathe it out if there were not this bliss in the heaven of one's heart?

The *Aitareya Upanishad* begins with the one Spirit creating the universe out of its being. As guardians for the worlds, Spirit made the *Purusha* (person). Out of the cosmic egg came speech, breath, eyes and sight, ears and hearing, skin, hair, and herbs; from the navel and outbreath came death, and from the organ of pleasure seed and waters were born.

In the concluding chapter of this short *Upanishad* the author asked who is this Spirit by whom one sees and hears and smells and speaks and knows? The answer is the following:

That which is heart, this mind—that is,
Consciousness, perception, discernment, intelligence,
Wisdom, insight, persistence, thought, thoughtfulness,
Impulse, memory, conception, purpose, life, desire, will
are all names of intelligence.

All things are guided by and based on this intelligence of Spirit *(Brahman).* Ascending from this world with the intelligent soul, one obtains all desires in the heavenly world, even immortality.

The *Kaushitaki Upanishad* begins by asking if there is an end to the cycle of reincarnation. The teacher answers that one is born again according to one's actions *(karma).* Ultimately the one who knows Spirit *(Brahman)* transcends even good and evil deeds and all pairs of opposites as a chariot-driver looks down upon two chariot wheels.A ceremony is described whereby a dying father bequeaths all he has to his son. If he recovers, it is recommended that he live under the lordship of his son or wander as a religious mendicant. This practice of spiritual seeking as a beggar became one of the distinctive characteristics of Indian culture.

A story is told of Pratardana, who by fighting and virility arrives at the beloved home of Indra, who grants him a gift. Pratardana asks Indra to choose for him what would be most beneficial to humanity, but Indra replies that a superior does not choose for an inferior. Pratardana responds that then it is not a gift. After bragging of many violent deeds and saying that anyone who understands him is not injured even after committing the worst crimes such as murdering a parent, Indra identifies himself with the breathing spirit *(prana)* of the intelligent soul *(prajnatman).* This breathing spirit is the essence of life and thus immortal. It is by intelligence *(prajna)* that one is able to master all of the senses and faculties of the soul. All these faculties are fixed in the intelligence, which is fixed in the breathing spirit, which is in truth the blissful, ageless, immortal soul. One does not become greater by good action nor less by bad action. One's own self *(atman)* causes one to lead up from these worlds by good action or is led downward by bad action. The soul itself *(atman)* is the world-protector and the sovereign of the world. Thus ultimately the soul is responsible for everything it experiences.

It is mentioned in the *Kaushitaki Upanishad* that it is contrary to nature for a Kshatriya to receive a Brahmin as a student. However, the *Upanishads* represent a time when the Kshatriya caste began to compete with Brahmins in spiritual endeavours. Though the Brahmins had control of the formal religion in the villages where the Kshatriyas controlled the government, by tutoring their sons and others in the forest the Kshatriyas developed a less ritualistic and traditional spirituality that is recorded in the mystical *Upanishads*.

CHAPTER

6

Philosophy of Hinduism

Among all the surviving customs Hinduism is the longest surviving philosophical custom in India. We can recognize several historical stages. The earliest, from around 700 BC, was the proto-philosophical period, when karma and liberation theories arose, and the proto-scientific ontological lists in the Upanishads were compiled. Next came the classical period, spanning the first millennium ad, in which there was constant philosophical exchange between various Hindu, Buddhist and Jaina schools. During this period, some schools, such as Sankhya, Yoga and Vaisesika, fell into oblivion and others, such as Kashmir Saivism, emerged. At last, after the classical period only two or three schools remained active. The political and economic disturbances caused by repeated Muslim invasions hampered intellectual growth. The schools that survived were the Logic school (Nyaya), especially New Logic (Navya-Nyaya), the grammarians and, above all, the Vedanta schools. The chief concerns of the Hindu philosophers were metaphysics, epistemological issues, philosophy of language, and moral philosophy.

Various schools can be distinguished by their various approaches to reality, but all regarded the Vedas (the sacred scriptures) authoritative, and all believed that there is a permanent individual self (atman). They shared with their opponents (Buddhists and Jainas) a belief in the need for liberation. They used similar epistemic tools and methods of argument. In direct contrast to their opponents, who were atheists, Hindu philosophers could be either theists or atheists.

In realwe can observe an increased tendency towards theistic ideas near the end of the classical period, with the result that the strictly atheistic teachings, which were more philosophically rigorous and sound, fell into disuse. Atma or soul was regarded as a part of larger reality in Hindu metaphysics.

These views of the world differed due to the fact that they had to be proved and properly established. Similarly, logical and epistemological tools were developed and fashioned as per the the needs and beliefs of individual philosophers. Most agreed on two or three sources of knowledge: perception and inference, with verbal testimony as a possible third. In this quest for philosophical rigour, there was a need for precision of language, and there were significant philosophical developments among the grammarians and the philosophers who explained the Vedas (the Mimamsakas). A culmination of these linguistic efforts can be seen in the philosopher of language Bharthari. One of his greatest accomplishments was the full articulation of the theory that a sentence as a whole is understood in a sudden act of comprehension.

It is customary to name six Hindu schools, of the more than a dozen that existed, thus lumping several into a single school. This is particularly the case with Vedanta. The six are listed in three pairs: Sankhya–Yoga; Vedanta–Mimamsa; Nyaya–Vaisheshika. This does not take account of the grammarians or Kashmir Saivism. In their quest for freedom from rebirth, all the Hindu schools operated within the same framework. Their ultimate goal was liberation. However they never doubted its real possibility that how much they were truly engaged in the quest for liberation apart from their philosophical preoccupations is not always clear.

Following the establishment of Vedic culture in the history of the Indian subcontinent, the development of philosophical and religious thought over a period of two millennia gave rise to what came to be called the six schools of aastika, or orthodox, Indian philosophy or Hindu philosophy. These schools have come to be synonymous with the greater religion of Hinduism, which was a development of the early Vedic Religion. Hindu Philosophy gives a clear understanding to the questions of cycle of life and death, the nature of Soul, the Universe and its creator and facts for joy and sufferings, happiness and sorrow, health and disease and the ultimate understanding of man's relationship with God. It also explains his duties during this birth as well as about his past and his future. It investigates and inquires the Truth and tempts us to think and fact in our search for a solution. Even though the Agamas and Vedas seem to be professing various doctrines, they both are written on the same philosophy but for various population group. The Agamas give us the Theological aspect of our practice with prayers to God in various expressions. The Vedas give us all the rituals and also the philosophy of our religious practice. All of them are based on the principle that the Soul is a part of the Divine spirit and is covered by the sheaths of "Upadhis" as an effect of ones Karma. It goes through endless rebirth as per the ones Karma to purify itself. Every one should follow his Dharma and perform their duties or Karma without attachment, as an offering to God to receive eternal salvation and liberation as Moksha.

MAIN FIGURES IN EARLY PERIOD

A number of Munis (Sages) and Rishis (Seers) of ancient India have, through the ages, compiled the scriptures that are today the binding force within Hinduism. Unfortunately, most of the lives of these great men are clouded by the mists of time and very little is known of them and their times. There are a few legends and myths that are based on the lives of a few of these great men but I have chosen not to include them here. Instead, I have only included the lives of those great religious figures that have definite historical records. In this section on Sages we have only included the name of one sage - Ved Vyasa who, though legendary, must be mentioned because of his paramount significance in the Hindu mythology and the ancient stories.

Ved Vyasa

The Great sage Ved Vyasa is a legendary figure in Hinduism. He is the great sage who has written down the Vedas as they were revealed to him by the Gods. Thus, he is the initiator of the sruti literature on which all of Hinduism is based. In fact, Hindu scholars hold, that which is derived from the Vedas - The Vaidika - is what constitutes True Hinduism.

Whatever else that has some other source is Avaidika and not Hinduism. Vyasa is popularly known as Ved Vyasa as he has written down the Vedas. He is also credited with composition of the Mahabharata. Some scholars even go to the length of asserting that it is he who has written down the Puranas and a number of other ancient texts. The chief legend says that Vyasa Dev is born at the beginning of every Yuga to write down what is revealed by the Gods for the religion of the people of that Yuga.

Maharshi Aitreya Mahidasa

Hindus believe that his mother was a maid named Itara. This Rishi is credited with the compilation of the Aitreya Brahmana and sections 1-3 of the Aitreya Aranyaka (the latter comprises the Aitreya Upanishad- one of the 10 canonical Upanishads for Hindus) belonging to the Rigveda.

Rishika Lopamudra

As per the the Hindu mythology Rishika Lopamudra was a Kshatriya princess from Vidarbha, who married Maharshi Agastya. She is the Seer of some verses of the Rigveda. Various edifying duologues between her and Sage Agastya are recorded in the Puranas.

Maharshi Vishwamitra

As per the hindu mythology he was originally a Kshatriya named Vishwaratha. He is credited with revealing the Gayatri Mantra, the Hindu prayer par-excellence. He was brought up to Brahminhood because of his spiritual luster.

Maharshi Valmiki

As per the the Hindu Mythology he basically was descendant from Sages but had become a chandaala (an outcaste) named Ratnakara, because he took to murder and highway robbery. He was reformed by Prajapati Brahma and was inspired by the divine Sage Narada to compose the Hindu epic par excellence- the Ramayana.

MAIN FIGURES IN MEDIEVAL PERIOD

In the medieval period of Hinduism Shankaracharya is the first of the five great acharyas who reformed Hinduism by delivering the essence of the sacred texts to the common people. It should be noted that "Acharya" means "Great Teacher". Before Shankaracharya the Vedic texts, the srutis, were orally studied and transmitted by and within a particular class of people, especially the Brahmins. They were written in a very esoteric language which was quite beyond the scope of the common people. The true catholicity of Hinduism was interpreted and revealed by Shankaracharya (788-820 A.D.), Ramanujacharya (11th century A.D.), Nimbarkacharya (11th century A.D.), Madhvacharya (13th century A.D.) and Vallabhacharya (1479-1531 A.D.) and it is to their credit that Hinduism is still such a respected religion in the world with numerous adherents. Being studied the world over today present-day Hindu thought and philosophy, owes much to these five great men.

It is widely believed that all these five great saints are believed to be Avatars sent down to earth to perform a definite mission - to deliver Humankind from the clutches of evil, a task they all performed impeccably well. They all preached various forms of the same basic philosophy and it is discouraged to treat one as being greater than the other. That they propounded various schools of philosophy is not thought to be a disadvantage within Hinduism. Instead they established various paths to the same goal - the Godhead. People from various levels of spiritual development can find succor and be benefited. Thus, their diversity serves diverse peoples. They all gave rise to various schools of Vaishnavism.

Shankaracharya

It is said that Shankaracharya was born of poor but pious Nambudiri Brahmin parents. From an early age he was inclined towards the ways of God. His father died when he was a very young boy. He was an only child and, when he decided to renounce the worldly life in favour of a holy one, his mother resisted piteously. He somehow persuaded her to allow him the life of an ascetic though she managed to extract a promise from him to visit her death-bed and see to her funeral. A pious Hindu cannot die and go to heaven unless his or her son performs the funeral rites. At that very early age Shankaracharya set out to find a teacher and found an ideal one in Govinda Bhagavadpada, a disciple of another great guru Gaudapadacharya who had advocated monism or Advaita.

The philosophy taught him by his guru befitted Shankaracharya perfectly. He was a very intelligent man. At that time Hinduism had degenerated into a mess of dogmas and rituals which all seemed meaningless to the common people but were perpetrated by the Brahmins, the priestly class, in whose interest it was to control the reigns of society by dictating the will of the Gods. There was such diversity of complex and expensive rituals that it seemed beyond the means of common people to achieve the grace of the Gods. In this bleak scenario more tolerant religions like Buddhism and Jainism, which themselves were reformist reactions against the evils of Hinduism, and which advocated simple personal devotion as a means of gaining salvation had gained much popularity to the detriment of Hinduism. Sankaracharya understood the common people's problems in adhering to Hinduism in its composite state and set out to reform the religion onto a very much personal level.

One of the other characteristics of Shankaracharya was that he was a brilliant and convincing orator. In those days in India dialectics, logic and semantics were regarded the only signs of great scholarship and the only way to win over others to one's point of view was to argue at scholarly debates and win the arguments. Shankaracharya studied the succinct aphorisms of Badarayana in his Brahma Sutras and wrote a brilliant commentary on them which was accepted all over India. He also wrote commentaries on the Bhagavad Gita, the Upanishads and other religious philosophical works. In his work Shankaracharya declared that the essence of the Vedas was that there was One God, who was without attributes, whose expression all else was. To make his doctrine available to everyone in India he traveled all over India with missionary zeal. He established four maths (monasteries) - at Kashmir in the North, Dwarka in the West, Puri in the East and Shringeri in the South. These institutions are still thriving today and millions of devotees flock to them to assume knowledge of this great man and his way to God. This had been Shankaracharya's chief objective and he achieved it in a very short time. He lived for only 32 years but within that period he managed to place Hinduism on a sound footing not only in India but also in other neighboring countries. In the present age he is much appreciated all over the world and his Absolute Monism - Kevala Advaita, though very hard to adhere to, is still a great source of inspiration not only to Hindus all over the world but also to theologians in general.

It can be concluded that this great sage's short biography that, in the end, he did not fail to keep his promise to his own mother. When it was time for her to die he was there by her side and, when she subsequently died, he, though an ascetic who had given up all contact with the outside world, arranged for her funeral.

Ramanujacharya

Ramanuja was born in the village of Perumbudur, in the state of Tamil Nadu in the year 1017 A.D. His father was

Keshava Somaji and his mother was Kantimathi, a very pious and virtuous lady. Ramanuja's Tamil name was Ilaya Perumal. At a very early age he lost his father. He persuaded his mother to let him set out of their village so that he could travel to one of the religious centers nearby and study under a Guru. He subsequently set out for Kanchipuram and started studying Advaita philosophy. His guru's interpretation of the Vedas was not quite to his liking and, after a rather colorful round of argument and insults, he left his guru for a better one in Kanchipurna, a Sudra who was much revered in the Vishishtadvaita community of Tamil Nadu.

The philosophy of Vishishtadvaita is Qualified Non-dualism. Ramanuja quickly found the philosophy to his liking and soon adopted it for his own. As per the interpretations of works left by him his Brahman is Sa-Visesha Brahman or Brahman with attributes. As per the Ramanuja's preachings Lord Narayana is Bhagwan or Supreme Being. The individual soul is Chit and all matter is Achit. The attributes are real and permanent but subject to the control of the Brahman. The attributes are called Prakaras or modes. Lord Narayana is the Ruler and Lord of the universe. All living things - Jivas are His servants and must worship Him and surrender to His will completely. The attributes are also called Shaktis and they are the manifest part of the Lord. He called his path of worship Bhakti. His followers are a particular sect among the chief sect of the Vaishnavites.

After thoroughly immersing himself in formulating his philosophy of God and the Causes of Creation set out of Kanchipuram to visit all the Vaishnavite Shrines in South India Ramanuja, he went about spreading his words and was widely accepted and revered wherever he went. Ultimately he reached Srirangam and settled there permanently. He lived a long and colorful life of 120 years full of holiness and religious zeal. He had several maths built and temples to his Lord established there. He formulated rules of worship and religious etiquette. He strove for the rest of his life to rid society of the evils that had crept into it subsequent to the degradation of Hinduism. He converted thousands of common people to his faith, alongwith a number of the outcastes of the time whom he lovingly welcomed to his community. He demolished barriers of caste and creed and welcomed all wholeheartedly. His religious precepts were easy to follow and keep. He advocated personal worship or Bhakti through which anyone could attain God. This was the main attractions of the branch of Hinduism he founded and thousands of people hungry for pointers to the right direction flocked to his maths to be converted. In this prominent quiet and singularly orderly manner he set about reforming Hinduism into a much more acceptable set of tenets that have stood the ups and downs of the a number of years that have passed from that time.

Alongwith the above qualities Ramanuja was an excellent controversialist and wrote commentaries on a number of ancient texts. His commentary on Badarayana's Brahma Sutras is known as Sri Bhashya. The Vishishtadvaita system was a very old one even at that time and Ramanuja followed the way of Bodhyana in this. Bodhyana had expounded this unique philosophy in his book Vritti written in 400 B.C. Ramanuja followed Bodhyana in his commentary on the Brahma Sutras. Ramanuja also wrote three other books - Vedanta Sara (Essence of the Vedanta), Vedanta Sangraha (Resume of the Vedanta) and Vedanta Deepa (Light of the Vedanta). Ramanujacharya's particular sect of Vaishnavites is called Sri Sampradaya and it still has an immense following today, particularly in South India, the birth place of this great sage.

Madhvacharya

As per the the Hindu texts and scriptures Madhvacharya was born in around 1199 A.D. at a small village called Velali near Udipi in South Kanara district in South India. He was of Tula Brahmin birth born to Madhya Geha and Vedavati, a virtuous woman. His father named him Vasudeva. Madhvacharya had an fantabulous physique and he could wrestle, run, jump and swim. People used to call him Bhima after the second Pandava brother in the Mahabharata. Madhva took up the study of the Vedas and the Vedangas early in his life and soon became well-versed in them. In his 25th year he took up Sanyash (Monkhood) and renounced the world. Achutaprakashacharya, a great guru at that time in Udipi, initiated him and thereafter he began to be known as Purna Prajna.

Madhva's command over the scriptures, especially of the components of the Vedanta, impressed Achutaprakashacharya so much that he soon made him head of his Math. Madhva now received the name Ananda Tirtha. He set out on a tour of Southern and Northern India. He preached to all and made a number of converts to his faith. He visited Badrinath, the Northern Dham, and, thereafter, returned to Udipi. Reinforced by both his studies and his travel experience he started to write his commentaries on the Bhagavad Gita and the Vedanta. He built several temples in Udipi to his Lord and acquired innumerable disciples. Upto this day Udipi is the center of the Madhva Sect and most orthodox Madhvas strive to visit Udipi at least once in a lifetime.

Advaita Philosophy was preached by Madhva. His sect is known as Sad Vaishnavism to distinguish it from the Sri Vaishnavism of Ramanujacharya. Madhva held that Vishnu or Narayana was the Supreme Being. This is the same as the doctrines of Ramanuja but Madhva's philosophy has certain distinctions.

Madhva laid much stress on Smarana - remembering the Lord at all times. He said – "Form a strong habit of remembering God. Then only will it be easy for you to remember Him at the moment of death." He performed a number of miracles before he died. He is still remembered for the gentle faith he preached to all. His emphasis on personal devotion, as of the other great teachers, drew in a number of of people to Hinduism while it made it easy for those who were already Hindus to understand their religion better.

Nimbarkacharya

At Vaiduryapattam on the banks of the River Godavari, in the state of Andhra Pradesh in Southern India, there was born a boy-child to a great ascetic Aruna Muni and his pious wife Jayanti Devi in the 11th century A.D. The learned Brahmins around named him Niyamanandacharya. He also became famous as Aruna Rishi and Haripriyacharya. He was sent to Rishikul to study the Vedas, Vedangas, Darshanas and other holy books. He mastered the scriptures in a short time. He was in his teens then and people were astonished at his knowledge and came to see and listen to him from miles around.

Niyamananda was visited by Brahma himself in the guise of a sanyasin and, pleased with his hospitality, given him the name Nimbarka - "Nim" – from the "Neem" tree, and "Arka" from the "Sun" or "Surya", is said by the Hindus. After that incident his disciples and others started calling him Nimbarkacharya. Sri Nimbarkacharya is believed to be an avatar of Vishnu's Chakra Sudarshan or discus. Sri Nimbarkacharya was an exponent of the Dvaitadvaita School of Philosophy. His followers worship Lord Krishna and His cowgirl lover Radha. For them the Bhagavad Gita is the most significant scripture. Sri Nimbarkacharya held that Jiva, living being, and the material world are both separate from yet identical to the Supreme Being, Brahman. The sect he founded thrives prosperously at Mathura and Brindavan, principal centers of Radha-Krishna worship.

Vallabhacharya

As per the the Hindu mythology Vallabhacharya was born to Lakshmana Bhatta and Illama, pious Telugu Brahmins, at Champaranya in the present-day state of Madhya Pradesh in 1479 A.D. His father died when he was only 11 years old but, the very next year, he completed his studies of the Vedas, the 6 Darshanas and the 18 Puranas at Varanasi, where he had been sent to study. He started for Brindavan and from there he set out on a Parikrama (Tour) of holy places in India. He returned to Varanasi and married Mahalakshmi and had two sons by her.

Vallabhacharya composed a number of works in both Sanskrit and Brij Bhasha, a local vernacular. His Sanskrit compositions are:

- Vyasa Sutra Bhashya.
- Jamini Sutra Bhashya.
- Bhagavata Tika Subhodhini.
- Pushti Pravala Maryada.
- Siddhanta Rahasya.

It is said that Sri Vallabhacharya was an avatar of Agni, the God of Fire. This great saint was an exponent of Pure Monism or Suddhadvaita. Lord Krishna is the Highest Brahman. He is called Purushottama, The Supreme Male and His body is Satchidananda. The sect of Sri Vallabhacharya is still thriving in the states of Rajasthan and Gujarat. His followers worship Bala Krishna, Lord Krishna as a boy. Vallabhacharya laid great stress on Pushti, divine grace, and Bhakti, devotion. Those who can achieve Maha Pushti, the highest grace, or Anuraga, attain the Godhead. All things are emanated from the Satchidananda or Akshara like sparks from fire. He was a contemporary of Sri Krishna Chaitanya Mahaprabhu. Sri Vallabhacharya died in 1531 A.D. at Varanasi.

Chaitanya Mahaprabhu

It is said about the Chaitanya Mahaprabhu that he was a monk and social reformer of the 16th century Bengal, (present-day West Bengal and Bangladesh) and Orissa in India. Sri Krishna Chaitanya was a notable proponent for the Vaishnava school of Bhakti yoga (meaning loving devotion to Krishna/God) based on the philosophy of the Bhagavata Purana and Bhagavad Gita. Mainly he worshipped the forms of Radha and Krishna and popularised the chanting of the Hare Krishna maha mantra. His line of followers, known as Gaudiya Vaishnavas, revere him as an avatar of Krishna in the mood of Radharani who was prophesised to seem in the later verses of the Bhagavata Purana. Sometimes he was also referred to by the names Gaura (Sanskrit for *golden one*) due to his light skin complexion, and Nimai due to his being born underneath a Neem tree. There are a number of biographies available from the time giving details of Chaitanya's life, the most prominent ones being the Chaitanya Charitamrita of Krishnadasa Kaviraja Goswami and the earlier Chaitanya Bhagavata of Vrindavana Dasa Thakura (both originally written in the Bengali language but now widely available in English and other languages) and the Chaitanya Mangala, written by Lochana Dasa Thakura.

Sai Baba of Shirdi

The scholars keep various views about the Sai Baba of Shirdi he is also known as Shirdi Sai Baba, was an Indian guru, yogi and fakir who is regarded by his Hindu and Muslim followers as a saint. Some of his Hindu devotees believe that he was an incarnation of Shiva or Dattatreya, and he was regarded as a satguru and an incarnation of Kabir. The name 'Sai Baba' is a combination of Persian and Indian origin; *Sai* is the Persian term for "holy one" or "saint", usually attributed to Islamic ascetics, whereas *Baba* is a word meaning "father" used in Indian languages.

The appellative thus refers to Sai Baba as being a "holy father" or "saintly father". His parentage, birth details, and life before the age of sixteen are obscure, which has led to a number of speculations and theories attempting to explain Sai Baba's origins. In his life and teachings he tried to reconcile Hinduism and Islam: Sai Baba lived in a mosque, was buried in a Hindu temple, practised Hindu and Muslim rituals, and taught using words and figures that drew from both customs. One of his epigrams which is widely known among both Hindus and Muslims says of God: "*Allah Malik*" ("God is Master").

Sai Baba in general and particular taught a moral code of love, forgiveness, helping others, charity, contentment, inner peace, devotion to God and guru. His philosophy was Advaita Vedanta and his teachings consisted of elements both of this school as well as of bhakti and Islam. Sai Baba remains a popular saint and is worshipped mostly in Maharashtra, southern Gujarat, Andhra Pradesh and Karnataka. Debate on his Hindu or Muslim origins continues to take place. He is also revered by several notable Hindu and Sufi religious leaders.

Sant Gyaneshwar

As per the the Hindu custom and the religious texts Sant Gyaneshwar was a 13th century marathi saint, poet, philosopher and a yogi of Nath custom. His works Bhavartha deepika teeka, popularly known as Gyaneshwari, and Amrutanubhav are regarded to be the milestones in Marathi literature. The Vaishnav Sampraday or the Vitthal Sampraday of Pandharpur, Maharashtra, India considers "Gyaneshwar as its spiritual leader and Gyaneshwari as its Dharmagrantha (holy book). In Alandi, Maharashtra he entered into Sanjeevan Samadhi at the age of 21.

Tukaram

As per the Hindu Mythology Tukaram was a prominent Marathi Sant and religious poet in the Hindu custom in India. He was born and lived most of his life in *Dehu*, a town close to Pune city in Maharashtra, India. He was born to a couple with the family name Moray - the descendent of the Mourya Clan. Through a custom in India in bygone days, Tukaram's family name is rarely used in identifying him. Rather, in accord with another custom in India of assigning the epithet sant to persons regarded as thoroughly saintly, Tukaram is commonly known in Maharashtra as Sant Tukaram. It is also said that he was spiritual guru of Shivaji.

It is also believed that Tukaram was a devotee of Lord Vittala – an incarnation of Lord Krishna, who in turn, regarded to be an incarnation of Lord Vishnu. Tukaram is regarded as the climactic point of the so-called Bhagawat Hindu custom, which is thought to have begun in Maharashtra with Namdev. Gyasneshwar, Namdev, Janabai, Eknath, and Tukaram are revered especially in the *warakari* sect in Maharashtra. He has recived guru-mantra comprising names of Krishna, Rama and Hari.

This was at the hands or by the media of a dream, of one Babaji Chaitanya – a possible indication that Tukaram had some connexion with prominent saint Chaitanya, and Gaudiya Vaishnavas believe that he was initiated and was a disciple of Chaitanya. Whatever information about the lives of the above saints of Maharashtra comes mostly from the works *Bhakti-Wijay* and *Bhakti-Leelamrut* of Mahipati. Mahipati was born 65 years after the death of Tukaram, (Tukaram having died 50 years, 300 years, and 353 years after the deaths of Ekanath, Namdev, and Dnyaneshwar, respectively.) Thus, Mahipati doubtlessly based his life sketches of all above "sants" primarily on rumours.

Public relgious preachings of Tukaram used to be mixed, by custom, with poetry, which included some of his own compositions. His discourses focussed on day-to-day behavior of human beings, and he emphasized that the true expression of religion was in a person's love for his fellow human beings rather than in ritualistic observance of religious orthodoxy, including mechanical study of the Vedas. His teachings covered a wide array of issues, including the significance of the ecosystem. Tukaram worked for his society's enlightenment in the warakari custom, which emphasizes community service and musical group worship.

Tukaram like Namdev, Janabai, and Eknath wrote in Marathi a large number of devotional poems identified in Marathi as *abhang*. A collection of 4,500 *abhang* known as the *Gatha* is attributed to Tukaram. *Mantra Geeta*, a Marathi translation in *abhang* form of the Sanskrit Bhagavad Geeta, is also attributed to him. It is an interpretation of Geeta from the perspective of *Bhakti* (devotion).

Vallabha Acharya

As per the Hindu Mythology Sri Vallabhacharya was a devotional philosopher, who founded the Pushti sect in India, following the philosophy of Shuddha advaita (Pure Non-dualism). He is regarded as an Acharya and Guru within the Vaishnava customs as promulgated and prescribed by the Vedanta philosophy. He is often associated with Vishnuswami, the founder of Rudra Sampradaya. Within Indian Philosophy he is known as the writer of sixteen 'stotras' (tracts) and produced several commentaries on the Bhagavata Purana, which discovers the a number of lilas (pastimes) of the avatar, Krishna. Vallabha Acharya occupies a unique place in Indian culture as a scholar, a philosopher and devotional (bhakti) preacher. He is widely regarded as the last of the four great Vaishnava Acharyas who founded the various Vaishnava schools of thought based on Vedantic philosophy, the other three (preceding him) being Ramanujacharya, Madhvacharya and Nimbarkacharya. He is especially known as a lover and a propagator of Bhagavata Dharma.

He was born in Champaranya near Raipur in the Indian state of Chhattisgarh. His education commenced at the age of seven with the study of four Vedas. He gained mastery over the books expounding the six systems of Indian philosophy. He also learnt philosophical systems of Adi Sankara, Ramanuja, Madhva, Nimbarka along with the Buddhist and Jain schools. He was able to recite hundred mantras, not only from beginning to end but also in reverse order. At Vyankateshwar and Lakshmana Balaji, he made a strong effect on the public as an incarnation of knowledge. He was now applauded as Bala Saraswati. It is believed that when Vallabhacharya entered Gokul, he thought about the significant question of fixing people to the right path of devotion.

He meditated on Krishna who seem ed to him in a vision in the form of Shrinathji, deity discovered by Madhavendra Puri and disclosed the 'Brahma Sambandha', a mantra of self dedication or consecration of self to Krishna. Vallabha Acharya related this experience to his worthiest and most beloved disciple. He became the first Vaishnava initiated by Vallabhacharya. He wanted to preach his message of devotion to God and God's grace called Pushti - Marga.

He contracted three pilgrimages of India. He performed the initiation ceremony of religious rite by conferring on them 'NamaNivedana' mantra or 'Brahma Sambandha' mantra. Thousands turned to be his disciples, but 84 devoted servants are most famous and their life has been documented in Pushti Marg literature as the 'Story of 84 Vaishnavas'.

Bhagwan Swaminarayan

Bhagwan Swaminarayan or *Sahajanand Swami* is the main figure in a modern form of Hinduism known as the Swaminarayan Faith and is the founder of the Swaminarayan Sampraday in which followers offer devotion to Bhagwan Swaminarayan as the final expression of god. In this particular custom, Sahajanand Swami is respectfully addressed as Bhagwan Swaminarayan by his followers. Sahajanand Swami was born in Chhapaiya, Uttar Pradesh.

He settled in the West Indian state of Gujarat, where he then preached his doctrine until his death in 1830. Sahajanand Swami is also known as Lord Swaminarayan, Ghanshyam Pande, Ghanshyam Maharaj, Shreeji Maharaj, HariKrishna Maharaj and Shri Hari. As per the legend, it was events that took place at Badarikashram (Abode of NarNarayan) that led to the incarnation of Swaminarayan. It is believed that Narayan took birth as Swaminarayan due to a curse of Rishi Durvasa.

With the advent of kaliyug, Adharm (immoral situation) had spread in Bharat Khand (India) and that Asur's (Evil people) had also tremendously increased. Hence he had accepted the curse, which was due to his own will, to take avatar on earth to demolish evil and establish Ekantik-dharm (Religion based on morality, knowledge, non-attachment and devotion). While there is indirect reference to Narayan taking birth in the form of Swaminarayan in the Geeta and Shreemad Bhagwad, there is a direct address to this in the Brahma Purana and Vishwaksena Samhita.

Swaminarayan Sampraday

Another Hindu prominent saint was Swaminarayan Sampraday. He established two gadis (seats), one in Ahmedabad (Shree NarNarayan Dev Gadi) and one in Vadtal (Shree LaxmiNarayan Dev Gadi) on Tuesday, November 21, 1825 AD. Bhagwan Swaminarayan then appointed an acharya to each of these two gadis to pass on his message to others and to preserve his fellowship, Swaminarayan Sampraday.

These acharyas came from his immediate family; he formally adopted a son from each of his two brothers, Rampratap and Ichcharam, and appointed them to the office of acharya.

Ayodhyaprasad, son of his elder brother Rampratap, was appointed Acharya of Ahmedabad Gadi, and Raghuvira, son of his younger brother Ichcharam, was appointed Acharya of the Vadtal Gadi.

Bhagwan Swaminarayan decreed that the office should be hereditary so that acharyas would maintain a direct line of blood descent from his family.

The institution of a hereditary line of religious specialists is common in Hinduism but what is unique in Bhagwan Swaminarayan's institution of this office is that he designated an administrative division of the followers into two territorial dioceses. This administrative division is set forth in minute detail in a document written by Sahajanand (Bhagwan Swaminarayan), known as Desh Vibhaag Lekh.

Hence, followers of the Swaminarayan Sampraday accept the acharyas as spiritual successors. The Shikshapatri Slokhs provides what followers of the Swaminarayan Sampraday believe to be direct scriptural references in which Bhagwan Swaminarayan recognizes acharyas as the rightful spiritual successors.

BASIC PHILOSOPHY

It is commonly said that philosophy is the rational aspect of the faith, in any culture or Religion. It is an integral part of Hindu religious beliefs and culture in India. It is a rational inquiry into the nature of truth or reality, giving clear solutions to A number of problems of life and human behaviour. It shows the ways to get rid of the pain and sufferings, to get happiness and peace of mind and to attain liberation and eternal bliss. Theology is regarded significant in most world religions. Philosophy is often agnostic and it is not part of the religious study. Hindus consider philosophy as an integral part of their religious experience. In Hindu culture, theology is well mixed in all aspects of life through its mythology, art, music and dance and they all carry a moral.

Hindu Philosophy is not merely a speculation or guess work of a solution for human problems and doubts, but an organized doctrine based on the mystical experience of the Sages and Seers. The teachings of Hindu philosophy are given to us in the Upanishads which are the wealth of our knowledge. The ethics and tenets are obtained from them through the Six Dharsanas and various later schools of philosophers.

The glory of Hindu philosophy is seen in the teachings of Hindu dharma, the theory of karma and rebirth, the six dharsanas, and the four yogas or spiritual disciplines. They not only create the questions in our mind to think but also give us the answers to the problems. Dharma means "that which holds" the people of this world and the whole creation. It is the eternal Divine law of God. That which brings well being to man and supports the world with prosperity is dharma. It is the absolute Truth and laws of righteous living. The four Vedas are the authority of Dharma. The truth about dharma can not be realised through any other knowledge and one's own facting through any analysis alone can not be that authority. So it is appropriate to say here that Vedas are the real authority of the Dharma.

ANCIENT RULES

As per the the ancient Indian Hindu rules Purushartha are the four kinds of human aspirations, which are dharma, artha, kaama and moksha. Among these, dharma is the foremost and is the gateway to moksha or immortality and eternal bliss. Practice of proper Dharma gives an experience of peace, joy, strength and tranquillity within ones-self and life becomes thoroughly disciplined. It is classified as SaA number ofa dharma or the general and Universal Dharma and Visesha dharma or specific personal dharma.

Samana dharma includes contentment, forgiveness, self-restraint, spiritual knowledge, absence of anger, non-greediness, non-stealing, truthfulness, purity, non-violence, control of senses and desire, discrimination between right and wrong and between real and unreal. Visesha or specific dharma includes duties due to one's birth, age and family and duties to society and family, due to one's career and job and spiritual life. They also include the specific dharmas for the four ashramas and four varnas. These are the regular duties including the rituals and services to the family, community, ancestors and God that every one is expected to perform. We have separate Dharma for each of the four Yugas or time periods. The 10 Rules of Dharma

Manusmriti written by the ancient sage Manu, prescribes 10 essential rules for the observance of dharma: Patience (*dhriti*), forgiveness (*kshama*), piety or self control (*dama*), honesty (*asteya*), sanctity (*shauch*), control of senses (*indraiya-nigrah*), fact (*dhi*), knowledge or learning (*vidya*), truthfulness (*satya*) and absence of anger (*krodha*). Manu further writes, "Non-violence, truth, non-coveting, purity of body and mind, control of senses are the essence of dharma". Hence dharmic laws govern not only the individual but all in society. The motive of dharma is not only to attain a union of the soul with the supreme reality, it also suggests a code of conduct that is intended to secure both worldly joys and supreme happiness.

Rishi Kanda has defined dharma in Vaisesika as "that confers worldly joys and leads to supreme happiness". Hinduism is the religion that suggests methods for the attainment of the highest ideal and eternal bliss here and now on earth and not somewhere in heaven. For instance, it endorses the idea that it is one's dharma to marry, raise a family and provide for that family in whatever way is necessary. The practice of dharma gives an experience of peace, joy, strength and tranquillity within one's self and makes life disciplined.

Rules Of Duty

The various rules of Dharma for people of various age groups, various family traits and various periods of time are given by the Vedas. The ashrama dharma gives the standards of living for various age groups of individuals. The Varna dharma is one that is most misinterpreted and misused. If properly interpreted and understood, it is the most efficient sociological system of the nation. It is indeed a splendid theory with a flawless rule. But, the defect came from somewhere else. Various dharma sasthras, or smrithis, written by Rishis like Manu, Parasara, and Yaagnavalkya, have varied for various periods of time as per the varying social and emotional surroundings of the Hindu society [Yuga-Dharma]. For philosophical guidance for daily living the Hindus often follow the teachings of various Dharma sasthras.

As per the the Hindu custom and its books the Divine is both in us and out of us. God is neither completely transcendent nor completely immanent. He is divine darkness as well as 'unencompassed light.' The philosophers with their passion for unity emphasize the immanent aspect, that there is no barrier dividing man from the real. Those who emphasize the Transcendence of the Supreme to the human insist on the specifically religious consciousness, of communion with a higher than ourselves with whom it is impossible for the individual to get assimilated. There cannot be a fundamental contradiction between the philosophical idea of God as an all-embracing spirit and the devotional idea of a personal God who arouses in us the specifically religious emotion. The personal conception develops the aspect of spiritual experience in which it may be regarded as fulfilling the human needs. God is represented as possessing the qualities we lack. The difference between the Supreme as spirit and Supreme as person is one of stand point and not of essence, between God as He is and as he seems to us. Justice, love and holiness are the highest qualities we know and we imagine God as possessing them, though these qualities exist in God in a various sense from their existence in us.

DIVINE LAWS

Law of Integrity

As per the the law of integrity the whole universe is imbued with divine presence. "All this is for the habitation of the Lord," thus begins the Isa Upanishad. All religions acknowledge that the God is omnipresent and is the ruler as well as dweller of the whole cosmos. Since God is present in each and every aspect of His creation, it logically follows that the whole creation is divine and sacred and that each and every object in it and each and every aspect of it, including ourselves, the good and the bad, the high and the low, deserve our unconditional love, respect and attention. It also becomes clear that we cannot deal with the world as per the our needs and desire or fear and expectations, but with a sense of equanimity as if we are playing hide and seek with God Himself in his gigantic world. We realize that self-realization is possible only by staying within and accepting the objective world as the twisted truth that need to be explored and resolved by consciously searching for God in its myriad objects not by going away or escaping.

It can be seen that people flock to religious places and places of worship as if God does not exist in their homes and hearts. It is rather unfortunate that a number of people put on their religious attitude or their feelings of reverence selectively on certain occasions, when they go to a religious place, meet with a pious person or celebrate a religious festival. This attitude and behavior is very much similar to those psychologists quote in their experiments with animals on the subject of conditioning. It is an attitude that comes not because of genuine love, but because of an attitude powered by fear, expectation, habit or desire. Knowing clearly that God is omnipresent and omniscient; it is interesting that we choose to worship God only on certain occasions or in a specific manner. What is worse most of us ignore the fundamental unity of life and indulge in discrimination and selfishness. The fanatics are in realthe worst instances. They are enemies of God, who use His very name to discredit Him and His creation. They in realneed the love of the humanity because they are deluded, devoid of genuine love for God and His creation. God is omnipresent and omniscient if we remember this fact we can bring this attitude into our day to day lives and reorient ourselves completely. We can treat everything in the universe as sacred and divine and make it not only as a source of inspiration but also as an object of veneration to experience the presence of God. We need not have to look to the heavens or ascend to it only after we die to experience the presence of God. We can celebrate life as a joyous offering to God each and every moment and feel His presence in every place. He, who is aware of this truth, would venerate the whole creation with unconditional love and respect. He would look upon the world with the mind of God and find himself in it. He would treat everything and everyone in it the way he would treat himself or expect others to treat him. He would deal with the world as if he is dealing with God.

The Buddha taught this to His followers when he advised them to cultivate friendliness towards the whole world. If we look at the world objectively from this point of view, we realize why the world is in conflicts and why human relationships fail so frequently. Why the world is mostly polluted, dirty and disease ridden. We realize the price we are in realpaying for not honouring the divine connection we have with the world we live in. If the world or conditions are unkind or are not favouring us, we need not have to look far for facts but into ourselves. The world is against us, because we are against each other, in competition with each other, suspicious of each other and cannot visualize and work for a united world. If we want the world to be with us, we need to reconnect ourselves with the world and live in harmony with it, with a sense of gratitude and reverence and with an awareness that you cannot really be happy if a part of your body is sick or disjointed and you use your body purely for your selfish desires without any concern for its wellbeing. So its better that we trust in the existence of God.

If we do not show any concern or love for the world in which we live, the world would become inhospitable for us. Man cannot find peace in his life, if he destroys life upon earth indiscriminately for his own survival. The same is true with plants and animals. If we indulge in the indiscriminate destruction of nature around us, nature would slowly make earth an inhospitable place for the mankind to live and propagate. It is very much true that the world is but a mirror in which we find ourselves. What you find in others is but what in realexists within you. What you give to others is what you receive in return. All religions preach this law. Those who seek the language of harmony and peace in life understand this principle very well and treat every thing in the world with due respect and a sense of sacredness. This law demands that you have to treat every one as how you would want to be treated by others. It says that you develop the vision of oneness of the universe and act accordingly.

People those who observe this law are forever linked to the presence of Divine with in themselves and with in others. They are connected to the flow of universal love that stems from the Oneness of the universe. But those who are self-centered find no true happiness. They find their match everywhere and find the world increasingly hostile. They may achieve temporary gains at the cost of others, but remain mostly unhappy, disturbed and unloved. When we accept this world as a true extension of ourselves, we will truly believe that what exists in us also exists outside. We will live with a sense of responsibility and objective to achieve life's goals in harmony with the world, rather than at the expense of others.

By just going to a Church or temple truth can not be brought as it is solace, but we can bring it in the love we spread and receive. If we are selfish and disconnected, however hard we may try, we cannot experience oneness with God. The love that we block in our hearts also blocks our consciousness to the love that comes from others. A person who experiences this ordeal has but an emptiness within from which he is rarely free. But if he can manage to shake off his pettiness, he will have the opportunity to experience the sacred presence of God in the world around Him. He will grow in the light of that awareness and learn to see the world as an aspect of God. He will find the world in harmony with his own aspirations and personal goals and live with the confidence that when the need arises, he would get the necessitated help or counsel from the stranger.

Law of Integral Equilibrium

Biologically human beings cannot tolerate extreme physical or mental conditions. Beyond a point, we cannot withstand the joys and sorrows or the comforts or discomforts of life. Excessive self denial is as harmful as excessive self indulgence. Overeating is as harmful to our wellbeing as obsessive dieting. Too much alcohol would burn the system. A little once in awhile would perhaps relax the muscles and serve the heart. Extreme inaction or extreme exertions are equally harmful to our professional and personal lives. This is true in case of other things concerning our lives. For instance in our relationships if we do not know where to stop, we may cause innumerable problems to ourselves and to others. If we do not know when to care and when to ignore our children or when to discipline them and when to pamper them, perhaps we may fail to bring them up as responsible adults. A certain degree of privacy and separation are necessitated for the relationships to survive even among the closest relationships.

Most of the time people become abnormal or lose sight of reality when they lose their inner balance. If ordinary individuals attempt to go the extremes in any matter, they put themselves in hard situations and suffer from serious problems. They may even develop some form of eccentricity or abnormality which may seriously interfere with their daily lives. Unless a person has trained himself well to withstand the rigors of working for an extraordinary objective or goal, it is better for him to remain with in balance and experience life in all its dimensions. To the degree we move towards the extremities, life become intolerable and painful. Whoever we are and whatever may be our achievements, if we swerve from the middle path, we will lose the sense of enjoyment. This in essence is the law of inherent balance. What we mean by this is that we must exert enough control on ourselves to ensure that we and our lives remain within bounds and in a state of balance so that we may be able to enjoy life in all its hues and colours without endangering our survival and happiness. We must know what is good for our lives and what is not and strictly adhere to them. We must know what is healthy for the body and the mind and what is not.

This principle runs the whole universe. There is an inherent balance in all creation. In some intricate and inexplicable way the diverse components of the universe remain with in their bounds. The visible and invisible forces of the universe hold their sway and keep the balance. And if there is an occasional disturbance or calamity in the universe or upon earth, it is basically to correct some imbalance or restore balance. Imagine what would happen to this balance if the earth tilts by a few degrees or moves away from the sun by a few thousand miles! We are safe on earth because the earth is in a state of balance, and is in harmony with itself and with other objects in the universe. We will vanish forever into some black hole of the universe the moment this balance is disturbed.

This is the foremost if we can learn anything from our experiences. Life on earth is conditioned by this principle of moderation. Our bodies and minds have evolved on the principle of balance and control. We are safe if we remain within bounds and avoid the extremes. If we know our limitations and stay with in our control we are at peace with ourselves.

Law of Wealth

On the principle of abundance the universe exists. It is by giving that you receive. This is the law of abundance, which stipulates that we cannot enjoy the riches of the universe unless we are willing to share them with others. Health and happiness need not always go together. Not all who accumulate wealth enjoy their lives. It is because they guard their acquisitions jealously unwilling to share them with others. Abundance does not mean mere accumulation of material wealth. Happiness, peace of mind and harmony in life are also part of this universal abundance. Abundance comes into a person's life only when he facilitates its free flow from him and through him. You can block the flow and you may accumulate wealth. But there is no guarantee that the wealth you amassed would bring you peace and harmony. You would enjoy the love and acceptance of others it can not be guaranteed.

Only the selfish accumulation of wealth only generates negative consequences of abundance- its overwhelming capacity to inflict pain and suffering. Remember, whatever that comes to you today will leave you some day. For every thing is here is so transient and fleeting. At the end of life all that is sought is lost and all that is given is gained. This is the basis of divine life and the secret of life.

Law of Personal Realism

The law of personal realism says that you are the creator of your life and your reality. Your thoughts become your actions and your actions create the circumstances in your life. You are responsible for everything that happens to you in your life.

This is the simple law of as you sow so you reap. It can also be called the law of motion and emotion. Every thought that we send out into the universe comes back to us with accumulated energy of its own kind. When negative thoughts go out of our minds, they will come back to us with redoubled negative energy and give us lot of pain and unhappiness. Positive thoughts on the other hand bring in positive energy and energize us, establishing in the process peace and harmony in our consciousness.

Our actions too yield the same results. Our positive actions bring in positive rewards and our negative actions bring negative rewards. The energy that we unleash either in the form of a thought or action always comes back to us with increased force. Thus through our actions and thoughts we are constantly creating our own realities. Whatever we give comes back to us. We should hence be very careful about our thoughts and actions as they have a lasting influence on the pattern of our lives. People blame others for what happens to them. Little do they know that if anyone is to be blamed it is the person himself who made it happen to himself. Wisdom is when something happens to you, instead of looking around for excuses and placing the blame on others, look into yourself and ask yourself why you made it happen? Why you invited those circumstances into your life either intentionally or unintentionally?

May be it is because you wanted to learn something out of that experience or you wanted to strengthen some aspect of your personality or resolve some long troubling relationship. When you start accepting responsibility for the events of your life, you begin to learn more about yourself, your inner thoughts, your fears and aspirations. Out of this awareness you also start expanding your consciousness, become aware of your thought processes, and through this awareness you ultimately learn to change the conditions of your life. And in its end it gives you the happiness and satisfaction.

Law of Compatibility

As per the the law of compatibility the ancient Aryans believed in 'rta' meaning the universal order or harmony. 'Rta' is an ancient word to which we can trace at least few significant words that are known to us today. One is the Sanskrit world 'ritu', which means season. The others are the Latin word 'rhythmus', the French word 'rhythme', the Greek word 'rhuthmos' and the English word 'rhythm', all meaning, beat, pulse, metre, pattern, order, flowing, and harmony. Let us understand why the concept of harmony and rhythm was regarded so significant by our ancient generations and why they elevated it to the level of highest divinity. They regarded Truth, harmony and order to be the Ultimate Reality lying beyond all realities, the hidden secret behind all manifest creation, or the Absolute Truth above all relative truths so they did so.

What is truth? Or how can Truth be defined? Truth does not necessarily mean only verbal truths. Truth is the fundamental reality where there are no conflicts and confusion, no divisions and separation, but only unity and harmony. Truth is where there is movement without obstruction and where there is order without confusion. Where there is conflict, separation and feeling of alienation, there is no truth. Where there is division and alignment of divisions into opposing parts there is no truth. There is no truth in ones life and ones being unless there is total harmony in ones whole being, which include ones activities, thoughts and environment. Truth resolves all conflicts, divisions and differences and establishes permanent peace, order and harmony in ones life. When you consider the world outside is various and separate from you there is always a conflict.

Again there is conflict when you consider others are various and separate from you. There is conflict when you consider that some one is good, or some one is bad; that some thing is this or some thing is that. There is conflict as long as you pass petty judgements about yourself or about the world around you. Unless you learn to resolve these differences, by expanding your consciousness, and learn to appreciate them in their own light, you cannot have real harmony and peace in your life.

The ordinary mind cannot understand this truth because it is still steeped in ignorance. But at the highest level of consciousness, all conflicts and confusion resolve themselves into one beautiful, harmonious whole. You may call it divine. You may call it God, This or That. The fact is, it is One, it is whole, and it is harmony and order, without any divisions and without any conflicts. At that level even in the seemingly chaotic conditions of life one can perceive harmony and certain order. That which we understand as good or that we understand as bad, become but the facets of the same Truth. He who realizes this fundamental reality of our existence no more suffers from inner confusion and conflicts. He suffers no more from the relative conflicts of his life or relationships. He stops judging things from the limited values of his mind and consciousness. He learns to forgive people. He learns to tolerate opposition. He learns to accept the conditions of his life without complaint. The people and their weaknesses without reservations are accepted by him.

There is nothing higher or lower, nothing sacred or evil for him. Nothing motivates him to take sides or judge the diversity of creation. He lives in harmony with himself and with others, with the world within himself and with the world external to him. He suffers not from fear or insecurity, or from worries and anxieties about himself or his life. If you want to live in peace, stop categorizing and grouping things and people, and it includes you also. Stop judging things from the relative state of your mind, against the partial truths you know and believe in. Understand that harmony comes when you live in peace with the world around you, and when you accept it whole heatedly and unconditionally without measuring it against your limited knowledge. It only happens when you become an embodiment of 'Rta', the rhythm of life and creation.

Law of Rationale and Feelings

One should learn to use appropriately the three forces of your personality namely emotion, fact and faith, to achieve peace and harmony in your life and move closer to God. Emotion, fact and belief are equally significant in human life. They serve various motives. But they are complimentary, which means that you need them all equally to conduct yourself in this world. Without the one the other two do not take you far be it your ordinary life or spiritual.

All these three help us to conduct ourselves in this world, but in their own various ways. It is hard to say which is more useful than the other two. He who has mastery over these three forces, is a master of himself and is qualified to reach God than any one else. Emotion, fact and faith in realemanate from the body, the mind and the inner spirit, or alternatively, the animal, human and divine components of the human personality. They are the Great Trinity, namely Lord Siva, Vishnu and Brahma, the divinities that exist at the microcosmic level also, where as the whole human personality can be contrasted withthe Cosmic Man (Purusha) or Supreme Being of the macrocosm. Without these three components, creation and our existence is not complete.

In a common paralance emotions connect us to the world; fact helps us to solve the problems of our existence, while belief helps us to transcend ourselves to reach the world beyond. Emotions bring people together through the power of love or the joy of being together. But do not help us maintain them for long. Fact helps us to understand the world around us intelligently, but does not take us far in building relationships that are based upon unconditional love, especially when the relationship are no more yielding the expected results. Fact merely can't explain properly the mysteries of our existence or the need for us to become spiritual. Its vision and its field of activity are limited to the tangible and to the sensory world.

In real sense it helps us to fact beyond facts to pursue the path of spirituality so that we may realize Truth in a various way where faith comes to our aid. It enables us to overcome our selfishness and petty mindedness so that we learn to love others unconditionally and sacrifice our selfish interests for the common welfare of all. When hardships surround us and we have exhausted our rationale means to deal with them, or when we are overwhelmed with the negative emotions of fear and hostility, faith provides us with some meaningful clues and the necessitated answers to sustain ourselves. When emotions and fact let us down, faith is the comforting and soothing companion. If you have faith in yourself and in God, you can withstand greater hardships and maintain your inner balance. Trust is an aspect of faith only.

Trust can bring diverse individuals and groups together so that they can work together and live in harmony, though this does not happen all the time as we do not have enough faith in each other. It is trust which is responsible for our social, political or economic institutions. But when people lose faith in them, they either use fact to change them or succumb to their emotions to destroy them. Emotions on their own destabilize our lives. Fact on its own leads us to unlimited ambition and selfishness and in the process endangers the very safety and survival of our existence. On its own faith binds us to blind dogmatism and superstition. Emotions may be harmful if used inappropriately or not regulated properly. The body can suffer from enormous damage because of negative emotions. But take emotions completely out of our systems and what you find will be automatons, devoid of any love for life or concern for themselves or others. If you take emotions completely of our consciousness, the institutions of family and society would collapse under the heavy burden of fact and conditional relationships alone. So we should know when and where to use these three instruments appropriately for the greater benefit of all instead of wasting these powers.

We should cultivate in ourselves the positive emotions of love, compassion, courage and inner joy, discarding wherever possible their corresponding negative emotions. Whether it is in your physical life, material life or spiritual life, learn to use three forces of your personality for your peace and inner happiness. Bring out the best of your emotions in your relationships. Use the best of your facting in times of hardships and when you stand alone in the contemplation of God, let the light of your faith shine through your heart.

Law of Misery

Just because of our inner imperfections suffering comes to us. To the extent we learn from our suffering and learn from it, our suffering is mitigated. Suffering is not a negative but a positive and dynamic force. Its objective is to open our eyes and correct our ways. It comes into our lives, not because we are destined to suffer, but because it has a message to deliver. When you pursue a wrong path, objective for a wrong goal, make some wrong choices or give expression to some inner imperfection, you suffer and in that suffering lays a warning that you need to change. Your suffering goes to the extent you become aware of it and respond positively to it and to the extent you correct yourselves or your actions.

The hidden motive of suffering hence is not to really subject to you physical or mental anguish, but to improve you in some aspect of your life. Those who refuse to listen to its message continue to suffer, perhaps more intensely, till good sense prevails and the necessitated change comes in them. The fact why every one suffers to some degree in the world is because every one is imperfect in some way and is in need of some improvement. It is because of the suffering that life evolves on earth.

Hence, when suffering comes into the life of an individual, he must look into himself deeply and find out the root cause. He must find out what its true message is, what it wants in him to change or improve. Once he identifies the cause, he must take necessary steps to change himself. He should strive sincerely to remove the cause. Suffering becomes not a dark affliction, but a beacon of light guiding us in the right direction towards the future in this way.

PRIMARY BELIEFS

Mainly the Hindu philosophy is divided into six orthodox (Sanskrit stika) schools of thought, or darshanas, discussed below.

Samkhya

In Hinduism Samkhya is the oldest of the orthodox philosophical systems. Samkhya postulates that everything in reality stems from purusha (Self or soul) and prakriti (Matter, creative agency, energy). There are a number of souls and they possess consciousness, but they are devoid of all qualities. Prakriti/Matter consists of three dispositions: steadiness (sattva), activity (rajas), and dullness (tamas), known as the three gunas, or qualities. Because of the intertwined relationship between the soul and these dispositions, an imbalance in disposition causes the world to evolve. Liberation occurs with the realization that the soul and the dispositions are different. Samkhya is a dualistic philosophy, but there are differences between Samkhya and other forms of dualism. Dualism is between the mind and the body in the West, whereas in Samkhya it is between the self and matter. The concept of the self is roughly equivalent to the Western concept of the mind. Originally Samkhya was not theistic, but in confluence with Yoga it developed a theistic variant.

Yoga

Yoga is the name of one of the six orthodox philosophical schools in Indian philosophy. The Yoga philosophical system is closely allied with the Samkhya school. The Yoga school as expounded by Patanjali accepts the Samkhya psychology and metaphysics, but is more theistic than the Samkhya, as evidenced by the addition of a divine entity to the Samkhya's twenty-five elements of reality. The parallels between Yoga and Samkhya were so close that Max Müller says that "the two philosophies were in popular parlance distinguished from each other as Samkhya with and Samkhya without a Lord." Heinrich Zimmer wrote about the intimate relationship between Samkhya and Yoga:

"These two are regarded in India as twins, the two aspects of a single discipline. Sekhya provides a basic theoretical exposition of human nature, enumerating and defining its elements, analyzing their manner of co-operation in a state of bondage (bandha), and describing their state of disentanglement or separation in release (moksha), while Yoga treats specifically of the dynamics of the process for the disentanglement, out outlines practical techniques for the gaining of release, or 'isolation-integration' (kaivalya)."

The foundational text of the Yoga school is the Yoga Sutras of Patanjali, who is regarded as the founder of the formal Yoga philosophy. The Sutras of the Yoga philosophy are ascribed to Patanjali, who, may have been, as Max Müller explains, "the author or representative of the Yoga-philosophy without being necessarily the author of the Sutras."

Nyaya

Basically the Nyaya school is based on the Nyaya Sutras. They were written by Aksapada Gautama, probably in the second century BC. The most significant contribution made by this school is its methodology. This methodology is based on a system of logic that has subsequently been adopted by the majority of the Indian schools. This is comparable to the relationship between Western science and philosophy, which was derived largely from Aristotelian logic. Nevertheless, Nyaya was seen by its followers as more than logical in its own right.

They believed that obtaining valid knowledge was the only way to gain release from suffering, and they took great pains to identify valid sources of knowledge and distinguish these from mere false opinions. As per the Nyaya, there are exactly four sources of knowledge: perception, inference, comparison, and testimony. Knowledge obtained through each of these is either valid or invalid. Nyaya developed several criteria of validity. In this sense, Nyaya is probably the closest Indian equivalent to analytic philosophy. The later Naiyanikas gave logical proofs for the existence and uniqueness of Ishvara in response to Buddhism, which, at that time, was basically non-theistic.

Vaisheshika

The school of Vaisheshika was founded by Kanada and postulates an atomic pluralism. All objects in the physical universe are reducible to certain types of atoms, and Brahman is regarded as the fundamental force that causes consciousness in these atoms. Although the Vaisheshika school developed independently from the Nyaya, the two eventually merged because of their closely related metaphysical theories. In its classical form, however, the Vaisheshika school differed from the Nyaya in one crucial respect: where Nyaya accepted four sources of valid knowledge, the Vaisheshika accepted only two—perception and inference. But both Vesheshika and Nyaya schools were not entirely identical.

Purva Mimamsa

Chief objective of the Purva Mimamsa school was to establish the authority of the Vedas. Consequently, this school's most worthful contribution to Hinduism was its conceptualisation of the rules of Vedic interpretation. Its adherents believe that one must have unquestionable faith in the Vedas and perform the yajñas, or fire-sacrifices, regularly. They believe in the power of the mantras and yajñas to sustain all the activity of the universe. In keeping with this belief, they place great emphasis on dharma, which consists of the functioning of Vedic rites. The Mimamsa assumed the logical and philosophical teachings of the other schools, but felt they did not sufficiently emphasise attention to right action. They believed that the other schools of thought that objectiveed for release (moksha) did not allow for complete freedom from desire and selfishness, because the very striving for liberation stemmed from a simple desire to be free. As per the Mimamsa thought, only by acting in accordance with the prescriptions of the Vedas may one attain salvation. The Mimamsa school later changed its views and commenced to teach the doctrines of Brahman and freedom. Its adherents then advocated the release or escape of the soul from its constraints through enlightened activity. Although Mimamsa does not receive much scholarly attention, its influence can be felt in the life of the practising Hindu, because all Hindu ritual, ceremony, and law is influenced by this school.

Vedanta

The Vedanta, or later Mimamsa school, focuses on the philosophical teachings of the Upanishads rather than the ritualistic injunctions of the Brahmanas. While the customal Vedic rituals continued to be exercised as meditative and propitiatory rites, a more knowledge-centred understanding began to emerge. These were mystical aspects of Vedic religion that focused on meditation, self-discipline, and spiritual connectivity, more than conventional ritualism.

The more recondite Vedanta is the essence of the Vedas, as encapsulated in the Upanishads. Vedantic thought drew on Vedic cosmology, hymns and philosophy. The Brihadaranyaka Upanishad seem ed as far back as 3,500 years ago. While thirteen or so Upanishads are accepted as principal, over a hundred exist. The most significant share of Vedantic thought is the idea that self-consciousness is continuous with and indistinguishable from consciousness of Brahman.

The aphorisms of the Vedanta sutras are presented in a cryptic, poetic style, which allows for a variety of interpretations. Consequently, the Vedanta broke into six sub-schools, each interpreting the texts in its own way and producing its own series of sub-commentaries. Four of them are as follows.

Advaita

Probably Advaita is the best-known of all Vedanta schools. Advaita literally means "non duality." Its first great consolidator was Adi Shankaracharya (788-820), who continued the line of thought of some of the Upanishadic teachers, and that of his teacher's teacher Gaudapada.

By analysing the three states of experience--waking, dreaming, and deep sleep--he established the singular reality of Brahman, in which the soul and Brahman are one and the same. Under the influence of an illusionary power called Avidya Ishvara is the expression of Brahman to human minds.

Visishtadvaita

The foremost proponent of the concept of the Supreme Being having a definite form, name, and attributes Ramanujacharya. He saw this form as that of Vishnu, and taught that reality has three aspects: Vishnu, soul (jiva), and matter (prakrti). Vishnu is the only independent reality, while souls and matter are dependent on Vishnu for their existence. Qualified non-dualism thus is known as Ramanuja's system.

Dvaita

Madhvacharya (1218-1317) like Ramanuja, identified Brahman with Vishnu, but his view of reality was pluralistic. As per the Dvaita, there are three ultimate realities: Vishnu, soul, and matter. Five distinctions are made: (1) Vishnu is distinguishable from souls; (2) Vishnu is distinguishable from matter; (3) Souls are distinguishable from matter; (4) A soul is distinct from another soul, and (5) Matter is distinguishable from other matter. Souls are eternal and are dependent upon the will of Vishnu. This theology attempts to addresses the problem of evil with the idea that souls are not created.

Dvaitadvaita (Bhedabheda)

Nimbarka proposed Dvaitadvaita, a 13th century Vaishnava Philosopher from the Andhra region. As per the this philosophy there are three categories of existence: Brahman, soul, and matter. Soul and matter are different from Brahman in that they have attributes and capacities distinct from Brahman. Brahman exists independently, while soul and matter are dependent. Thus soul and matter have an existence that is distinguish yet dependent. Further, Brahman is a controller, the soul is the enjoyer, and matter the thing enjoyed. Also, the highest object of worship is Krishna and his consort Radha, attended by thousands of gopis, or cowherdesses; of the celestial Vrindavana; and devotion consists in self-surrender.

Shuddhadvaita

Vallabhacharya (1479 - 1531) proposed Shuddhadvaita, who came from the Andhra region but eventually settled in Gujarat.

Achintya Bheda Abheda

A devotee of Krishna, Chaitanya Mahaprabhu (1486-1534), proposed a synthesis between the monist and dualist philosophies by stating that the soul is both distinct and non-distinct from God, whom he identified as Krishna, and that this, although unthinkable, may be experienced through a process of loving devotion (bhakti). This philosophy of "inconceivable oneness and difference" is followed by a number of modern Gaudiya Vaishnava movements, including ISKCON, sometimes called the Hare Krishna movement. ISKCON has recently took part in bringing the academic study of Krishna-related philosophies into Western academia through the theological discourse on Krishnology.

ETHICS

With other philosophical trends and schools Hindu schools of philosophy developed in close, lively dialogue. As early as

400–300 BC, both Panini and the author of Manusmriti (a third century BC book of laws) identified two major intellectual trends, one involving belief in the sacred texts known as the Vedas, and one involving their rejection. Those who regarded the Vedas as their authority later developed into what we know as the Hindu schools. With a few exceptions, most of the religious and philosophical movements objectiveed at liberation, complete freedom from life and rebirth. From about the eighth century BC, belief in rebirth was found among most philosophical and religious leaders.

At first, the mechanism of rebirth was thought to be prompted by bad actions. It was also believed that by good actions a person became good and by evil actions a person became evil. Since with time this must have come to be perceived as rather simplistic, the idea of rebirth became more complicated. A person was reborn just by acts, regardless of whether those acts were good or evil. Liberation from rebirth could be attained by an absence of desire; desire of any sort, whether a craving for food, say, or for a new thing, entangled a person in the worldly repetition mechanism.

Various thinkers and teachers were specifically concerned with effective ways of achieving liberation. This meant establishing the basic presuppositions of the theory, such as what it is that truly exists, how this could be proved, and how liberation was to be viewed, and, moreover, how to promulgate such beliefs. There were constant discussions, an ongoing search for better ways of arguing with opponents. The formal necessitatements for building an argument were much disputed; each school believed that only its tools for debate were necessary, and that any others were useless.

An axiom held by most followers of the Vedic custom was that there is a self (atman) which travels from life to life. The 'life' in question need not be human; it can also be that of an animal. In the early philosophical sources, the Upanishads, there is little room for any sort of agency beyond individuals with selves. It is only later that we find the idea of God or gods actively creating the universe and directing individual persons towards liberation or towards realizing some sort of aspiration towards the divine. Both these objectives were combined in many instances.

The concept of atman was crucial in a number of debates, because there were a number of people who either had a various understanding of it or who claimed to need no such concept. Argument helped towards a more precise articulation of the term, although a number of Hindu thinkers held that knowledge of atman is only a partial understanding of reality; the individual self is only a part of the larger scenario of the universe. The universe was thought to be an all-encompassing spiritual entity, of which atman is a minute fragment. Experiencing this spiritually, through meditative practices, frees a person from the ordinary way of things: such a person is not reborn, and does not repeat the anguish, pain, disease, old age and death of ordinary mortals, but is instead forever free. This can be accomplished through one's own efforts, although often the guidance of a teacher, a guru, is necessitated. These efforts may necessitate to be extended over various lifetimes in order to work off all the accumulated karmic impressions. Karmic impressions, which may result from physical activities, speech or mental acts, are what in realbind people to the rotating process of rebirth.

Step by step, notions of divine intervention in the process of liberation found their way into numerous teachings. It was a compounding of one's own efforts plus divine grace which would grant final deliverance, which was now not only freedom from repeated cycles of lives, but also either an identification with the divine, or companionship with a god as a lover or eternal servant. Some Advaita philosophers postulated a single ultimate principle, whereas others argued for the existence of an ultimate cause of the universe, namely God. As it is to this day the worship of a multitude of gods was still widely practised.

One of the most prominent thinkers of the School of Logic (Nyaya), Udayana (eleventh century), constructed an elegant set of arguments for the existence of God. Put crudely, his claim is that this multifarious world must obviously be the effect of some cause, and that cause must be nothing other than God. On the other hand, not all thinkers felt a need to trace the world to one primary cause, even though most took it for granted that causal chains are of prime significance in interpreting the world. The nature of the causal relation was much debated. Some claimed that an effect somehow already exists in latent form in its cause, just as yoghurt is potentially already present in milk even before the milk turns sour. In the same way, this whole manifold world somehow pre-existed in an unvariousiated primeval watery mass, into which it will dissolve itself again at the end of its existence. There are repeated existences and dissolutions.

Many other philosophers, such as Sankara (eighth century), interpreted the relation between cause and effect in a slightly various way. The difference between the two is only apparent, because in reality the universe is only superimposed onto an unchanging, everlasting, universal and unvariousiated principle, the Brahman of the Upanisadic thinkers. We superimpose things out of ignorance. A favourite analogy is that of a man walking along the road, half-blinded by the brilliant sunshine at noon. Suddenly he jumps across an elongated shape in the road, out of fear that he may step on a snake. A passer-by laughs and asks, 'Are you afraid of a dirty old piece of rope?' The person who jumped with fear was superimposing a snake onto the old rope. In the same way, we superimpose the whole universe onto Brahman. In reality, there are no causal relations at all. We talk of such concepts to facilitate debate, but they have no place on the final level.

Epistemic Concerns

The reasearchers and philosophers differed in their views about the number and characteristics of the various means of knowledge. The most widely accepted evidence was perception. Inference and verbal testimony (such as an utterance by a competent speaker or a statement from the Vedas) were also regarded significant. Some schools added analogy and other special kinds of inference. Because of their differing ontologies, schools also disagreed about the objects of knowledge. Nyaya held that these were self, body, sense organs, mind, rebirth, pain and freedom (moksha). Sankhya linked the objects of cognition to the sense organs: the eye has colour as its object, the ear has sound, the tongue taste, and so on; inference has as its objects things beyond sensory perception, such as consciousness, the unvariousiated material stuff of the universe, and causal relations. 'Perception' was usually confined to sensory or external perception. Some thinkers also recognized a sort of mental perception for mental states (such as joy or anguish). Sometimes this was classed as belonging to a larger category of internal perception which also included yogic perception. Yogic and other types of perception in turn could be classed as 'extraordinary', as in the Nyaya system, especially its later form (Navya-Nyaya, 'New Logic'). Precise definitions of perception varied widely. Some thought it was direct awareness of colour; others argued that it was a cognition arising from the relation of an object with the senses, which is not verbal and not erroneous, but definite. An exchange of ideas arose over whether perception is a direct experience, that is, non-propositional, and whether one can postulate a propositional level of perception. Nyaya and the classical Sankhya claimed to understand perceptions of two levels: non-propositional (roughly what we call 'sense data') and propositional.

Anumana or inference was the next most significant instrument of knowledge. In the classical period, three kinds of inference were usually enumerated. Their definitions betray certain confusion between old and new ideas of inference. Inference is used as a source of knowledge in cases where objects cannot be apprehended directly. The foundation of inference is the consistent relation between the fact and the thing-to-be-proved.

The coherent relation is not explicitly stated in the syllogism, although it is quite obvious: where there is smoke, there is fire. Verbal testimony was thought to be another decisive source of knowledge of things beyond sensory apprehension. A competent testifier is a reliable person who has direct knowledge, wants to communicate it and is also capable of expressing it. It was argued that the revealed sacred literature could be classed as testimony. There was also some discussion about whether to subsume this source of knowledge under inference. Other suggested pramanas were analogy and presumption. An instance of presumption is the following: it is observed that Devadatta is fat; nobody sees him overeating during the day; so (the presumption is that) he must eat all night. Indian philosophers also discussed an argument known as tarka, a kind of facting that we call reduction ad absurdum.

There was a preoccupation with language in Indian culture from the earliest times. 'Language' here means Sanskrit. A concern with the power and limitations of language is already clear in the Rigveda. Of the six theoretical branches of learning listed in the Vedas, four are closely related to language: grammar, etymology, lexicography and poetry. The level of accomplishment eventually attained in these is demonstrated in Panini's descriptive grammar, the Astadhyayi. Patanjali's commentary on this, the Mahabhasya (second century BC) can be thought of as a kind of a bridge between grammatical and philosophical concerns. The fifth-century philosopher Bharthari stands out among those who studied language. In his Vakyapadiya, he considers the faculty of speech to be an instinct or intuition. He compares it to animal instinct and does not believe that language is learned. Language, as per the Bharthari, accompanies cognition - there is no cognition without language. He equates language with Brahman as his understanding of language is rather metaphysical.

The theory of sphoma is particularly associated with Bharthari, although the notion had been formulated some centuries before him. As per the this theory, a sentence is an integral unit. Analysing a sentence in terms of phonemes, morphemes or words is useful for learning motives, but the whole sentence alone is meaningful. When those who know a language hear an utterance in that language, they hear a sentence, not single words or phonemes; only those who do not know the language will hear individual bits of sound. Bhartrihari holds that it is permanent and natural, not based on convention as for the relation between word and meaning.

However, all schools of philosophy were concerned with language, perhaps the earliest was Mimamsa. The followers of this school were concerned with the interpretation of the Vedas, and in particular with the problem of the relation between words and sentences. The Mimamsakas argued that, for a word to be intelligible, each utterance of it has to be identical with an earlier utterance that is now remembered. By extrapolation, words must be eternal. The meaning of words is eternal, as is the relation between word and meaning in the same manner.

Panini observed the need for a capacity for mutual connection between the meanings of words, and the Mimamsakas similarly developed a set of conditions for meaningful and correct sentences. They named the capacity for mutual connection between the meanings of words 'mutual expectancy'. For instance, 'he rides an elephant' fulfils the condition of mutual syntactic expectancy, but a string of words such as 'elephant, house, riding' does not. But as per the this condition, the sentence 'he rides a house' is also a sentence. So another condition, 'semantic compatibility', was added. In a sentence like 'he rides a house', the semantic compatibility is absent. The Mimamsakas also necessitated that the condition of 'contiguity' be fulfilled: words must not be spoken at long intervals or be separated by other words. Another condition was 'the intention of the speaker', about which there were varying opinions. All chief branches of the Mimamsa school developed its own theory regarding the semantic relationship between words and sentences.

The adherents of Prabhakara believed that the meaning of a sentence arises directly from its collection of words. Conversely, words convey meaning only in the context of a sentence. Each word in a sentence conveys both its isolated meaning and the syntactic meaning. On the other hand, Kumarila Bhatta and his followers believed that the meaning of a sentence arises circuitously. Each word gives its individual meaning, and this uses up its significative power; hence the syntactic relation must be obtained by means of a secondary significative power. This view was also shared by the Advaita Vedantins, who, in order to be able to express truths about the Absolute, could not always use words with their primary meaning, but had instead to use the secondary meaning.

The Advaitins of course were not the only ones who distinguished between the primary and secondary meanings of words. This practice was well known among other philosophers, grammarians, and especially literary critics. In his Mahabhasya, Patanjali distinguished primary and secondary meanings, while Bhartrihari discussed transfer of meaning (upacara) through such tropes as simile, metonymy, and synecdoche and so on. By the ninth century, Anandavardhana, in his exposition of literary criticism, was discussing the 'suggestive power' of words. He observed that a text does not yield its full meaning to every reader, since the ideal reader must be trained in the symbolism and conventions of a text, and familiar with the realities to which the text refers. Such a reader has an intuitive grasp of the text that untrained reader's lack.

At first primarily the school of Nyaya was concerned with theories of the relation between a word and its meaning. The Naiyayikas did not consider this relation to be natural, but saw it as just a matter of convention. This conventional relation is called 'significative power' (Shanty). Shanty applies to primary meaning only; although secondary meaning is accepted, it is regarded only in terms of its relation to the primary meaning and can apply only to single words, not to whole sentences. The Naiyayikas and the grammarians stayed active for a number of centuries, in the course of which their teachings were transformed. The Naiyayikas especially developed new terminology and techniques of argument; this change was reflected in their adoption of a modified name, Navya-Nyaya.

Moral Issues

The two significant principles govern Indian moral philosophy: karma and dharma. The theory of karma was articulated early in Upanisadic times (which are usually placed from 700 BC onwards, but were possibly earlier). It concerns the causal relation between acts and their results, although neither was always understood in a uniform way. In general, the workings of karma were not interpreted as a fatalistic mechanism. With the exception of a few schools, most Indian thinkers came to conceive of karma in terms of a kind of naturalistic law of causation.

The best-known philosopher of the Upanishads, Yajñavalkya, was the first one to teach karma, which soon became discernible in almost all intellectual developments, as well as being a governing principle in everyday ethics. The principle of dharma is closely connected with karma. Dharma literally means 'to uphold what is correct', what we may call today 'morality'. The precise translation of the term depends on the context. For instance, we can translate dharma as 'justice' in cases where something that was unlawfully taken away is to be regained. Thus, in the epic Mahabharata, it is justice for the Pandavas to regain their kingdom, which was illegally taken from them by their cousins, the Kauravas. There is also dharma as 'individual duty', as per the a person's social and economic status in society. This could be contrasted with a certain extent with the Kantian idea of duty (duty for duty's sake). Then as a guide in moral and social issues there is general dharma which applies to society as a whole.

A significant ideal in Hindu moral philosophy that of the stages of life, is described in the body of literature known as the Dharmauastras. This endorses the determination of social status by birth, and prescribes for each individual (at least, each male of the two highest classes, namely priests and royalty) the various stages to progress through in life. The prescribed sequence is as follows: first, the socially responsible person should study and abstain from sexual relations; next, he should marry, bring up offspring and accumulate material possessions; third, he should become a religious seeker, leaving behind the comforts of home, family and riches (although his wife may still provide some familiar comfort); ultimately, he should leave the companionship of his wife and roam alone as an ascetic until death. Two value systems, one socially engaged, the other with an ascetic tendency, seem to be combined here. Closely related are the four objectives of human life (purushartha): material wellbeing, pleasure and enjoyment, morality and social responsibility, and, the ultimate goal, liberation from repeated birth. Here, too, two value systems are combined: the first three objectives guide the socially engaged, whereas the last is the objective of a person in the final stage of life.

Metaphysics

Still Vedanta survives and is the most influential school of modern times, having great intellectual and political figures among its adherents. 'Vedanta' describes several schools and numerous thinkers, and means 'the appendage to the Vedas', referring in this way to the body of texts known as the Upanishads. The Upanishads have been a source of inspiration and dogma since their beginnings around 700 BC. Embedded in them are ideas that came to dominate Indian thought, namely karma, rebirth, and liberation from the ever-revolving cycle of rebirth. The means of liberation is to experience the identity of the individual self (atman) with a larger cosmic entity (Brahman). Individual thinkers each had a various interpretation of these tenets, but all essentially agreed on the means of liberation. Curiously, the development of Vedanta did not take place until more than a millennium after the earlier Upanishads. The most authoritative thinker of whom we know today was Sankara.

Like other Vedantins, Sankara built on an earlier custom. The work to which they all responded was Badarayana's Brahmasutra (or Vedantasutra) of around ad 50. It stimulated A number of interpretive commentaries, which gave occasion for new schools to arise. The most prominent interpretation of the Brahmasutra is known as Advaita Vedanta. It focuses on Brahman, which is understood as identical with atman. Out of ignorance, the material world is superimposed on the ultimately empty Brahman; this superimposition is sometimes described as an illusory projection (maya). The first spectacular name in this custom is Gau apada, who taught Uankara's teacher.

Sankara was prolific in his philosophical output. He commented on all the major Upanishads and the Bhagavad Gita ([Upanishad, or Secret Teaching] Recited by the Lord Krishna), and a number of other works are ascribed to him. His Advaitism can be characterized as a strict nondualism: there is nothing other than Brahman, either real or unreal, and the goal is to know this through a trance-like experience which grants liberation from rebirth. Were it not for this experience of truth, which is the vision of identity between atman and Brahman, we would always superimpose this colourful world on transparent Brahman. This superimposition is an act of mistaking an unreal object for a real one, just as we superimpose silver on a piece of a glittering shell or a snake on a rope. If we could lift the superimposed object away from the real one, underneath we would find something altogether of varied form.

The significance of a personal God is diminished by this doctrine as it is austere. It failed to stimulate the imagination of a number of people, and with time there was a strong reaction to such an abstract portrayal of reality. The form of Vedanta that flourished subsequently tended to have a more theistic cast. The earliest work of theistic Vedanta was Bhaskara's interpretation of the Brahmasutra, whereby the individual self is both various and not various from God (Brahman). This doctrine was called 'the teaching of difference with no difference' (Bhedabhedavada). The Brahmasutra was often seen in the light of theology devoted to the god Vishnu.

The eleventh-century philosopher Ramanuja, commenting on the Brahmasutra in his Sribhasya, claims that everything is Brahman, yet acknowledges the reality of individual selves and the material world. This teaching is called 'qualified monism' (Viœicmadvaitavada) because Brahman is described as Knowledge and as being merciful, all-powerful and all-pervading. Everything that exists is contained in Brahman, understood as a personal God who should be approached with constant devotion. Other interpreters of the Brahmasutra postulated devotion to God; to a number of them, he was some form of Vishnu, which indicates that they too had a problem with absolute monism. Hence they introduced a modified monism: Nimbarka, for instance, combined both dualism and nondualism.

The extreme position of disavowing monism was taken in the thirteenth century by Madhva (not to be confused with Madhava), who claimed that there is an absolute difference between Brahman and individual selves (Dvaitavada). Another extreme position was expressed by Vallabhacharya in his teaching of pure nondualism (Uudhadvaitavada). Still other thinkers with other interpretations, such as Chaitanya (1486–1534) of the Bengal Vaisnavism, did not leave a corpus of literature behind them.

With respect to epistemology and some ontological issues Sankhya and Vedanta are similar. Sankhya was an old dualistic school reaching back to the ontologies of Upanisadic times. It postulated an irreducible duality of consciousness and material stuff. Originally, the material stuff existed in an unvariousiated form, until it was disturbed by an intangible prodding of consciousness. Once disturbed, it produced twenty-three parts of the universe, with the human individual's parts in preponderance. Altogether, with consciousness and the unvariousiated material stuff, there are twenty-five things that exist. The goal of Sankhya was to experience the basic duality in a trance-like state, to discriminate between 'spirit' and 'matter'. Perhaps this dualism reflected vacillation between idealistic/metaphysical tendencies and naturalistic/ materialistic tendencies.

Vaisheshika was another old school, which in some respects was close to Sankhya. Like Sankhya, it strove to list all the things that exist in reality, to name everything there is. Such a proto-scientific enumeration of categories marks the antiquity of these systems. The number of ontological categories as per the classical Vaisesika of Prauastapada is six. Other philosophers enumerated as A number of as ten, others only seven. Among these categories, such as substance, quality and activity, we find a category of relation, inherence. Inherence is a relation between things that do not exist in isolation. It holds between qualities and substances, and between particulars and universals; a quality inheres in its substratum, a substance, so that, with a red apple, the red colour is a quality of the substance apple. This red colour cannot exist on its own, but always has to inhere in something, whether an apple or a hibiscus flower.

The Vaisheshika are known as the Indian atomists. Motion inheres in the atoms, which, in their varying compositions as whole objects, are the substratum of motion. The Vaisheshika school is frequently lumped together with the Nyaya ('Logic') school. The fact for this might be that later Nyaya philosophers took it upon themselves to comment upon and revise the old atomistic school. The word nyaya is often used for a maxim or an instance in an argument, which is perhaps why it was adopted for the Logic school; earlier, however, it was used to refer to the system of Mimamsa.

The Nyaya school also had a list of basic categories. Their sixteen categories are quite obviously the parts of a rigorous argument: for instance, instruments of knowledge, objects of knowledge, doubt, motive, instance, and so on. Thus the list consists of epistemological or proto-epistemological tools. The chief preoccupation among the Naiyayikas was to build proper arguments. They used a five-member syllogism based on the constant relation between logical fact and thing-to-be proved (sadhya). This relation came later to be known as concomitance or pervasion (vyapti).

The Naiyayikas also tried to safeguard against possible mishaps in argument by distinguishing three kinds of fallacy in facting. The early Mimamsakas were completely engaged in interpreting the scriptures, which conveyed injunctions for ritual actions such as sacrifices and ceremonies. These actions should be performed because the Vedas say so – the Vedas are authoritative. Other pursuits, such as acquiring knowledge of oneself or engaging in philosophical debates about God, serve no motive. Furthermore, any philosophical pursuit may give rise to doubts, and the doubts may extend to the authority of the Vedas. It was centuries before Mimamsa was freed from such dogmatism, by the philosophers Kumarila and Prabhakara (both seventh century).

They maintained atheistic positions, and made fun of inconsistencies in arguments for the existence of God. Prabhakara put forward a theory of the self-verifying nature of simple (non-propositional) perceptual knowledge which was heavily criticized by philosophers of other schools. Yoga was a practical discipline of physical postures, breathing techniques and meditation whose origin we are unable to trace to any precise time, place or event. It went hand-in-hand with the ascetic life, no matter what the value system or outlook of its practitioners.

Yoga is classically grouped with Sankhya. There may be two reasons for this. First, both systems date back to the ancient encounter in Indian history between Aryan nomadic conquerors and a settled agricultural people (which lasted several centuries from 1500 BC onwards). There are speculations that Sankhya developed within the newcomers' custom, whereas Yoga was practiced among the original inhabitants. Perhaps just as the worldviews of these groups grew together, so were the schools assimilated one to the other. The second fact may have been that Yoga needed a theoretical background to become a system.

Sankhya is the oldest recognizable proto-philosophical bundle of ideas. But what Sankhya and Yoga share is not really significant in view of the fact that a number of other schools adopted Yoga techniques. As per the the Yogasutra, the objective of Yoga is to be able to attain a state of deep concentration (samadhi) by stopping the activity of the mind. Yoga differs significantly from Sankhya in requiring the grace of God for liberation. Yoga can be seen as a practical discipline capable of being adapted by various theoretical systems, especially those whose adherents are supposed to undergo spiritual experiences to attain liberation from pain, anguish, longing and rebirth.

CHAPTER 7

Hinduism and New Millennium

HINDUISM AND SPIRITUAL FREEDOM

India is the land where Sanatana Dharma took root and flourished. So whatever her present condition, the rise of Hindutva in India will have a major impact on the history and politics of this century. It is therefore of fundamental importance to understand it role in the growth of the Indian nation. It is a uniquely spiritual ideology founded on spiritual freedom. In the light of this, 'conversion' to Hinduism entails accepting a way of looking at the world and not simply changing faith and adopting a new mode of worship. *Above all it means acknowledging spiritual freedom and rejecting exclusivism.* It is like accepting the scientific method, which also is a way of looking at the world. But ultimately, every Hindu must place truth and knowledge above faith. There is no dogma. This is why people who are initiated into Hinduism are made to recite the Gayatri Mantra, which is an assertion of this spirit of intellectual freedom. *The only enemies of Sanatana Dharma (Hinduism) are those that oppose spiritual freedom.* Protecting and nurturing Sanatana Dharma and the society founded on it is the responsibility of Hindutva. Rights like spiritual freedom come with responsibility.

INDIA'S UNITY IS OF UNTOLD ANTIQUITY

After a long and dark period in its history, Hinduism is again on the rise. This is true in the national as well as the spiritual sense, for India cannot exist without its spiritual foundation. There are many Western scholars as well as Western educated Indians who hold that India was never a nation but only a collection of clans and groups in a geographical 'subcontinent'. They further claim that Indians were united as a people for first time by the British. This has two fallacies. First, the British did not rule over a united India. Their authority extended over roughly two-thirds of India while the remaining portion was ruled by hereditary rulers – like the Maharajas and Nawabs – who acknowledged the British monarch as their chief but ruled according to their own laws and tradition. *This means it is not India per se, but British India that was not a nation, but a patchwork or states.* Second, although often politically divided, the goal was always to unite all of India under a single rule.

In spite of this history, it was claimed by the British, and faithfully repeated by the Leftist intellectuals, that the British unified India. This is completely false. *The unity of India, rooted in her ancient culture, is of untold antiquity.* It may have been divided at various times into smaller kingdoms, but the goal was always to be united under a 'Chakravartin' or a 'Samrat'. There was always a cultural unity even when it was politically divided. This cultural unity was seriously damaged during the Medieval period, when India was engaged in a struggle for survival – like what is happening in Kashmir today. Going back thousands of years, India had been united under a single ruler many times. The earliest recorded emperor of India was Bharata, the son of Shakuntala and Dushyanta, but there were several others. Some examples from the *Aitareya Brahmana*.

"With this great anointing of Indra, Dirghatamas Mamateya anointed Bharata Daushanti. Therefore, Bharata Daushanti went round the earth completely, conquering on every side and offered the horse in sacrifice.

"With this great anointing of Indra, Tura Kavasheya anointed Janamejaya Parikshita. Therefore Janamejaya Parikshita went round

the earth completely, conquering on every side and offered the horse in sacrifice."

There are similar statements about Sudasa Paijavana anointed by Vasistha, Anga anointed by Udamaya Atreya, Durmukha Pancala anointed by Brihadukta and Atyarati Janampati anointed by Vasistha Satyahavya.

Atyarati, though not born a king, became an emperor and went on to conquer even the Uttara Kuru or the modern Sinkiang and Turkestan that lie north of Kashmir. There are others also mentioned in the *Shatapatha Brahmana* and also the *Mahabharata.* This shows that the unity of India is an ancient concept.

As previously noted, the British did not rule over a unified India. Far from it, for their goal was *divide and rule.* They had treaties with the rulers of hereditary kingdoms like Mysore, Kashmir, Hyderabad and others that were more or less independent. The person who united all these was Sardar Patel, not the British. But this unification was possible only because India is culturally one. Pakistan, with no such identity or cultural unity, is falling apart.

The spiritual tradition of Sanatana Dharma, which we call Hinduism, includes the code of *Raja Dharma* and *Kshatra Dharma* needed to defend the nation.

This is also part of Hindutva. This is needed to defend society against hostile forces seeking to destroy society, especially its spiritual foundation. This is what happened during the medieval period when Islamic warriors tried to uproot Hinduism from its soil. But thanks to the heroism of both rulers and the common people, Hindutva defeated these forces and saved Sanatana Dharma. It is now being called upon to defend again in the face of cries of Jihad by fanatics across the border and intellectuals and politicians hostile to the concept of nationalism. It is therefore of paramount importance to understand what the role of Hindutva is in defending the country. This is what we need to look at next.

VOLUMINOUS IDEA OF HINDUISM

The elaborate presentation of alternative points of views draws attention to the plurality of perspectives and arguments, and this tradition of accom-modating heterodoxy receives...extensive support within well-established Hindu documents (for example in the fourteenth-century study *Sarvadarsanasamgraha* ('Collection of All Philosophies'), where sixteen contrary and competing viewpoints are sequentially presented in as many chapters).

In contrast with this large view, many Hindu political activists today seem bent on doing away with the broad and tolerant parts of the Hindu tradition in favour of a uniquely ascertained - and often fairly crude - view which, they demand, must be accepted by all. The piously belligerent army of Hindu politics would rather take us away from these engagingly thoughtful discussions and would have us embrace instead their much-repeated public proclamations...

It is sufficient to note here that there is a well-established capacious view of a broad and generous Hinduism, which contrasts sharply with the narrow and bellicose versions that are currently on political offer, led particularly by parts of the Hindutva movement.

The Emergence of Hindutva

In the early years after independence, the broad and comprehensive concept of an Indian identity which had emerged during the long struggle for freedom commanded sweeping allegiance. The determi-nation to preserve that capacious identity was strengthened by the deep sense of tragedy associated with the partitioning of the subcon-tinent, and also by considerable national pride in the fact that despite the political pressure for 'an exchange of people, the bulk of the large Muslim population in independent India chose to stay in India rather than move to Pakistan.

It is this spacious and absorptive idea of Indianness that has been severely challenged over recent decades...it can be said that the movement sees Hindutva (liter-ally, 'the quality of Hinduism') as a quintessential guide to 'Indianness'.

The Bharatiya Janata Party (BJP), the political party that represents the Hindutva movement in the Indian parliament, was in office in New Delhi between 1998 and 2004, through leading a coalition govern-ment, until its electoral defeat in May 2004...Although Hinduism is an ancient religion, Hindutva is quite a recent political movement. A political party called the 'Hindu Mahasabha' did exist before India's independence, and its successor, the 'Jan Sangh', commanded the loyalty of a small proportion of Hindus. But neither party was a political force to reckon with in the way the BJP and its associates have now become.

Even though the BJP is no longer dominant, in the way it was over the last few years, it remains a politically powerful force, and is work-ing hard to return to office before long.

The BJP gets political support from a modest minority of Indians, and, no less to the point, a limited minority of the Hindus....the proportion of total votes in Indian parliamentary elections that the BJP has maximally managed to get has been only about 26 per cent...in a country where more than 80 per cent of the total population happen to belong to the Hindu community. It is certainly not the party of choice of most Hindus - far from it. The Hindutva movement has had a strong effect on recent political developments in India, and has added very substantially to the poli-tics of sectarianism. It is therefore important to investigate the nature of the intellectual claims it makes and the arguments it presents.Since the Hindutva movement has been accompanied by violent physical actions, including the killing and terrorizing of minorities (as happened in Bombay in 1992-3 and in Gujarat in 2002), it is difficult to have patience with its intellectual beliefs and public proclamations.

Numbers and Classification

The first difficulty is that a secular democracy which gives equal room to every citizen irrespective of religious background cannot be fairly defined in terms of the majority religion of the country.

There is a difference between a constitutionally secular nation with a majority Hindu population and a theocratic Hindu state that might see Hinduism as its official religion (Nepal comes closer to the latter description than does India). Furthermore, no matter what the official standing of any community as a group may be, the status of individ-ual citizens cannot be compromised by the smallness (if that is the case) of the group to which he or she belongs.

While the statistics of Hindu majority are indeed correct, the use of the statistical argument for seeing India as a pre-eminently Hindu country is based on a conceptual confusion: our religion is not our only identity, nor necessarily the identity to which we attach the greatest importance.

History and Indian Culture

Certainly, the ancientness of the Hindu tradition cannot be disputed. However, other religions, too, have had a long history in India, which has been, for a very long time indeed, a multi-religious country, making room for many different faiths and beliefs. Aside from the obvious and prominent presence of Muslims in India for well over a millennium (Muslim Arab traders settled in India from the eighth century), India was not a 'Hindu country' even before the arrival of Islam. Buddhism was the dominant religion in India for nearly a millennium. Indeed, Chinese scholars regularly described India as 'the Buddhist kingdom'.

Inventing the Past

History is an active field of intellectual engagement for the Hindutva movement, and parts of that movement have been very involved in the rewriting of history...What is its specific relevance in contemporary Indian politics, and why is Hindutva poli-tics so keen on redescribing the past? The rewriting of India's history serves the dual purpose of playing a role in providing a common basis for the diverse membership of the Sangh Parivar, and of helping to get fresh recruits to Hindu political activism, especially from the diaspora. It has thus become a major priority in the politics of Hindutva in contemporary India. Following the electoral victory of coalitions led by the BJP in 1998 and 1999, various arms of the government of India were mobilized in the task of arranging 'appropriate' rewritings of Indian history. Even though this adventure of inventing a past is no longer 'official' (because of the defeat of the BJP-led coalition in the general elections in the spring of 2004), that highly charged episode is worth recollecting both because of what it tells us about the abuse of temporal power and also because of the light it throws on the intellectual underpinning of the Hindutva movement.

HISTORY OF HINDUISM THROUGH

The world today is looking to a new millennium, with the year 2000 having just arrived (though will little of the fanfare or catastrophes predicted of it!). As modern culture is dominated by western civilization, which has a Christian basis, it looks to the Christian calendar as defining time for humanity. That most of humanity today and most of history has not been Christian is seldom emphasized.

However, a new millennium is nothing new for Hinduism, which is now in its sixth millennium of the present Kali age, not to speak of its recognition of longer ages or yugas before that. The Hindu tradition has crossed many thousands of years, going back to the very origins of civilization as we know it some ten thousand years ago at the end of the last Ice Age. From the early beginnings of civilization in India on the banks of the now dry Sarasvati River up to the present technological age, Hinduism has remained as a steady flame of spiritual light in the world. It is the most enduring religion and culture in the world, continuing remarkably age after age. Over the course of time Hinduism has seen numerous civilizations come and go. It witnessed the fall of Egypt, Babylonia and Rome, as well as the arising of Christianity and Islam, and the coming of the modern age. What is the secret behind Hinduism's ability to endure? It has not continued age after age simply because of a conservative culture that has preserved old customs. It has endured because of its ability to adapt to time changes and to reinvent itself in a dynamic way in successive eras.

The Hindu tradition is not based upon any particular historical revelation that would tie it down to a particular era or cause it to look to any end of time or end of the world. It accepts the existence of different ages (yugas) of humanity and different civilizations, of which our current cycle of civilization is only one. Hindu Dharma sees history according to the cycles of nature, with the rising and falling of cultures like the coming and going of plants and animals through the seasons of the year. Hinduism positions itself above time in the eternal, looking to link humanity with what transcends time.

The Hindu tradition is not based upon any specific savior or prophet or historical personality. It recognizes many sages and seers, known and unknown, both inside its tradition and outside of it. It accepts many great teachers of the past but also those of the present and of the future. It has no chosen people but addresses all living beings, not merely humans but plants and animals as well. Nor is it simply an earth tradition but looks to beings of all worlds, including the denizens of subtle worlds beyond the physical.

Hinduism defines itself as Sanatana Dharma, the Eternal or Universal Dharma. Dharma means universal law, the fundamental principles behind this marvellous universe like the law of karma. Sanatana means perennial, referring to eternal truth that manifests in ever new names and forms. Hinduism is the oldest religion of the world because it is based on the eternal origins of creation. But it is also the newest religion in the world because it adjusts its names and forms to every generation and looks to living teachers, not old books, as its final authority.

Because of this background, Hinduism views the new millennium in a different way than most people today. Christians view the new millennium as either bringing the end of the world along with salvation for the faithful that they have long prayed for, or as marking a new era to spread their religion further in the world through renewed evangelical and missionary efforts. Other people look to a new millennium as defined by the inventions of science and taking us into a new era of technological wonders and space travel.

From the Hindu perspective no religion owns time and no revelation defines history. Each person and each culture has its own time or duration, which should be used for self-discovery and self-realization. Hindu sages look at the new era for humanity arising today through science and globalism as but the dim beginnings of a greater age of consciousness and spirituality that is as yet only touching the horizon. They don't see this new era defined by the year 2000 but by the events of the past few decades and yet many more decades to come. The industrial revolution gave way to the information revolution but the information revolution must in turn give way to an age of consciousness that is the real goal of human striving. Humanity is still in transition between an era of materialism and one of spirituality and the decisive turn has not yet been made. The coming century is bound to bring ecological and cultural crises that will force us to move in a more conscious direction. This will bring not only great new discoveries and breakthroughs as we advance in knowledge, but also suffering and karmic reckoning for our immature and arrogant way of dealing with our environment.

INDIA AT A CROSSROADS

What is the secret of this great and enduring culture of India? The unique feature of Indian or Bharatiya culture is unity-in-multiplicity or what could be called 'Vedic pluralism.' The oldest Indian text and perhaps the oldest book in the world, the *Rigveda* boldly proclaims: "That which is the One

Truth the seers teach in many different ways (*Rigveda* I.164.46)," and "May noble aspirations come to us from every side (*Rigveda* I.89.1)."

The Indic view is that though Truth is One the paths are many. There is no need for any religious exclusivism or cultural uniformity. Many different religions and philosophies must exist relative to the different levels and temperaments of individuals. Even atheism has a place as one possible view of reality for the human mind. A free discussion and representation of all views is necessary to arrive at truth. Even errors and mistakes must be allowed in a free inquiry into truth. Truth can never be destroyed through scrutiny or examination. It is only behind closed doors or in fixed dogma that truth cannot stand.

Vedic pluralism, however, is not mere polytheism or separatism. It is a recognition of a unity that transcends name and form. The Hindu sense of the One is also that of the infinite. Its unity is of the universal, not of one thing as opposed to another, but as the one thing, like a single thread, that links all things together. Such a deep inner unity can embrace a multiple expression, just as the ocean can hold many waves and not get disturbed by them. This bedrock of Indic pluralism gave rise to the many different sects of Hinduism, which remains the most diverse religious tradition in the world with its Vedic, Tantric, Shaivite, Shakta, Vaishnava and other sects both ancient and modern. It also provided the ground for Buddhist, Jain, and Sikh traditions, which themselves have much diversity. It spawned perhaps the greatest diversity of spiritual teachings in the entire world. It respects science and art as part of our spiritual quest, building a great material culture as well as wonderful temples. On its basis people in India could even come to appreciate the spiritual aspects of less tolerant religious groups who invaded them from across the border. Though still largely misunderstood in the West as polytheism or a worship of many Gods, this Bharatiya (Indic) pluralism reflects an open quest for truth and a free flowering of all true human potentials such as the world desperately needs today.

Unfortunately, over the first fifty years since independence India has not discovered its real roots or reclaimed its true soul as a civilization. Its intellectuals have mimicked western trends in thought, particularly Marxism, even after these have been discredited in the West, following them with an almost uncritical Hindu type of devotion. In an excessive pursuit of secularism they found it necessary to denigrate their own pluralistic traditions and favour foreign ideologies of religious or political exclusivism. They have forgotten their great modern sages like Swami Vivekananda and Sri Aurobindo who projected futuristic views of the Indian tradition and instead adulate western thinkers devoid of any spiritual realization. They look at India with jaded eyes and find its salvation in foreign lands. While many westerners come to India seeking spiritual knowledge, Indian intellectuals look to the West with admiration, pursuing materialistic ideologies that have left them unable to understand their own more spiritual traditions. The result is that after fifty years of independence India has not truly awakened; though it may be stirring in its sleep.

We are now entering into a global age in which pluralism must be the foundation of world culture. We can no longer pretend that only one race, one culture or one religion alone is true. The dawning century is no longer a missionary and colonial era in which one group can be allowed hegemony in the world. It is a new age of dialogue and respect in which we learn to honor and cherish all the cultures of the world. This should start with the honoring of tribal cultures that are the custodians of the Earth and the wisdom of nature that we so quickly losing in this artificial age. It must include not just dominant western religions, but the great traditions of the East, like Hinduism and Buddhism, which have a firm foundation in tolerance and synthesis. We must learn to embrace all human beings and their cultures as part of one great family (Vasudhaiva kutumbakam). We can certainly have our differences but should respectfully allow others to be different as well. Let our differences be a cause for admiration and celebration, not for mistrust, hatred and a seeking to eliminate them.

The dharmic traditions of India emphasize an organic pluralism as the model for human development. Just as the human body is one but has different organs that perform various functions for the benefit of the whole, so human society is one in essence but diverse in function, with each person like each cell of the body playing a vital role. This is not a model of democratic uniformity. It recognizes that the male an the female, the young and the old, the artist, thinker, businessman, politician and yogi, with all their differences, all have their special place in society, which is enriched by their diversity.

Yet Bharatiya Pluralism is not a relativism of anything goes. Its foundation lies in universal values like ahimsa, not wishing harm to any other creature and not seeking to interfere with the natural order. It is a pluralism that reflects a respect for the sacred in all things. It is not a pluralism of hedonism or materialism like that of the West that is insensitive of the environment or of other cultures. It is a pluralism of the spirit, not simply of the body; a pluralism of spiritual teachings, not merely of material choices.

It is time for India once more to be a leader and an innovator in world culture, rather than a follower and imitator as at present. To accomplish this, India must discover its own voice and initiate its own action in the global forum. Sri Aurobindo once remarked that India's real role was to be the guru among the nations of the world. At present it can hardly keep order within its own frontiers. The country is crushed by its own bureaucracy, though this grip is gradually loosening. Perhaps because of long foreign rule India developed a sense of apathy and resignation and a tolerance for oppression and inequality. This must go.

A new vitality and creativity is necessary for India that honours the spirit of the country's venerable traditions but does not restrict itself to previous outdated forms. This requires a new generation of thinkers who are global in outlook but grounded in the spirituality of Yoga and Vedanta. Indic thinkers must return to their cultural wellsprings, not to stop there, but to create a new vision of the future. *Out of the old Upanishads they need to envision new Upanishads.* Such a new India would combine science and spirituality in a global perspective, combining the wisdom of ancient rishis with that of modern creative thinkers. It would set forth a new spiritual or yogic science showing us how to realize the consciousness that is the foundation of the entire universe and the basis of universal law. It would develop our material potentials but for the greater glory of the Spirit, the Self of all beings. It would protect the earth which reaching into outer space. It would raise the downtrodden, not to convert people to a belief but to help all people realize their highest potential. Such an awakened India is crucial for world culture, which presently remains trapped between a destructive consumerism on one side and a rigid religious exclusivism on the other.

We can already see how such traditional Indian disciplines as Yoga, Ayurveda and Vedanta are gaining respect worldwide for their global vision. Such an Indic or Dharmic perspective should be added to religion, philosophy, science and medicine all over the world. The new India and the new generation of Indians should take up this task of world-making as their goal. The new world order of the computer and the information revolution gives the country a new chance in the global arena and offers a situation more favorable to its unique talents. But for this to occur India must stand up and speak out according to its real essence—which is as a spiritual superpower—regardless of whether this pleases everyone else in the world.

Today there is only one superpower in the world, the United States. But it is a superpower in the outer world only. Its wealth hides a spiritual poverty and growing psychological and social unrest. No technological superpower can properly guide the world in the planetary age. Only a spiritual superpower can do this. India has the potential to be the world's spiritual superpower, but it requires a great labour to bring it forth. The question is whether the country and its leaders are willing to make the effort. This requires looking back to the inspiration of the great rishis and yogis of the region, not merely following current political and economic compulsions—but looking back only to go forward with a renewed sense of mission and power.

THE CRISIS IN THE PSYCHE OF INDIA

A defeatist tendency exists in the psyche of modern Indians perhaps unparalleled in any other country today. An inner conflict bordering on a civil war rages in the minds of the country's elite. The main effort of its cultural leaders appears to be to pull the country down or remake it in a foreign image, as if little Indian and certainly nothing Hindu was worthy of preserving or even reforming. The elite of India suffers from a fundamental alienation from the traditions and culture of the land that would not be less poignant had they been born and raised in a hostile country. The ruling elite appears to be little more than a native incarnation of the old colonial rulers who haughtily lived in their separate cantonments, neither mingling with the people nor seeking to understand their customs. This new English-speaking aristocracy prides itself in being disconnected from the very soil and people that gave it birth.

There is probably no other country in the world where it has become a national pastime among its educated class to denigrate its own culture and history, however great that has been over the many millennia of its existence. When great archaeological discoveries of India's past are found, for example, they are not a subject for national pride but are ridiculed as an exaggeration, if not an invention, as if they represent only the imagination of backward chauvinistic elements within the culture.

There is probably no other country where the majority religion, however enlightened, mystical or spiritual, is ridiculed, while minority religions, however fundamentalist or even militant, are doted upon. The majority religion and its institutions are taxed and regulated while minority religions receive tax benefits and have no regulation or even monitoring. While the majority religion is carefully monitored and limited as to what it can teach, minority religions can teach what they want, even if anti-national or backward in nature. Books are banned that offend minority religious sentiments but praised if they cast insults on majority beliefs.

There is probably no other country where regional, caste and family loyalties are more important than the national interest, even among those who claim to be democratic, socialist or caste reformers. Political parties exist not to promote a national agenda but to sustain one region or group of people in the country at the expense of the whole. Each group wants as big a piece of the national pie as it can get, not realizing that the advantages it gains mean deprivation for other groups. Yet when those who were previously deprived gain power, they too seek the same unequal advantages that causes further inequality and discontent.

India's affirmative action code is by far the most extreme in the world, trying to raise up certain segments of the population regardless of merit, and prevent others from gaining positions however qualified they may be. In the guise of removing caste, a new castism has arisen where one's caste is more important than one's qualifications either in gaining entrance into a school or in finding a job when one graduates. Anti-Brahminism has often become the most virulent form of castist thinking. People view the government not as their own creation but as a welfare state from they should take the maximum personal benefit, regardless of the consequences for the country as a whole. Outside people need not pull Indians down. Indians are already quite busy keeping any of their people and the country as a whole from rising up. They would rather see their neighbours or the nation fail if they are not given the top position. It is only outside of India that Indians succeed, often remarkably well, because their native talents are not stifled by the dominant cultural self-negativity and rabid divisiveness that exists in the country today.

Political parties in India see gaining power as a means of amassing personal wealth and robbing the nation. Political leaders include gangsters, charlatans and buffoons who would stop short at nothing to gain power for themselves and their coteries. Even so-called modern or liberal parties resemble more the courts of kings, where personal loyalty is more important than any democratic participation. Once they gain power politicians routinely do little but cheat the people for their own advantage. Even honest politicians find that they cannot function without some deference to the more numerous corrupt leaders who often have a stranglehold on the bureaucracy.

Politicians divide the country into warring vote banks and place one community against another. They offer favors to communities like bribes to make sure that they are elected or stay in power. They campaign on slogans that appeal to community fears and suspicions rather than create any national consensus or harmony. They hold power based upon blame and hatred rather than on any positive programs for social change. They inflame the uneducated masses with propaganda rather than work to make people aware of real social problems like overpopulation, poor infrastructure or lack of education. Should a decent government come to power, the opposition pursues pulling it down as its main goal, so that they can gain power for themselves. The idea of a constructive or supportive opposition is hard to find. The goal is to gain power for oneself and to not allow anyone else to succeed.

To further their ambitions Indian politicians will manipulate the foreign press to denigrate their opponents, even if it means spreading lies and rumors and making the country an anathema in the eyes of the outside world. Petty conflicts in India are blown out of proportion in the foreign media, not by foreign journalists but by Indians seeking to use the media to score points against their own opponents in the country. The Indians who are responsible for the news of India in the foreign press spread venom and distortion about their own country, perhaps better than any foreigner who dislikes the culture ever could.

The killing of one Christian missionary becomes a national media event of anti-Christian attacks while the murder of hundreds of Hindus is taken casually as without any real importance, as if only the deaths of white-skinned people mattered, not the slaughter of the natives. Missionary aggression is extolled as social upliftment, while Hindu efforts at self-defence against the conversion onslaught are portrayed as rabid fundamentalism. One Indian journalist even lamented that western armies would not come to India to chastise the political groups he was opposed to, as if he was still looking for the colonial powers to save him!

Let us look at the type of leaders that India has had with its Laloo Prasad Yadav, Mulayam Singh Yadav, Jayalalita or Subrahmanya Swamy to mention but a few. Such individuals are little more than warlords who surround themselves with sycophants. Modern Indian politicians appear more like colonial rulers looting their own country, following a divide and rule policy, to keep the people so weak that their power cannot be challenged. Corruption exists almost everywhere and bribery is the main way to do business in nearly all fields. India has an entrenched bureaucracy that resists change and stifles development, just out of sheer obstinacy and not wanting to give up any control. The Congress Party, the oldest in this predominantly Hindu nation, has given its leadership to an Italian Catholic woman simply because as the widow of the last Gandhi prime minister, she carries the family torch, as if family loyalty were still the main basis of political credibility in the country. And such a leader and a party are deemed progressive!

The strange thing is that India is not a banana republic of recent vintage but one of the oldest and most venerable civilizations in the world. Its culture is not trumpeting a militant and fundamentalist religion trying to conquer the world for the one true faith but represents a vaster and more cosmic vision. India has given birth to the main religions that have dominated East Asia historically, the Hindu, Buddhist, Jain and Sikh, which are noted for tolerance and spirituality. It has produced Sanskrit, perhaps the world's greatest language. It has given us the incredible spiritual systems of Yoga and its great traditions of meditation and Self-realization. As the world looks forward to a more universal model of spirituality and a world view defined by consciousness rather than by religious dogma these traditions are perhaps the most important legacy to draw upon for creating a future enlightened civilization.

Yet the irony is that rather than embracing its own great traditions, the modern Indian psyche prefers to slavishly imitate worn out trends in western intellectual thought like Marxism or even to write apologetics for Christian and Islamic missionary aggression. Though living in India, in proximity to temples, yogis and great festivals, most modern Indian intellectuals are oblivious to the soul of the land. They might as well be living in England or China for all they know of their own country. They are isolated in their own alien ideas as if in a tower of iron. If they choose to rediscover India it is more likely to occur by reading the books of western travellers visiting the country, than by their own direct experience of the people around them.

The dominant Indian intelligentsia cannot appreciate even the writings of the many great modern Indian sages, like Vivekananda or Aurobindo, who wrote in good English and understood the national psyche and how to revive. It is as if they were so successfully brainwashed against their own culture that they cannot even look at it, even if presented to them clearly in a modern light!

Given such a twisted and self-negative national psyche, can there be any hope for the country? At the surface the situation looks quite dismal. India appears like a nation without nationalism or at least without any national pride or any real connection to its own history. Self-negativity and even a cultural self-hatred abound. The elite that dominates the universities, the media, the government and the business arenas is the illegitimate child of foreign interests and is often still controlled by foreign ideas and foreign resources. It cannot resist a bribe and there is much money from overseas to draw upon. Indian politicians do not hesitate to sell their country down the river and it does not require a high price. Fortunately signs of a new awakening can be found. There is a new interest in the older traditions of the country and many people now visit temples and tirthas. Many young people now want to follow the older heritage of the land and revive it in the modern age. The computer revolution and the new science are reconnecting with the great intelligence of the Indian psyche that produced the unfathomable mantras of the *Vedas*. Slowly but surely a new intelligentsia is arising and now several important journalists are writing and exposing the hypocrisy of the anti-Hindu Indian elite. Yet only if this trend grows rapidly can there be a real counter to the defeatist trend of the country. But it requires great effort, initiative and creativity, not simply lamenting over the past but envisioning a new future in harmony with the deeper aspirations of the region.

One must also not forget that the English-educated elite represents only about three percent of the country, however much power they wield. The remaining population is much more likely to preserve the older traditions of the land. Even illiterate villagers often know more of real Indian culture than do major Indian journalists and writers.

Meanwhile overseas Hindus have become successful, well educated and affluent, not by abandoning their culture but by holding to it. They see Hindu culture not as a weakness but as a strength. Free of the Indian nation and its fragmented psyche, they can draw upon their cultural resources in a way that people born in India seldom can. Perhaps they can return to the country and become its new leaders.

However, first this strange alienated elite has to be removed and they will not do so without a fight. The sad thing is that they would probably rather destroy their own country than have it function apart from their control. The future of India looks like a new Kurukshetra and it requires a similar miracle for victory. Such a war will be fought not on some outer battlefield but in the hearts and minds of people, in where they choose to draw their inspiration and find their connection with life.

Yet regardless of outer appearances, the inner soul of the land cannot be put down so easily. It has been nourished by many centuries of tapas by great yogis and sages. This soul of Bharat Mata will rise up again through Kali (destruction) to Durga (strength). The question is how long and difficult the process must be.

EQUALITY OF HINDUISM

In the scheme of Manu the Brahmin is placed at the first in rank. Below him is the Kshatriya. Below Kshatriya is the Vaishya. Below Vaishya is the Sudra and Below Sudra is the Ati-Sudra (the Untouchables). This system of rank and gradation is, simply another way of enunciating the principle of inequality so that it may be truly said that Hinduism does not recognize equality. This inequality in status is not merely the inequality that one sees in the warrant of precedence prescribed for a ceremonial gathering at a King's Court. It is a permanent social relationship among the classes to be observed-to be enforced-at all times in all places and for all purposes. It will take too long to show how in every phase of life Manu has introduced and made inequality the vital force of life. But it will illustrate it by taking a few examples such as slavery, marriage and Rule of Law. Manu recognizes Slavery. But he confined it to the Sudras.

Only Sudras could be made slaves of the three higher classes. But the higher classes could not be the slaves of the Sudra. But evidently practice differed from the law of Manu and not only Sudras happened to become slaves but members of the other three classes also become slaves. When this was discovered to be the case a new rule was enacted by a Successor of Manu namely Narada. This new rule of Narada runs as follows: "In the inverse order of the four castes slavery is not ordained except where a man violates the duties peculiar to his caste. Slavery (in that respect) is analogous to the condition of a wife."

Recognition of slavery was bad enough. But if the rule of slavery had been left free to take its own course it would have had at least one beneficial effect. It would have been a levelling force. The foundation of caste would have been destroyed. For under it a Brahmin might have become the slave of the Untouchable and the Untouchable would have become the master of the Brahmin. But it was seen that unfettered slavery was an equalitarian principle and an attempt was made to nullify it. Manu and his successors therefore while recognising slavery ordains that it shall not be recognised in its inverse order to the Varna System. That means that a Brahmin may become the slave of another Brahmin. But he shall not be the slave of a person of another Varna i.e. of the Kshatriya, Vaishya, Sudra, or Ati-Sudra. On the other hand a Brahmin may hold as his slave any one belonging to the four Varnas. A Kshatriya can have a Kshatriya, Vaisha, Sudra and Ati-Sudra as his slaves but not one who is a Brahmin. A Vaishya can have a Vaishya, Sudra and Ati-Sudra as his slaves but not one who is a Brahmin or a Kshatriya.

A Sudra can hold a Sudra and Ati-sudra can hold an Ati-Sudra as his slave but not one who is a Brahmin, Kshatriya, Vaishya or Sudra. Challenge Conversion and Hindu Response: Again at a moment of history of our ancient nation when the Hindu foundation of the nation is being challenged and sought to be undermined. But never before in our history has the challenge been as dangerously deceptive, pernicious, and sophisticated as it is now. It is therefore difficult to respond to this challenge since it cannot be easily perceived.

Hence, the response to this challenge and the implicit threat has to be well thought out and profound, but as before in our history, the response to be fruitful has to be designed and structured by the confluence of spiritual guidance and political resolve. Such a confluence has been the fundamental basis of our past responses to such challenges in history, from the installation by rishis of Adi Raja Prithu as King of Bharatvarsh, Chanakya's founding of the Mauryan kingdom, the establishment of the Vijayanagaram empire at Hampi by Sringeri Shankaracharya, to inspiring the fighting armies of Shivaji by Swami Ramdass. Even Mahatma Gandhi and Jayaprakash Narayan in their respective struggles for independence of the nation from colonialism, and for the restoration of democracy in a nation that was drowned in the darkness of the Emergency, had followed this unique Hindu model of spiritually guiding a political movement without seeking the fruits of office for themselves. The Hindu foundation of modern India is why India has been and is even today referred to, in India and abroad, as Hindustan. Hindustan is defined as a nation of Hindus and those who accept that their ancestors are Hindus. The concept also includes refugee minorities who accept the core values of the Hindu culture and therefore recognised as a part of the Hindustan nation. Thus, when the Dwarka Mutt Shankaracharya gave the arriving Parsi refugees in Sanjaan [Kutch coast] a five-point requirement for settling in the country, they readily accepted and have not deviated from it even today.

These five points were: Giving up Persian language and adopting Gujarati; wearing Indian clothes instead of Persian; treating the cow as sacred; reciting some select Sanskrit shlokas in their marriage ceremony; and laying down of weapons. Despite being the smallest minority, with disproportionate share in offices of power and national wealth, and perhaps also the wealthiest community, there is and has been no tension or conflict between Hindus and Parsis. Today Hindus despite de facto in power and in the organs of the state, are victims of that same targeting, but of course in a very subtle and sophisticated manner. In furthering the objective of this targeting, Islam and Christianity, more so the latter, have been able to leverage the influence of prominent Hindus themselves.

Parsis and Jews do not threaten the Hindu character of the nation. They do not seek to proselytise or convert Hindus by monetary inducements or by obscurantist preachings such as curing persons who convert, of incurable terminal diseases. But on the other hand, the preachings of the religious leaders of Islam and Christianity in India, altogether for a thousand years, had targeted Hindus and sought the religious conversions to their faiths by creating deprivation and loss of self-esteem, through the abuse of the power of the state against Hindus.

They were not subtle about it. For example, in 1545, King John III of Portugal gave a command to the then Governor of Goa that neither public nor private 'idols' of Hindu heathens be tolerated on the island of Goa and that severe punishment be meted out to those who persist in keeping them. Thereafter, a terrible inquisition followed during which Hindus were killed, brutalised and their temples razed to the ground. Still we must not forget only a minority of Hindus converted to Christianity. No other religious community other than Hindus suffered such prolonged and atrocious persecution and survived as a religion of a vast majority on their own soil. Let us not forget this defiance in our past. Today Hindus despite de facto in power and in the organs of the state, are victims of that same targeting, but of course in a very subtle and sophisticated manner. In furthering the objective of this targeting, Islam and Christianity, more so the latter, have been able to leverage the influence of prominent Hindus themselves, who wittingly for money or unwittingly because of a programmed mindset of being defensive about being a Hindu [thereby ready to ape the West] are tools of this targeting. What is the nature and scope of this targeting, and is there a way for us to end it by conciliation with Christians and

Muslims? In other words, can we seek to end religious conversion in India today by the ancient Hindu way of shashtrarthas as Hindu saints did, as for example Adi Sankara did with Buddhism and Uttara Mimamsa theologies and Azhwars and Nayanars saints in the south did with Jainism? Will indeed Christians and Muslims recognise the sanctity of shashtrarthas?

There is a serious problem here because as an interesting study of Sarah Claerhout and Jakob De Roover titled: The Question of Conversion in India concludes, Hindus and Christians have fundamentally different and mutually exclusive concepts of religion and thus also in their approaches to the question of conversion. Hence, say the authors, for Hindus and Christians to dialogue on conversion would be fruitless because they will have "great difficulties making sense of each other's statements and arguments". This is because Hindus do not consider any religion as wholly false, and as Gandhiji put it, all religions have some errors in them. Since all religions lead to God, hence there is no need for forcing a conversion. Christians [and Muslims] think that their's is the only true religion, and it is God's work to convert heathens and kafirs to their only true religion. Therefore, either Hindus will have to capitulate on this question by permitting religious conversion in India, or in the alternative be united and assertive to ensure that laws are enacted and effectively enforced against religious conversion of Hindus. There is no third way.

It is urgent now that Hindus be mobilised to assertively oppose any further conversion from Hinduism to any other non-Indian religion. There is no room for indifference here. This is because that status quo is damaging to the Hindu faith, since the Christian missionaries and Muslim mullahs are already fully at work, funds being no constraint, to convert Hindus. If conversions are not explicitly opposed, then Hindus are implicitly acquiescing in the atrocity. There is a fundamental disconnect between the religious outlook of Hindus and the Christians and Muslims which makes it impossible for a fruitful debate and mutual understanding on the question of religious conversion.

WESTERN MONOCULTURE AND INDIC PLURALISM

The Spread of the Monoculture

Western civilization, in spite of claims to support diversity, is promoting a worldwide monoculture—the same basic values, institutions and points of view for everyone—which it calls 'globalization'. Western commercial culture with its pursuit of markets and commodities eliminates all true culture, which is based on quality, not quantity. It creates a culture of money that submerges any true culture of refinement or spirituality, in which everything can be bought and sold, possessed or capitalized on. If we visit shopping malls in America today, for example, it is hard to tell what state in the country we are located in.

The shopping malls in Florida, California, New York or the Midwest have the same basic stores and sell the same basic products. The streets look the same, as do the houses, apartment buildings and office buildings. People eat the same basic types of food and have the same habits of work, sleep and relaxation. Almost everything is mass-produced and follows the same economy driven forces. These same types of businesses pioneered in America are spreading worldwide, whether it is Coca Cola, McDonalds, blue jeans or Barbie dolls. One finds the same multinational corporations operating in nearly every major city of the world, whether Tokyo, Shanghai, Mumbai or London. While one finds foreign stores like Chinese restaurants in shopping malls even in America, which have their niche in the global scene, these operate according to the same commercial approach as standard western businesses. They do not represent real globalization but a co-opting of foreign businesses by the western commercial culture. The world media is yet more of a monoculture. News services worldwide provide what are essentially the same stories from the same cultural slant. They are standardized in a western model and promote a western point of view with western ideals of free trade, social equality, democracy and affluence. People all over the world watch Hollywood movies, listen to the pop music of the US and Europe, and adulate American athletes.

Similarly, in the universities of the world, it is mainly western civilization that is taught, even if there is an old and profound civilization. In a country like India, Shakespeare is a much better known and quoted poet than Kalidas, the equivalent great Sanskrit poet. The West honours the Japanese for enthusiastically taking up western culture, music and entertainment. But it regards as close-minded or communal, cultures that try to hold their own ground and avoid the consumerist assimilation.

The Danger of Monoculture

This consumerist monoculture is a great leveler of culture. Wherever it goes it either destroys or co-opts the local culture. It destroys local culture by ending native traditions and replacing them with western business, political, religious or intellectual models. It co-opts them by turning local arts and crafts into exotic ware for mass marketing, for example, how Native American culture has been turned into a big business in the US, though the money seldom goes to the natives! Monoculture results in 'deculturalization' in which entire cultures and civilizations are subverted or eliminated. Modern commercial culture is monopolistic and seeks hegemony, though it allows a diversity within its ranks so long as it doesn't interfere with its expansionist aims.

We can compare this social monoculture with plant monoculture. Monoculture in farming occurs when the same crops are planted over and again in the same soil. The result is that the soil gets exhausted. Monoculture in nature occurs when the diversity of plant species is destroyed by deforestation and a few species, often of foreign origin, are planted instead or simply flourish as weeds. Monoculture in agriculture and forestry result in the loss of both plant and animal species. Similarly, monoculture in human culture brings about the loss of cultural and individual diversity. Today we are witnessing, generally silently, an appalling and rapid disappearance of traditional cultures. Languages, the hallmark of culture, are passing away in the world at a rapid rate. Monoculture with its standardization and uniformity is the rule. Franchise is the game in businesses of all types. Local and home owned stores are disappearing, just as the family farm has given way to global agribusiness run by large oil companies (like Exxon owning vast tracts of farmland in California)!

We can draw a further analogy between the monoculture and the use of terminator seeds, which when planted render native seeds sterile. The real purpose of such seeds is not to increase food production but to make farmers worldwide dependent on seed banks for further crops that puts them under control of the global agribusiness.

The monoculture tries to control the rules of debate and the presentation of ideas worldwide, which all goes back to it for validation. People only gain validity in their field when famous or recognized by the monoculture and its media. Representatives of other cultural traditions don't count for anything. The result is that people go to monoculture institutions to gain credibility even in their local cultural disciplines. In the Indian context, Indian scholars seek their credentials not in their own temples and ashrams of their own country but in western institutions like Heidelberg, Oxford or Harvard, or in westernized departments of their own countries like at JNU (Jawaharlal Nehru University), the centre of leftist thought in India. Such scholars become opponents of their own cultural traditions, supplanting native schools of thought with the cultural seeds of the West, putting an end to their own independent traditions of thought which they are supposed to represent!

The destruction of cultural diversity, like that of biodiversity, is devastating to living systems. The loss of cultural diversity does to human beings what the destruction of biodiversity does to the world of nature. Just as we are destroying our outer landscape of forests and wilderness, so we are destroying our inner landscape of art and spirituality. Our minds are as polluted as our rivers.

Monoculture and the Quality of Life

Monoculture claims to improve life by raising 'living standards'. People all over the world make what is on paper a much higher income than that of their parents. With this income they can buy computers, televisions, stereos, or whatever the latest technological equipment happens to be. They can afford to go to restaurants, watch movies or travel and stay in expensive hotels. However, this increased 'paper wealth' is deceptive. Their houses, which on paper are worth phenomenally more than those of their parents, are usually smaller and much more expensive to maintain. In fact, housing shortages are everywhere. The beautiful scenery of nature that used to surround human habitats is replaced by a bleak urban environment of cement, glass and steel, in which the garden is but a few potted plants on a terrace overlooking the street!

The quality of air and water has been greatly reduced all over the world. Our cities have air that is unhealthy to breathe. Most of our water is unfit to drink. Even fish cannot live in most of our streams. The quality of food is significantly less in spite of advances in corporate farming. Fast food and over-spiced restaurant food replace the home grown or freshly cooked food of previous generations. Good quality fresh fruit and vegetables, which used to be commonly available, are now only rarely found in special natural food stores in the West at a special price. The monoculture person has less real leisure time than previous generations. We are busy all week long working, using our spare time for shopping or other chores. There are few local cultural events of music, plays, festivals and dance and even these have been commercialized and are spectator events, not the participatory events of earlier times. They have no aura of the sacred that the rituals of previous generations often had. The real victim of monoculture, therefore, is the individual who is deprived of any direct contact with nature, the universe, a community, himself or herself.

The movement toward monoculture arose through the industrial revolution and the printing press that could standardize information. It mushroomed in the twentieth century with global industrialization. Now with the computer and media age it is far advanced, moving forward at times almost like a blind steamroller crushing everything in its path.

Monoculture and Monotheism

The roots of monoculture in western civilization can be traced to monotheism, particularly of a missionary type—the effort to impose a belief in only One God of a certain type on all people, ignoring all other spiritual paths, however old or rich in ideas and experiences. This One God appears as a tyrannical, if not militant being who has a severe set of rewards and punishments—which necessitates a single savior, bible and church for the entire world. Whether this was the original intent of the prophets or a deviation, it has come to represent the dominant trend in western religious thinking and the orientation of western culture both religious and secular.

Under early Christianity, monotheism allied itself with Roman imperialism and an allegiance to the state—which was a political monoculture—turning a religious rigidity into a military weapon. In the colonial era, western monoculture became a cult of church and empire as a means of conquering the world, to make everyone western and Christian in civilization. Monoculture extends from an expansionist monotheism, which is monoculture in religion and destroys religious diversity and individual spiritual experience that is only possible apart from any church and its dogma. It leads to other forms of monoculture politically, economically, socially and intellectually.

Western monotheism is essentially an authoritarian tradition and monotheistic institutions like the Vatican are authoritarian hierarchies to the present day, with orders being imposed upon the masses from on above. The dogma of the book, prophet or savior and One God cannot be questioned. Anti-blasphemy laws remain in effect in so-called Islamic 'republics', making it a crime, if not a capital offense, to even question the book or the prophet. Anti-apostasy laws are also there, making it a crime for a Muslim to convert to another religion (but allowing members of other religions to convert to Islam). Such laws were present in medieval Christianity where they were used to oppress science and stop any freethinking.

Today, however, Christians have put a new spin on their monotheism. They would equate monotheism, if not Christianity itself, with unity, equality and democracy—One God and one humanity. However, this is done without changing the exclusive and monopolistic nature of Christian beliefs or institutions, making one doubt its sincerity. The current pope, for example, though really a conservative figure, has used this form of propaganda to justify Catholic conversion efforts in the world. He would have us believe that promoting an authoritarian church and its antiquated dogma was somehow liberal and would advance political freedom, particularly in non-Christian countries, where the church would come in to save people from anti-democratic governments and social inequalities! He speaks out against the lack of freedom and democracy in various countries without introducing these into his own church first!

Monotheism and Christianity are being equated in the West with democracy and human rights, though this was certainly no part of their colonial rule. We should look at Central and South America, where an alliance of the church with dictators and military rulers has been long standing, and which continue to have a great inequality between the rich and the poor, those of European blood and the native Indians. We must remember that the fascist dictators of Europe and America, including Mussolini, were good Catholics that the church did not seriously oppose. Yet those who oppose the missionaries today in the third world are called fascists or communalists, not the missionaries, completely ignoring the facts of history!

Monoculture, in turn, has no real problem with monotheism, though western monotheism is largely authoritarian and anti-democratic. There is no one person, one vote idea in these religions but only fiats and fatwas from on high. Monoculture treats the monotheistic church with the same dignity of any country or corporation that has economic or political clout.

This is because western monotheism has adopted the corporate model and used its numbers and resources to gain political influence and favors. It has created a global multinational religious business using the media and the Internet for proselytizing, spreading a religious message like an advertising campaign. The world media does not challenge such religious aggression, any more than it does the aggression of the fast food industry.

Nineteenth century colonial rulers, like the British in India, found missionaries to be useful, even though Europe at the time had many free thinkers questioning the church and the Bible.

So too, the modern monoculture finds missionaries to be a helpful tool—even though they represent a more conservative form of Christianity than practiced by most people in the West. Such backward religious beliefs appeal to the poor and uneducated, which is why the most devout Christian countries like those in South America are among the most backward in the world. This means that Christianity can be provide a first stage in the westernization of poorer cultures, particularly those like India that have deep religious roots.

Monoculture and Democracy

Monoculture has made a home with democracy. This may be surprising at first because democracy appears as the ultimate form of pluralism, with each individual a free and equal member of society. After all, democracy allows each person, even the poor, weak or elderly, the same one vote. However, current democracies only have the appearance of pluralism. If we look deeper, only an educated democracy can be truly pluralistic. An uneducated democracy can create its own form of totalitarianism or mob rule. The masses are easy to manipulate by money, the media or an appeal to prejudices and vote banks. Getting elected for a politician in a modern democracy is not a matter of encouraging pluralism but of manipulating public opinion with slogans and promises that are seldom kept. Charismatic movie stars can easily defeat seasoned diplomats. The modern politician resembles more a Roman emperor controlling the masses through bread and circuses than any true representative of the people or of an enlightened culture.

In addition, promoting democracy worldwide is a good tool to destroy political diversity. No other political systems are allowed today in the world but democracy of a western-style nature—which means the rule of business, the media and the monoculture, along with the promotion of western civilization. Groups agitating for a western style democracy systematically undermine other governments as if anything else were immoral, just as monotheistic religions cannot tolerate other religious views. Modern democracy does not allow for pluralism in governmental systems but requires that it is the only acceptable form, just as monotheism claims all morality for itself and equates other forms of spirituality with the devil.

Modern democracies give the vote to the isolated individual, who is easy to manipulate. Other power centers of a local kind get marginalized, just as multinational corporations and their franchises put an end to local businesses and native crafts under the guise of free trade.

Modern democracies are largely state run governments and have little place for the local rule found in traditional societies, where the village, tribe or community had the rights of self-determination over the most important issues of life, health and work. The state, like the churches previously, doles out its favors and makes the individuals dependent upon it for their livelihood. Leaders pretend to be doing the will of the people when they are only making the people subservient and keeping them ignorant.

Democracy has created an atomization of society, the reduction of all social groups to the isolated individual, who removed from more intimate social support becomes exposed and easy to influence. Without the social support of family and community, for example, the elderly end up as wards of the state, on Medicare.

Such state care, though deemed compassionate, is impersonal, often cruel and masks a fundamental destruction of natural social orders. The social isolation created by modern democracy is resulting in an epidemic of depression in the West that is striking all age groups but particularly those in middle age. The prescription drug industry has become the compassionate savior of modern society, but is really getting an entire culture addicted to drugs as the solution to their mounting physical and psychological problems! Governments debate on how much money to spend on prescription drugs for the elderly, but they never ask why an entire generation is dependent upon drugs for its well-being.

Monoculture and Free Trade

Monoculture does quite well with free trade and the spread of global consumerism, which is monoculture economics. Other economic systems are not allowed and are systematically undermined. The economic might of the monoculture levels any economic diversity, moving towards a single financial standard or currency worldwide. A uniform world economy destroys local economies and their rich diversity of expression and interactions based on an organic dependency. The rule of multinational businesses takes the place of local economies. Global corporate solutions are applied to local management issues, often with disastrous results.

Corporate agriculture, the new agricultural monoculture, for example, is advertising its ability to feed the world and end world hunger, portraying itself in the benefic aspect of the church or a socialist government selflessly aiding the poor. What it is really doing is undermining the most basic of human rights, the right to feed oneself and to control one's food sources. What the global agribusiness envisions is control of the world food market, so that it can force entire countries to bow down before it, who cannot even eat without its favour. Among its tools are genetically engineered crops, including terminator seeds that destroy local plant varieties, fertilizers that weaken the soils and breed dependency, and patents on plants that afford corporate ownership to nature's bounty. Meanwhile, those who oppose the global food business are deemed backwards, causing hunger and starvation in the world, as if apart from the agribusiness no one could feed themselves!

Should any group oppose the monoculture, the religious, political, intellectual and economic forces of monoculture will attack it, often mercilessly. Monoculture ideas of monotheism, democracy, social equality and free trade are used as the moral torch to consume all other cultural views. They are deemed 'universal', meaning that no one can question them or look to what is really working behind them. Such 'universalism' is simply a new mask of intolerance. The very forces that try to resist monoculture are denigrated as communal, undemocratic and unprogressive, even if they are pluralistic in their approach or reflect a deep spiritual wisdom or love of nature.

For example, the Hindu effort to resist missionaries in India is portrayed in the media as a form of religious fundamentalism, while the Christian missionary aggression and intolerance of Hindu pluralism is deemed progressive.

Similarly, when Hindu economic activists used the slogan of 'computer chips yes, potato chips no', resisting the American fast food industry, the western media deems the response to be backward and confused.

SOCIAL CLASSES IN HINDUISM

The pattern of social classes in Hinduism is called the "caste system." The chart shows the major divisions and contents of the system. Basic caste is called *varna*, or "colour." Sub-caste, or *jati*, "birth, life, rank," is a traditional subdivision of *varna*. The *Bhagawad Gita* says this about the varnas: The works of Brahmins, Kshatriyas, Vaishyas, and Shudras are different, in harmony with the three powers of their born nature. The works of a Brahmin are peace; self-harmony, austerity, and purity; loving-forgiveness and righteousness; vision and wisdom and faith.

These are the works of a Kshatriya: a heroic mind, inner fire, constancy, resourcefulness, courage in battle, generosity and noble leadership. Trade, agriculture and the rearing of cattle is the work of a Vaishya. And the work of the Shudra is service. There are literally thousands of sub-castes in India, often with particular geographical ranges, occupational specializations, and an administrative or corporate structure. When Mahatma Gandhi wanted to go to England to study law, he had to ask his sub-caste, the Modh Bania, for permission to leave India. ("Bania", means "merchant," and "Gandhi" means "greengrocer"—from *gandha*, "smell, fragrance," in Sanskrit—and that should be enough for a good guess that Gandhi was a Vaishya.) Sometimes it is denied that the varnas are "castes" because, while "true" castes, the jatis, are based on birth, the varnas are based on the theory of the gunas (the "three powers" mentioned in the Gita). This is no more than a rationalization: the varnas came first, and they *are* based on birth.

The gunas came later, and provide a poor explanation anyway, since the guna *tamas* is associated with both twice born and once born, caste and outcaste, overlapping the most important religious and social divisions in the system. Nevertheless, the varnas are now divisions at a theoretical level, while the jatis are the way in which caste is embodied for most practical purposes. Jatis themselves can be ranked in relation to each other, and occasionally a question may even be raised about the proper varna to which a particular jati belongs. As jati members change occupations and they rise in prestige, a jati may rarely even be elevated in the varna to which it is regarded as belonging.

Associated with each varna there is a traditional colour. These sound suspiciously like skin colours; and, indeed, there is an expectation in India that higher caste people will have lighter skin—although there are plenty of exceptions (especially in the South of India). This all probably goes back to the original invasion of the Arya, who came from Central Asia and so were undoubtedly light skinned. The people already in India were quite dark, even as today many people in India seem positively black. Apart from skin colour, Indians otherwise have "Caucasian" features—narrow noses, thin lips, etc.—and recent genetic mapping studies seem to show that Indians are more closely related to the people of the Middle East and Europe than to anyone else.

Because Untouchables are not a varna, they do not have a traditional colour. Since this is otherwise not found, and it is traditionally used for the skin colour of Vishnu and his incarnations. Chief among those is *Krishna* whose *name* actually means "black" or "dark," but he is always shown blue rather than with some natural skin colour. The first three varnas are called the *twice born*.

This has *nothing* to do with reincarnation. Being "twice born" means that you *come of age* religiously, making you a member of the Vedic religion, eligible to learn Sanskrit, study the Vedas, and perform Vedic rituals. The "second birth" is thus like Confirmation or a Bar Mitzvah. According to the *Laws of Manu* (whose requirements may not always be observed in modern life), boys are "born again" at specific ages: 8 for Brahmins; 11 for Kshatriyas; and 12 for Vaishyas. A thread is bestowed at the coming of age to be worn around the waist as the symbol of being twice born.

The equivalent of coming of age for girls is marriage. The bestowal of the thread is part of the wedding ceremony. That part of the wedding ritual is even preserved in Jainism. Ancient Iran also had a coming of age ceremony that involved a thread. That and other evidence leads to the speculation that the *three* classes of the twice born are from the original Indo-European social system—the theory of George Dumezil. Even the distant Celts believed in three social classes.

The three classes of Plato's *Republic* thus may not have been entirely his idea. Although there must have been a great deal of early intermarriage in India, nowhere did such an Indo-European social system become as rigid a system of *birth* as there. The rigidity may well be due to the influence of the idea of *karma*, that poor birth is morally deserved. According to the *Laws of Manu*, when the twice born come of age, they enter into the four *ashramas* or "stages of life."

1. The first is the *brahmacharya*, or the stage of the student (*brahmacharin*). For boys, the student is supposed to go live with a teacher (*guru*), who is a Brahmin, to learn about Sanskrit, the Vedas, rituals, etc. The *dharma* of a student includes being obedient, respectful, celibate, and nonviolent. "The teacher is God." For girls, the stage of studenthood coincides with that of the householder, and the husband stands in the place of the teacher. Since the boys are supposed to be celibate while students, Gandhi used the term *brahmachari* to mean the celibate practitioner that he thought made the best *Satyagrahi*, the best nonviolent activist.
2. The second stage is the *garhastya*, or the stage of the householder, which is taken far more seriously in Hinduism than in Jainism or Buddhism and is usually regarded as mandatory, like studenthood, although

debate continued over the centuries whether or not this stage could be skipped in favour of a later one. This is the stage where the principal *dharma* of the person is performed, whether as priest, warrior, etc., or for women mainly as wife and mother. Arjuna's duty to fight the battle in the *Bhagawad Gita* comes from his status as a householder. Besides specific duties, there are general duties that pay off the "three debts": (1) a debt to the ancestors that is discharged by marrying and having children; (2) a debt to the gods that is discharged by the household rituals and sacrifices; and (3) a debt to the teacher that is discharged by appropriately teaching one's wife, children, and, for Brahmins, other students. The three debts are sometimes associated with the three Gods of the Trimurti—the ancestor debt with Brahma, the gods debt with Vishnu, and the teacher debt with Shiva.

3. The third stage is the *vanaprastya*, or the stage of the forest dweller. This may be entered into optionally if (ideally) one's hair has become gray, one's skin wrinkled, and grandchildren exist to carry on the family. Husbands and wives may leave their affairs and possessions with their children and retire together to the forest as hermits. This does not involve the complete renunciation of the world, for husbands and wives can still have sex (once a month), and a sacred fire still should be kept and minimal rituals performed. This stage is thus not entirely free of *dharma*. The Forest Treatises were supposed to have been written by or for forest dwellers, who have mostly renounced the world and have begun to consider liberation. The modern alternatives seem to consist of the more stark opposition between householding and becoming a wandering ascetic. Nevertheless, forest dwelling is an institution that doesn't really develop as such in Jainism and Buddhism. The idea that husbands and wives would

engage in ascetic practices together, without celibacy, would appear extraordinary. In those terms, it is an unfortunate loss if the institution does not continue in modern Hinduism.

4. The fourth stage is the *sannyasa,* or the stage of the wandering ascetic, the *sannyasin* (or *sadhu*). If a man desires, he may continue on to this stage, but his wife will need to return home; traditionally she cannot stay alone as a forest dweller or wander the highways as an ascetic. The *sannyasin* has renounced the world completely, is regarded as dead by his family (the funeral is held), and is finally beyond all *dharma* and caste. When a *sannyasin* enters a Hindu temple, he is not a worshipper but one of the objects of worship. Not even the gods are *sanyasins* (they are householders), and so this is where in Hinduism, as in Jainism and Buddhism, it is possible for human beings to be spiritually superior to the gods. It has long been a matter of dispute in Hinduism whether one need really fulfil the requirements of the *Laws of Manu* (gray hair, etc.) to renounce the world. The Mahabharata says that Brahmins may go directly to Renunciation, but it also says that the three debts must be paid—and the debt to the ancestors could only be paid with husbands and wives living together either as householders or, if renunciates, as forest dwellers (indeed, the Pandavas are all born in that way). There are definitely no such requirements in Jainism or Buddhism. The Buddha left his family right after his wife had a baby, which would put him in the middle of his *dharma* as a householder. Buddhism and Jainism thus developed *monastic* institutions, with monks and nuns, but these did not really develop as such in Hinduism: While wandering ascetics are rather like mendicant monks, we lack monasteries and nuns, and the ascetics are, traditionally, supposed to have already lived something like a normal, lay life.

The four stages of life may, somewhat improbably, be associated with the four parts of the Vedas: the samhitas with the stage of the student, who is particularly obligated to learn them; the Brahmans with the stage of the householder, who is able to regulate his ritual behaviour according to them; the aranyakas with the stage of the forest dweller, who regulates his ritual behaviour according to them and who begins to contemplate liberation; and finally the upanishads with the stage of the wandering ascetic, who is entirely concerned with meditation on the absolute, *Brahman*.

The twice born may account for as much as 48% of Hindus, the number put at more like 18% – quite a difference but more believable. The Shudras (58% of Hindus) may represent the institutional provision that the Arya made for the people they already found in India. The Shudras thus remain once born, and traditionally were not allowed to learn Sanskrit or study the Vedas – on pain of death. Their *dharma* is to work for the twice born. But even below the Shudras are the Untouchables (24% of Hindus), who are literally "outcastes," without a varna, and were regarded as "untouchable" because they are ritually polluting for caste Hindus. Some Untouchable sub-castes are regarded as so polluted that members are supposed to keep out of sight and do their work at night: They are called "Unseeables." In India, the term "Untouchable" is now regarded as insulting or politically incorrect (like *Eta* in Japan for the traditional tanners and pariahs). Gandhi's *Harijans* ("children of God") or *Dalits* ("downtrodden") are preferred, though to Americans "Untouchables" would sound more like the gangster-busting federal agent Elliot Ness from the 1920's. Why there are so many Untouchables is unclear, although caste Hindus can be ejected from their jatis and become outcastes and various tribal or formerly tribal people in India may never have been properly integrated into the social system. When Mahatma Gandhi's sub-caste refused him permission to go to England, as noted above, he went anyway and was ejected from the caste.

After he returned, his family got him back in, but while in England he was technically an outcaste. Existing tribal people as well as Untouchables are also called the "scheduled castes," since the British drew up a "schedule" listing the castes that they regarded as backwards, underprivileged, or oppressed. The Untouchables, nevertheless, have their own traditional professions and their own sub-castes. Those professions (unless they can be evaded in the greater social mobility of modern, urban, anonymous life) involve too much pollution to be performed by caste Hindus: (1) dealing with the bodies of dead animals (like the sacred cattle that wander Indian villages) or unclaimed dead humans, (2) tanning leather, from such dead animals, and manufacturing leather goods, and (3) cleaning up the human and animal waste for which in traditional villages there is no sewer system.

Mahatma Gandhi referred to the latter euphemistically as "scavenging" but saw in it the most horrible thing imposed on the Untouchables by the caste system. His requirement on his farms in South Africa that everyone share in such tasks comes up in an early scene in the movie *Gandhi*. Since Gandhi equated suffering with holiness, he saw the Untouchables as hallowed by their miserable treatment and so called them "Harijans" (*Hari=Vishnu*). Later Gandhi went on fasts in the hope of improving the condition of the Untouchables, or at least to avoid their being politically classified as non-Hindus. Today the status of the Shudras, Untouchables, and other "scheduled castes," and the preferential policies that the Indian government has designed for their advancement ever since Independence, are sources of serious conflict, including suicides, murders, and riots, in Indian society.

Meanwhile, however, especially since economic liberalization began in 1991, the social mobility of a modern economy and urban life has begun to disrupt traditional professions, and oppressions, even of Untouchables. Village life and economic stasis were the greatest allies of the caste system, but both are slowly retreating before modernity in an

India that finally gave up the Soviet paradigm of economic planning.

THE INDIC MODEL OF PLURALISM

The Indic model of culture is not one of monoculture but of cultural diversity, like India's landscape of many wide rivers and towering mountains. Indic civilization is based upon a pluralistic model and a synthetic approach to life's problems. It acknowledges that different points of view may be valid for different individuals and communities and encourages these to develop unhindered by any overriding church, state or business concerns. Its sense of unity arises through interdependence. We see this in Indic religions that offer many sages, yogis, teachings, a diversity of Gods and Goddesses, and a recognition of both the One and the many.

Western civilization as it has developed over the past centuries, on the other hand, is monolithic and singularistic. It imposes a single point of view on everyone. Its sense of unity arises from uniformity. We see this in western religions that require a single God, book, savior, prophet or church for everyone. The one God of western monotheism reflects this need for control, uniformity, power, retribution and revenge.

In the colonial era, western powers sought to impose their religion on Asia using force, intimidation and incentives and denigrating Indic religions as primitive, promoting conversion as a necessity for civilized growth. In the post-colonial era, western religions use the guise of democracy and human rights to continue the same proselytizing efforts. When Indic religions oppose them, they are labeled communal, intolerant or anti-democratic. Democracy itself has become the instrument of a consumerist totalitarianism. The masses are easily manipulated by the ability to promote and fulfil their material desires, their needs for greater entertainment or new conveniences. The Asian view is not one of democratic uniformity but of an organic order that recognizes different individual, class and cultural needs. We must look at society like the human body in which there is a unity of being but a diversity of functions. For true freedom in the world, there must be both material and spiritual freedom, which requires freedom from any cultural domination whether economically, politically or religiously.

However, certain aspects of Hindu thought and culture can become popular, trendy or commercially viable in the monoculture today. This is most obvious in the Yoga movement that is already being mass marketed and turned into franchises. Yet whether this serves to spiritualize western culture to corrupt the spiritual traditions of the East remains to be seen.

This rising interest in spirituality has occurred because the materialist monoculture leaves people inwardly empty. Material affluence has resulted in spiritual poverty and psychological malaise. It is also because western religions are rather bland affairs compared to exotic Hinduism and all of its gurus, deities and Yoga practices. Those who have gone through the monoculture and seen its limitations are more likely to be attracted to the dharmic traditions of the East.

The question then arises whether Hindu culture is rich and diverse enough overcome the monoculture or assimilate it over time. No doubt it can do so eventually. The issue is how much time and effort and obstructions along the way will be required to change the monoculture. But for this to occur, Hindu thought and its pluralistic sense of the Divine must become part of the new paradigm. Over time, the natural human urge for diversity will also arise to counter monoculture that must lead to sterility, like monoculture in agriculture.

The movement toward global uniformity must be abandoned, not only materially but also spiritually. True globalism is not that of monoculture consumerism but based on a respect for local environments, which also means honoring local cultures. True culture is not a commercial commodity but is priceless. It is rooted in a consciousness, a state of mind, and harmony with the natural world. Keeping up with the latest trends in the market place will never take us there. To discover it we must turn our machines off and look within.

Bibliography

Aiyar, R. Krishnaswami: *Outlines of Vedaanta*, Chetana, Bombay, 1978.

Arthur, A.: *Tantrik Texts: Kalivilasa Tantra*, Luzac and Co., London, 1917.

Aurobindo, Sri : *Essays on the Gita*, SriAurobindoAshram Publication Dept, 2000.

Bansal, J. L.: *Srimad Bhagavadgita (The Vedanta Text)*|, JPH, Jaipur, India, 2013.

Bazaz, Prem Nath. *The Role of Bhagavad Gita in Indian History*. New Delhi: Sterling, 1975.

Berreman, Gerald D.: *Hindus of the Himalayas*, University of California Press, Berkeley, 1963.

Bhattacharya, Narendra Nath: *A Dictionary of Hindu Mythology*, Munshiram Manoharlal, Delhi, 2001.

Brodbeck, Simon. "Introduction." In *The Bhagavad Gita*. Translated by Juan Mascaró, xi–xxxii. London: Penguin, 2003.

Brooks, E.: *The Original Analects: Sayings of Confucius and His Successors*. Columbia University Press, New York, 1988.

Cornille, Catherine: *Song Divine: Christian Commentaries on the Bhagavad Gîtâ*, Peeters Publishers, 2006.

Davis, Richard H.: *The "Bhagavad Gita": A Biography*, Princeton University Press, 2014.

Deusse, Paul: *The System of Vedanta*, Motital, Delhi, 1985.

Easwaran, Eknath: *The Bhagavad Gita*, Nilgiri Press, 2007.

Flood, Gavin: *An Introduction to Hinduism*, Cambridge: Cambridge University Press, 1996.

Goldman, R.: *The Ramayana of Valmiki*, Berkeley Hills Books, New York, 2000.

Harlan, B.: *From the Margins of Hindu Marriage*, Oxford University Press, New York, 2000.

Jain, G.: *The Hindu Phenomenon*, UBSPD, Delhi 1994.

Krishnamurthy, Visvantha: *Essentials of Hinduism*, Narosa Pub. House, New Delhi, 1989.

Lamotte, Étienne. *Notes sur la Bhagavadgîtâ*. Paris: Paul Geuthner, 1929.

Mahendranath, S.: *Comparative Studies in Vedaantism*, Humphrey Milford, Bombay, 1927.

Mitchell, Stephen: *Bhagavad Gita: A New Translation*, , Bantam Books, Varanasi, 2002.

Paramahansa, P.: *Autobiography of a Yogi*, Self-Realization Fellowship, Los Angeles, 1984.

Pratyagatmananda, Swami: *Science and Sadhana*, Sri K. P. Maitra, Calcutta, 1966.

Reuchenbach, Hans: *The Philosophy of Space and Time*, Dover Publications, New York, 1958.

Robinson, Catherine A. *Interpretations of the Bhagavad-Gîtâ and Images of the Hindu Tradition: The Song of the Lord*. London: Routledge, 2006.

Rocher, L.: *The Puranas*, , Motilal Banarsidass, Delhi, 1984.

Samdup, Lama Kazi, Dawa: *Chakrasambhara Tantra*, Luzac and Co., London, 1910.

Sharpe, Eric J. *The Universal Gîtâ: Western Images of the Bhagavadgîtâ; A Bicentenary Survey*. London: Duckworth, 1985.

Shearer, Alistair, and Peter Russell: *The Upanishads*, Harper and Row, New York, 1978.

Singh, Ram Pratab: *The Vedanta of Shankara: A Metaphysics of Value*, Bharat Publishing House, Jaipur, 1949.

Sushil, K.: *The Ethics of the Hindus*, Calcutta University Press, Calcutta, 1952.

Trilok, C.: *Sadhus and Saints of India and Nepal*, Tecpress, Bangkok, 1996.

Venkatarama, A.: *Advaita Vedanta, according to Sankara*, Asia Publishing House, New York, 1965.

Visvantha, K.: *Essentials of Hinduism*, Narosa Pub. House, New Delhi, 1989.

Wendy, D.: *The Rig Veda: An Anthology*, Penguin, New York, 1981.

Zimmer, Heinrich: *Myths and Symbols in Indian Art and Civilization*, Joseph Campbell, Delhi, 1946.

Index

S

T

U

V

W

Y

❑❑❑